THE FARALLON COOKBOOK

THE VERY BEST *of* SAN FRANCISCO CUISINE

THE FARALLON COOKBOOK

THE VERY BEST of SAN FRANCISCO CUISINE

By **MARK FRANZ** and **LISA WEISS**   Desserts by **EMILY LUCHETTI**

Photographs by **PAUL MOORE**   Forewords by **JEREMIAH TOWER** and **PAT KULETO**

CHRONICLE BOOKS

SAN FRANCISCO

DEDICATION

To Louise and Charles with love.

To the memory of my father, who turned on the light for me when I was nine years old, and nurtured that light with nightly repasts of exotic and unusual foods of the world—Mark

To Dan, Jordan, and Jodie, my own fan club—Lisa

To the memory of Joe Weiss, a greatly missed friend and brother-in-law who is in our hearts daily—Mark and Lisa

Text copyright © 2001 by Ocean Club LLC dba Farallon Restaurant.
Photographs copyright © 2001 by Paul Moore.
Library of Congress Cataloging-in-Publication Data available.

ISBN 0-8118-2919-7

Printed in Hong Kong

Styling by George Dolese
Design by Sara Schneider
Composition by Suzanne Scott

The photographer wishes to thank his assistants Martin Dunham and Jesse Leake for their great effort, George Dolese for his unerring eye, and Mark Franz for the inspirational food.

Distributed in Canada by Raincoast Books
9050 Shaughnessy Street
Vancouver, BC V6P 6E5

10 9 8 7 6 5 4 3 2 1

Chronicle Books LLC
85 Second Street
San Francisco, California 94105

www.chroniclebooks.com

ACKNOWLEDGMENTS

Books and restaurants require a tremendous amount of teamwork. We'd like to thank everyone who directly and indirectly contributed to this project.

To my mother for allowing me to pursue a goal that she wasn't so sure of and backing me all the way. | To Pat Kuleto for being my best friend as well as the greatest partner anyone could have. | To Jeremiah Tower—fourteen years together in the trenches, teaching me to think of food the way he does: purely, simply, elegantly, and historically. | To Lisa Weiss for putting my thoughts and visions into words, giving them clarity, and paring down hours of babble into distinct and coherent statements and recipes. | To Dan Weiss for allowing this book to be born in his home and for nurturing this baby's parents with some great wines. | To my chefs George Francisco, Parke Ulrich, Bradford Barker, Nathan Powers, Don Hall, Emily Luchetti, Brian Erskin, Heather Ames, and James Sommerville for making it possible for me to spend time away from the restaurant to complete this book. | To Amy Klingelhofer for fulfilling all my last-minute requests for "picture perfect" ingredients. | To the entire staff and management at Farallon, headed up by the formidable Lori Theis. | To Peter Palmer, who not only shares my same passion for wine and food, but also created an amazing cellar for the restaurant. | To Paul Moore, George Dolese, and Jesse Leake for being great professionals and even greater friends. | To Lucienne Francisco and Ingrid Ulrich for all their invaluable assistance in Lisa's kitchen and with the manuscript. | To Richard Miyashiro for running a great organization and blocking downfield. | To Jovan Lozares for keeping everything in order, as it should be. | To the memory of Elizabeth David and Richard Olney; I am forever grateful for the times spent with them in Paris, London, and Toulon where they shared with me their passion for food, introduced me to the old guard, and taught me the value of learning from the past.

—MF

To Mark Franz—what can I say? You are a brilliant chef, loyal friend, all-around good guy, and I thank you for all that you've done for me. | To all the staff at Farallon who made me feel at home and were so generous with their knowledge and assistance. | To Ingrid Ulrich, who was there from the beginning and who was really responsible for getting all these non-existent recipes into print. | To Lucienne, without whom I could never have completed this project and whose friendship I value immensely. | To Louise Franz for her tremendous enthusiasm and willingness to contribute even when she had no time. Your glossary will not go to waste. | To Emily Luchetti, a most incredible cook and mentor. Your advice and help were above and beyond the call of duty. | To Peter Palmer, whose good humor and enthusiasm are reflected in these incomparable wine notes. | To George Francisco, Parke Ulrich, Bradford Barker, Randy Sommerville, Nathan Powers, and Don Hall, who so graciously shared their tremendous knowledge with me and always went the extra mile to answer my questions. | To Ann Byington for her encouragement with this project as well as her invaluable work on the proposal. | To Mark (Drew) Knoble for sharing his wealth of knowledge of ingredients with me. | To our home recipe testers who were so precise and thoughtful in their comments: Sebia Petrovich, Elaine Adamson, Don Caruso, Duke and Jan Lang, Greg Leon, and Lindsay Wheelock. Also, Lia Huber for her help testing and for her wonderfully entertaining emails. | To Jeremiah Tower for starting this whole thing and influencing an entire generation of chefs. | To Pat Kuleto for his heartfelt foreword and Nancy Ganner for getting it to us on time. | To Jane Dystel, who was there every step of the way with advice and encouragement. | To Bill LeBlond, a terrific person and even better editor, who supported and believed in this book before I did. | To Paul Moore, George Dolese, and Jesse Leake, for the photography that really captured the spirit of Mark's food. | To Amy Treadwell and the gang at Chronicle Books for their good humor and hard work on this really huge project. To Sara Schneider for an elegant design that made it all fit. | To Carolyn Miller for her awesome and astute editing skills. | To Emma Ulrich and William Francisco, who were born during the course of this project and were very cooperative with their timing and temperaments. | To Bruce Aidells: your encouragement made me believe that I was up to this project. | And a special thanks to Hal, Patti, Joanne, Mike, Nicole, Rusty, Katharine, Marlene, Steve, Mary, Michael, Marsha, Sebia, Renee, Jim, and the rest of my extended family and friends: you are why I cook.

—LW

TABLE OF CONTENTS

Jean Cocteau was once asked what he would save from his studio if it were burning. "The fire," he replied. For me, the studio is the easy part, so let's look at the fire, and how to keep it burning. At Chez Panisse I started the fire. The Santa Fe Bar & Grill, with Mark, was literally all about fire, and at Stars we kindled it again. And whenever the fire seemed in danger of going out, we always found a way to refuel it. One of the most dramatic and memorable of those times was in the early nineties, when I rented a villa just south of Florence for six months. The purpose was to give the staff of Stars time to reinspire themselves in the Tuscan countryside and the Florentine markets. I knew that seeing the local foods and cooking them would fan the embers.

As did lunch. A swim in the pool surrounded by olive trees wasn't bad either, nor were the ubiquitous chilled Antinori whites. The great marble-slab table with a view for miles over the Castellina in the Chianti Valley. But the greatest find was an outdoor wood oven in the wall of the villa, which was found covered in vines and filled with old paint pots. We cleaned it out, built a fire for twelve hours with herbs to baptize its new incarnation, and shoved a massive loin of white veal into it. The tastes were sublime, revealing to us again that old familiar formula for great food: perfect ingredients, cooked with little interference by a cook, using classic techniques. From then on, we cooked everything in that oven, and I have never seen Mark so fulfilled and at peace. The oven was the inspiration for all our cooking in the next couple of years. It became the benchmark for the restaurant's kitchen, because we had learned that the further a restaurant's food gets from home-hearth cooking, the more dangerously strange and unsatisfying it becomes.

Our earlier efforts at inspiring each other tended to be more grand. I remember the Labor Day dinner in 1985 that Mark and my other chefs from the Santa Fe Bar & Grill and Stars put on for us. They served Iranian Molossol caviar with hot buttered brioche toasts made every few minutes, as I had taught them. With that we drank our frozen pepper vodka, Champagne Salon le Mesnil 1971, and Taitinger Grande Annee 1977. I had always gone on about the mastery of a menu by serving consommé after a rich first course, so they made one from squab and floated it with black truffles. The next course was ravioli stuffed with brandade, bathed in a lobster sauce, and Meursault 1977. Then a roast saddle of lamb with a potato galette and flageolets, knowing, thanks to Richard Olney, how surprisingly marvelous two starches are together, particularly potatoes and beans. We had two red wines with the lamb, a Chateau Latour 1961 and a Jordan Cabernet Sauvignon 1976. This was followed by another palate cleanser, a garden salad with walnut oil and Meyer lemon, and no wine. Mark already knew of the delights of teasing the diner with subtle repetition that doesn't really repeat, so the next course was a liver mousse made from the squabs, and a Richebourg from the Domaine de la Romanée Conti from my favorite year, 1969. Then blancmange and raspberries with the dessert wine, a Chateau Suduiraut 1966; this marriage was our homage to the lesson taught to me by Elizabeth David years before. With the vintage port we had warm pistachios and some cheeses. It was a Croft 1963—another lesson in perfection. And just to show we did not take ourselves too seriously, we ended the meal with a Jell-O mold, marshmallows, and Cool Whip, with Glenfiddich 1973.

It happened for me last summer, when a high, fragrant hedge of lavender surrounding a lapis-colored pool was baking in the evening summer sun, the Champagne was chilling, and in front of me on the old beige stones of a French village was a chapon de Bresse, the real thing, turning on a spit over a fire fueled with dried vine cuttings from Cahors, while inside was waiting the first course of five-minute eggs with truffle-butter sauce. I thought of Mark. I remembered the night at Stars when Mark told me that if he heard one more word about those damn French chickens he would hit me. Obviously I had been going on again about the sorry lack of decent poultry in the United States, let alone being able to choose from five or so different grades. So I hit him instead, with a plane ticket to Paris. On the way there, I waxed lyrically about the chickens at the Rungis market, and about spit-roasting in Richard Olney's fireplace, the fragrance of the hillside herbs grown in impoverished soil, and the intense pleasures of the simple local wine.

When Jack Lang was France's minister of culture, he initiated "*La Semaine du Goût,*" sending off to the schools around France missionaries of taste armed with various perfect products—an apricot picked ripe, unpasteurized cheese, real bread—to give the young students a taste lesson and to build their benchmark-food memory. At the California Culinary Academy in 1979, I did the same, and Mark was my star pupil. At the school, I wanted to lay a foundation so that the cooks of the future could avoid the clouded thinking that came later in the eighties when chefs began to cultivate newness for its own sake, serving up oddity instead of authenticity. At the Academy, I lined up blind tastings of various ingredients like America's favorite beers, chocolates, butters, vinegars, sugars, olive oils, Scotches, brandies, and so on. Each time, the students were amazed to find their old favorites replaced with a brand chosen for its taste and not its advertising. "Authenticity," I told them, "and balance. You will all be high-wire artists," I said, "and the higher you go, the more dangerous it is to assume or preconceive. Read (Escoffier's chapter intros, Boulestin, Colette, Nignon, Elizabeth David, Richard Olney, anything out of Australia) and cook with impeccable foods. Do that, and as a cook you will never be guilty of the cardinal sin of thinking that you are in charge. The painter does not change the basic colors," I told them. "Remember when you were a child graduating to the watercolor box that had fifty colors instead of twelve? And of going wild mixing them all together—only to get muddy brown? Ditto with cooking."

What makes a great book, like a great chef, is honesty. So in *The Farallon Cookbook*, Mark lets the ingredients guide the dish. The recipes are created by the marketplace, and the cooking techniques are modernized classical. A year after Farallon opened, Mark cooked for me one of the best lunches I have ever had. It was simple and direct, using fabulous ingredients with just the right amount of his interference.

When he came to the table at espresso time, I complimented the sure-handed simplicity of the dishes and the menu. He smiled, knowing what was forming in my mind. Like the count in Norman Douglas's *South Wind*, who said that "the ideal cuisine should display an individual character," he was a chef who could "take the food back to that directness, to what was really in his heart, rather than in the part of his mind influenced by trends." Neither one of us had to say anything more. Mark understands the complexity of Escoffier's *"faites simple."* And the tremendous ongoing discipline of tending the fire. It takes guts to tweak your act when you're playing to a full house. But that's this book.

Incredible as it may seem, Farallon was an accident.

I had known Mark Franz for years through his exceptional cuisine at Stars in San Francisco, and his cooking and determined character had always impressed me. We talked a lot about our common interests in not only food and wine, but also our passions for sailing and fishing. One evening, after an incredible dinner at Stars, I thought to myself how great it would be to have Mark as a partner someday.

A few years later, in 1994, the day finally arrived, when the two of us were having lunch in a Mexican restaurant in Sonoma. Mark and I, after a few preliminary conversations, had decided to look for a space for our new venture and were taking a look at this restaurant, which we knew was for sale, with the idea that we would create the ultimate food and wine-country experience on the North Coast. We were both excited about the design concept, which incorporated an old adobe courtyard theme in honor of Sonoma's first vintner, Gen. Mariano Guadalupe Vallejo. After a few hugs, we began the long and painful process of negotiating a lease and planning the project. For over a year, both of us put in hundreds of hours, until the day finally arrived when we were ready to begin the development. Unfortunately, at the last hour, our permits were denied due to insufficient parking.

I was devastated—and sure that I had lost Mark as a partner. As we left the Planning Commission meeting and were walking through the dark parking lot that evening, Mark gave me a big hug and said, "No problem, Pat. It wasn't meant to be. We'll still be partners; I'm in for the long haul with you."

I knew then that I had an extraordinary partner in Mark. We decided not to appeal the decision, but to move forward and do something together in San Francisco. As luck would have it, we found an amazing spot just off Union Square in the old Elks Club building. Part of the space included the antique, arched mosaic ceiling that once soared over earlier generations of Elks as they swam in their heated swimming pool. Mark loved this old Union Square location, and being in the heart of San Francisco made it feel like home for both of us.

When we began to toss around ideas for our new venture, we kept asking ourselves, "What is San Francisco known for? What do people think of when they hear 'Golden Gate?'" The answer seemed obvious, especially due to our mutual love of the ocean. We said, almost in unison: "Seafood." San Francisco is the greatest seaport on the West Coast. We have a wealth of seafood here: salmon, halibut, sturgeon, rock cod, sole, sand dabs, lingcod, tuna, crab, oysters, mussels and clams, abalone—just about everything you can possibly think of. For a chef and restaurateur, the possibilities were endlessly exciting.

Envisioning the image for this new space, I started thinking about an underwater fantasy world—part Captain Nemo, part Star Trek. It began with the hand-painted mosaic ceiling that looked like old-world, traditional architecture: a 1920s classic in the style of Julia Morgan.

I decided to make the bar area at the entrance into a magical, underwater experience. All of the fantasies I had—of giant jellyfish floating overhead, of huge illuminated sea kelp columns coming up from the floor, of sole and crabs swimming on the bottom of the sea, of a giant sunset around the perimeter of the water and a midnight sky above, and of jellyfish tentacles hanging down from the ceiling—would prove to be hugely upsetting to Mark. I knew it could be hokey and "Disney-esque" if I couldn't pull it off with authenticity and style. I would excitedly try to explain these things to Mark, and he'd just shake his head and say, "It sounds crazy and it absolutely scares me to death, but I totally trust you."

Mark may not have believed that I could follow through with all those ideas that made him so nervous. The task of creating the giant sea creatures was a far greater one than I had imagined, even after thirty-five years of doing this kind of thing. We used the top artists on the West Coast and also had to go to New York to find more "reality-challenged" people who could pull off the illusions on such a grand scale, and who were capable of making the giant lighting elements.

The spiral staircase to the mezzanine, which we call the "caviar staircase," was fabricated simultaneously on both coasts—all the steel was made here in the West, while the bronze bull-kelp railings were being finished on the East Coast—and it was almost an impossible task to complete. My vision for the bar was a giant clamshell swallowing the world, and at the same time I wanted it to mimic the ribs on the inside of a huge blue whale. I also chuckled at the idea of people sitting on top of bronze octopus barstools. In the Nautilus Room, just off the bar and preceding the dining room, I conjured up a gigantic nautilus shell almost thirty feet in diameter, sliced in half so you're sitting right in it and you can see chambers along the coral floor. I wanted all of these elements to have a realistic feel and patina to them— a texture that would make it all feel alive.

One of the most difficult challenges was to restore the mosaic ceiling. It had almost completely deteriorated and was peeling off, and you could barely make out the intricate pattern underneath. We finally did it as Michelangelo would have—we had artists lying on their backs atop scaffolding for months. The end result was magnificent. The paintings in Farallon are also an integral part of its illusion. I wanted to extend the feeling of being underwater by looking out through the portholes under the sea, and to have all the creatures looking back in. Some had to be whimsical, while others had to be absolutely authentic.

I knew that no one in the entire world would be able to understand where I was going with this, except of course, for Mark. As the restaurant began to take its physical shape and the giant jellyfish lights and the eight-foot sea urchins began to appear, it began to sink into Mark what kind of challenge lay ahead of him. How could he create a cuisine to match this wild and crazy environment? He'd need to come up with something that would be able to stand up to, and be compatible with, this design. Little did we know that this craziness was to become one of the West Coast's highest-grossing fine restaurants.

Mark and I spent endless hours trying to conceive the perfect cuisine for the restaurant. We kept thinking of what San Francisco really wanted and how we would do it. Mark wanted it to be a blend of classic and traditional timeless cuisine, unlike what anyone else offered. I agreed, and at the same time, I wanted it to have an element of splash; more contemporary, and on the cutting edge. We talked and talked until we were blue in the face, trying to shape our concepts so we could blend them together in the physical manifestation of this restaurant. That's when we came up with what we call coastal cuisine: classically pre-pared but stunningly original seafood dishes from all over the world. It fit the bill perfectly.

In so many ways, I found the perfect partner in Mark. Not only was he able to grasp my image of this restaurant, but he dramatically embellished it with his abilities as one of the country's best chefs, and together we pulled it off. When he started lining up his team, I recognized his uncanny ability to organize and motivate people to work with him to help him realize his culinary visions. He pulled together a remarkable group of talented and extremely individual people, and he inspired them to reach their own personal heights as a team. He's the Pied Piper of chefs, and people came from everywhere for the opportunity to work with him.

I've always loved the sea, and my Farallon adventures with Mark Franz have been nothing short of a dream come true. It's been a joy and a privilege to work with such a fantastically gifted chef.

This collection of dishes and recipes should be an inspiration to anyone who values the vivid, fresh flavors that come from maritime cuisine. It is a book that honors the ocean and the talents of a chef who has captured its essence.

INTRODUCTION *by Mark Franz*

I cook for many reasons. I cook because I love to eat and I love to feed people. I cook because I need to eat and because I need to earn a living. I cook for the creative fulfillment it gives me and because I love the adrenaline rush I get at show time. Sometimes I cook breakfast at home just for myself, and then I'll go to work and cook dinner for hundreds of people. But whether I'm cooking at the restaurant or cooking at home for my family and friends, I get as much pleasure from the process as I do the result.

I love cooking because it's a physical activity that employs all of my senses. It's about taste, of course, but it's also about smell—think of bread baking or chicken stock simmering. It's about touch, like feeling a steak for doneness, or gently tossing salad greens with my hands. It's about listening for the bubbles to subside in a pan of oil, telling me when the frying is complete. And it's about the great sense of satisfaction I feel when I send a plate out of the kitchen that's stunning to behold.

There's an aspect to the way I approach cooking, however, that appeals to the adventuresome, and I admit, somewhat rebellious part of my nature: improvisation. The servers at Farallon actually hate it when I cook. They'll serve a dish, come back to the line to pick up another order of the same dish, and I've already changed it. When I cook, I like to taste, smell, feel, and look at my ingredients, and when I start out to prepare a meal, I love the idea that I don't know where it will end up. It's always been that way with me. From the very beginning of my culinary career, I've always let my ingredients drive the creation of the meal.

In the mid-seventies, compelled by a desire to nurture an emerging creative impulse and give my twenty-five-year-old life some direction, I enrolled at the California Culinary Academy. It was there, in my very first class, that I met Jeremiah Tower, who was teaching a class called "Taste." Every day for four weeks, we tasted a mind-boggling variety of ingredients: vinegars—how many people in 1976 had even *heard* of balsamic?—olive oils, nut oils, sugars, chocolates, chilies, salts, peppers, and spices from all over the world. We learned how the tongue and palate perceive only salt, sweet, bitter, and sour; how a great dish is all about the balance of flavors; and about how textures, like crunchy and crispy, smooth and greasy, can add to or detract from our overall satisfaction with a dish.

But learning how to taste was only the beginning. Though Jeremiah taught me a profound respect for ingredients, and gave me a foundation in classic French techniques, the experience that really defined how I cook to this day was as far from a kitchen or classroom as I could get. After graduating from CCA and spending months working fifteen-hour days at Ernie's, a highly acclaimed French restaurant in San Francisco, I began to seriously question my choice of careers. Frankly, I was burned out, and when a friend suggested that I come to Alaska to help him build a lodge and take wealthy clients on fishing trips in the Alaskan wilderness, I jumped at the chance.

Thousands of miles from nowhere for several weeks at a time, I was on my own, with no communication from my base camp. For meals, I was provided only basic provisions, and it was expected that I would hunt, fish, or forage for the rest. Guests were flown in, and I was responsible for piloting them up the river and onto the lake to fish for trout (the biggest I've ever seen), salmon, and bass. After several months of a steady diet of fish cooked every way I could think of—foil-wrapped, over pine needles, with beer, with bourbon, and au naturel—I started to get bored. Soon, I rigged up a smoker, and we began to dine lavishly on meals like smoked salmon and trout with foraged wild greens and mushrooms. And slowly I began to recall what it was that I loved about cooking. Fending for myself, often without human contact for days at a time, I had developed a very deep respect and visceral connection to the wild creatures and plant life that had sustained me—I truly *got* that cooking was all about the food.

I returned to the Bay Area in 1982, feeling a profound sense of who I was and, for the first time in my life, a real direction and purpose. I was confirmed in my dedication to my career and knew, without a doubt, that I was going to be a chef. At the time, Jeremiah had just taken over the kitchen at the Balboa Cafe. He didn't have anything to offer me there, but needed another cook at his new Santa Fe Bar & Grill in Berkeley, where he was experimenting with one of the first mesquite grills in California. I joined Steve Vranian and Noreen Lam to work at Santa Fe.

The three of us began by throwing out all the rules of kitchen hierarchy and establishing a working relationship whereby no one person was in charge and we were all responsible for some aspect of production. Our days began with local purveyors showing up at our door with all kinds of new and wonderful products: Bruce Aidells brought us his unique handmade sausages, Warren Weber brought us mixed baby salad greens, Laurel Chenel brought her artisan goat cheeses, and Paul Johnson of Monterey Fish brought impeccable seafood. We all shared a naive, wide-open, improvisational approach that allowed us to experiment. For me, it was a kind of continuation of my approach to cooking in Alaska. Each day, we would simply see what were the freshest ingredients available, plan our menu, and start cooking, without any preconceived ideas. The most gratifying part, though, was that our customers were eating it up. Literally. They seemed to share and embrace our pioneering culinary spirit. In fact, sometimes the more unusual our food became, the more they loved it—chili-braised goat on hominy, for instance. For several weeks we sold twenty pounds of brains a night. It was during that time at the Santa Fe that I developed a total confidence in my techniques and really learned how to cook, unencumbered by recipes or kitchen dogma. After two years, Jeremiah asked me to be the chef at Stars, the new restaurant he was opening in San Francisco.

From the day we opened on July 4, 1984, a block from the San Francisco Civic Center, Stars became a social gathering spot, and before long, it was an institution. On any given night, as I peered through the steam of the open kitchen into the bar and past the piano player, I could see singles and socialites, politicians and celebrities, locals and tourists, all mingling, eating, drinking, and partying. We were producing seven hundred covers a day, four hundred of those at night. When I actually had time to reflect, I was truly amazed to think that over the course of two years, I had gone from a solitary existence, preparing freshly caught fish over a campfire in the Alaskan wilderness, to preparing sautéed foie gras with truffles for diners like Rudolph Nureyev, James Beard, Richard Olney, and Julia Child. I really learned how to cook at Santa Fe, but it was during my decade-long tenure at Stars that I was able to hone my skills, further develop my palate, and evolve as a chef.

While I was at Stars I met Pat Kuleto, a talented and gregarious bear of a man whom I had long admired for his spectacular restaurant designs as well as his entrepreneurial spirit and business acumen. Often, when he'd come into the restaurant we'd sit and talk, and eventually a friendship formed based on our shared passions for food, wine, hunting, sailing, and fishing. In 1994, after I had made the decision to leave Stars and strike out on my own, Pat and I discussed the possibility of becoming partners in a new restaurant venture. Two years after weathering a discouraging and futile attempt to get our first project off the ground, we found a perfect space just off Union Square in San Francisco. In 1997, our dream came true when we opened Farallon, named for the islands off the Golden Gate, in the ocean where we both love to sail and fish.

I have to admit to a certain amount of skepticism when Pat described to me his initial design ideas for the restaurant interior, but I'm glad that I trusted him. Farallon is a tasteful blend of fantasy and comfortable elegance, unique in the world of fine dining. Coming up with a menu that could stand next to Pat's fanciful and incredible interior, however, was no easy assignment.

Going back through three years of menus while we were culling recipes for this book, I was struck by the evolution of our food. Farallon's first menus reflected the need I felt at the time to compete with six-foot jellyfish, eight-foot sea urchins, and massive glowing kelp columns, in addition to what I perceived to be our diners' expectations. The dishes on those menus were loaded with truffles, foie gras, and caviar, rich with hollandaise and butter, and complex. You'll still find a lot of sexy ingredients on our menus and in these recipes, but we've eliminated much of the richness, and the dishes are more refined and less complex. I've learned to relax and have gone back to the food that resonates with me on a more personal level. You'll also find that our current dishes showcase diverse culinary backgrounds of my very talented chefs, George Francisco, Bradford Barker, Parke Ulrich, Nathan Powers, and Don Hall.

This book came about for one reason: I decided it was time to share the Farallon recipes that our guests have been requesting since we opened. Ah, if only it were that easy. As is often the case, this project became much more complicated than I ever could have imagined. The major difficulty, of course, was in translating the Farallon kitchen dishes into recipes that could be used with ease by the home cook. Along with the recipes, I'd like to offer the two principles that I think are most important to the act of turning out good food: Using the best ingredients available, and preparing them for use in the kitchen.

If there is any one common quality that characterizes the good cooks of the world, I firmly believe it's a fanatic dedication to using only the best ingredients available—availability being the key. I realize that what is available to me, here in California, during any particular season, might be different from what is available to people in the Midwest or on the East Coast. But what all good cooks do, no matter where they live, is actively seek out the freshest and highest quality ingredients and then build their meals around them.

The thing that most impressed me on my first trip to France many years ago was that the act of going to the market to gather ingredients for a meal was at least as important as the process of preparing the meal, and almost as important as the meal itself. It was a revelation to me that people actually *enjoyed* going grocery shopping. And they did it daily. How else were they to find out which fish was freshest, and whose strawberries were sweetest? And how else were they to catch up on the local gossip? In France, life revolves around the table, and by extension, going to the market is an integral part of their social fabric.

That trip was almost thirty years ago, and while Americans still have not adopted the European attitude towards the pleasures of the table, I've seen a tremendous revolution in the way we eat and, more specifically, shop for our food. Yes, I know, we're still a nation addicted to fast foods, supermarkets, and now even mega-markets, full of convenience foods that are all designed to get us out of the kitchen as quickly as possible. But around the corner from that warehouse store, you're just as likely to find a farmers' market. Supermarkets today carry once-exotic ingredients like arugula and lemongrass. Now, not only can you purchase your cereal and bananas from an online grocer, you can order fresh white Italian truffles in season as well. There's no reason to accept rock-hard tomatoes or day-old fish today. Local farmers' markets are springing up all over the country and are a gold mine for enthusiastic and curious cooks. Thanks to the Internet, impeccably fresh, organically grown, high-quality foods and unusual ethnic ingredients are now available to cooks in all parts of the country, not just in the major metropolitan areas.

As a cook, every dish I create is dependent on the ingredients I find, and no amount of technique can disguise poor-quality food. And at the restaurant, the quality of our ingredients is dependent on our purveyors, whether foragers, farmers, or fishermen. As a home cook, it's just as important to go out and establish relationships with your own local suppliers—butchers, fishmongers, supermarket managers, produce buyers, and local farmers. These are the people that you will, hopefully, turn to, who often have a wealth of knowledge about their products and are anxious to share their knowledge with anyone who shows an interest in good food or cooking. Seek to learn from them. In the process, you'll be developing your palate, making friends, and strengthening your ties to the community.

Recipes are merely guides, and the best cooks are the ones that use them for inspiration at the market. When shopping for a meal, always have a few ideas in mind. Think of the season and what might be freshest and most reasonably priced. If your fishmonger doesn't have Prince Edward Island mussels, imagine how the bisque would taste with fresh oysters instead, and if he's just received some pristine ahi, consider making tartare as a first course rather than soup.

The second principle of good cooking, I think, is to prepare your components and organize your ingredients before making the actual dish. In the professional kitchen, this is known as *"mise en place,"* the French phrase meaning "put in place." It means that all your ingredients are prepped and utensils set out and ready to go before beginning the cooking and assembly of the meal. *Mise en place* is the cornerstone of an efficient professional kitchen and includes *all* the prep work that can be done ahead of time. *Mise en place* ranges from simple tasks like peeling and chopping vegetables, to more complex ones like filleting fish and making stocks and sauces. It also includes having everything ready at the cooking stations: garnishes within reach, pots of water boiling for pasta, plates warming in the oven.

Mise en place is as much a state of mind as it is a procedure, because when the *mise en place* is done, the chef is mentally prepared to deal with any situation that may arise and can focus on the more immediate task of cooking and plating the meal. If you're a home cook, you should understand that *mise en place* is about more than just doing things ahead of time or making your own stock from scratch. *Mise en place* is a tool, like any other kitchen tool, but one that can give you peace of mind, because a good cook is an organized cook. When you have your *mise en place* set, the pressure is off, and once you're relieved of the anxiety of making last-minute decisions, you can take your cooking to a more complex and creative level.

People who know me well were surprised when they heard I was writing a cookbook. "But you never use recipes," they said. That's true. Since the time I graduated from cooking school, I've rarely looked at a recipe. I cook from my gut, and now after twenty-five years, from my experience. Recipes have always seemed to be in direct conflict with a process that for me is inherently experiential and often extemporaneous.

So as someone who's confessed to rarely using recipes, you're probably wondering why I would want to write a cookbook. Simply put, because I love cookbooks. Because just as a meal shared with friends is about more than the food, a cookbook is about more than recipes. Cookbooks can do many things: teach skills and techniques, introduce new ingredients, and show how to combine them. Some of my favorites offer lessons in history and philosophy, or are personal guides to other cultures; many are memoirs of well-fed lives. The cookbooks that I most treasure, however, have two things in common: They've either taught me or inspired me, and the best of them have done both. I hope this one will be that kind of cookbook for you.

NOTES TO THE HOME COOK FROM LISA WEISS

Included in this book are fifty-five savory dishes and fourteen desserts from Emily Luchetti. With the exception of one dish that Mark created while we were testing (the Black Bass and Sea Urchin Tartare in a Nori Sandwich), all were culled from Farallon's menus. Though Mark and Emily selected them with an eye towards including their customers' as well as the staff's own favorites, they also wanted to include a broad range, a little something for everyone. So some dishes are quite easy to prepare, like George's Sake-Pickled Salmon or the Oyster Stew, and a few are quite challenging, like the Seafood Pyramid or the Monkfish Chaussons.

From the beginning of this project, I was well aware of the inherent difficulties in writing recipes for dishes born in restaurant kitchens, and the resulting problems in trying to cook from those recipes at home. So in an effort to write user-friendly recipes that still accurately represent the dishes served at Farallon, Mark and I worked together in my kitchen, along with Ingrid Ulrich and Lucienne Francisco, writing, measuring, analyzing, testing, and tasting each and every recipe to make sure they would be as accurate and unambiguous as possible. In some cases we made adjustments to make them easier for the home cook, but never were they compromised.

Chefs' recipes tend to be daunting because of their length and complexity. But it's important to realize that just as a chef can build a dish, a home cook can break a dish down into more manageable parts. Though the dishes in this book are presented the same way as they are at Farallon, giving you a feel for the way Mark puts things together, you should feel free to play around with the recipes, depending on your time and inclination.

No recipe in this book, or any other, should be followed slavishly. However, if you're a novice in the kitchen, take your time, carefully read your recipe through once or twice before you begin, and if you've shopped well, your meal will be a success. No matter what your level of expertise, we've written the recipes in a way that reflects Mark's free-wheeling spirit in the kitchen, and that we hope will inspire you and encourage your own spontaneity.

In Improvisations you'll find suggestions for substitutes for the ingredients called for in the recipe. Most foods can be exchanged for ones that are available to you.

Advance Prep is particularly useful if you're entertaining. Here's where you'll find out how far ahead the components of a dish can be prepared, relieving a lot of last-minute anxiety.

In Simplifying you'll find alternate serving suggestions if you don't have the time or desire to make all the components of a dish.

What's a great meal without wine? Mark consulted with Farallon's excellent sommelier, Peter Palmer, in order to provide suggestions for wines that complement all the dishes in the book.

In addition to all of the above, and for those of you who, like Mark, don't like to use recipes, Paul Moore's photos should provide all the inspiration you need.

RECIPES

Simply Raw

With seafood, simple is indeed best. Pluck an oyster from its bed, shuck it, slurp it down, and taste that briny-sweet essence of the sea. The simplest way to serve seafood is of course au naturel, or uncooked, and from day one, Farallon's menu has begun with a section we call "Simply Raw," which contains everything from oysters on the half shell to tartares, ceviches, and carpaccios.

In this chapter, you'll find a few of my personal favorites. I love raw seafood and can think of no better way to begin a meal than with a few raw oysters and a glass of Champagne. When I'm in a more indulgent mood, I like to top the oysters with caviar. If it's a celebratory occasion at home, however, and I want an appetizer course that's dramatic as well as delicious, I'll present my guests with a huge platter laden with ice and an array of raw and cooked seafood. At the restaurant we call this Iced Atlantic and Pacific Shellfish Indulgence—a dish inspired by the classic French *plateaux de fruits de mer*, or "platters of fruits of the sea," served in bistros and brasseries all over the south of France—a spectacular two- or three-tiered display of pristine raw oysters and clams, poached mussels, prawns, crab claws, periwinkles, and lobster.

The best part about serving "simply raw" seafood, besides the fact that it's sweet, delicate, and delicious, is that it's easy on the cook. If you have access to impeccably fresh ingredients, you can make an immediate impression on your guests with some quickly shucked oysters, served with a mignonette sauce or a squeeze of lemon. For something a little more complex but just as easy, try Oyster and Wild Salmon Tartare with Roasted Beets and Crisp Giant Capers, or Maine-Diver Scallop Ceviche with Green Peppercorns, Grapefruit, and Chili Vinaigrette. For a more formal occasion, it's not difficult to put out a traditional platter of Caviar, Smoked Salmon, and Gravlax with Buckwheat Blini and Sour Cream.

The Japanese have long appreciated the delicate and pure taste of raw fish, and some of the most popular items on our raw menu include Asian-inspired dishes like beautiful Onaga Carpaccio with Cucumber Consommé, and Black Bass and Sea Urchin Tartare in a Crisp Nori Sandwich (which also makes a great cocktail hors d'oeuvre).

It's hard, though, to overstate the importance of using impeccably fresh fish in any raw preparation. Make sure you read "Buying and Storing Fish and Shellfish" (page 221), so you'll be an educated shopper.

Although this dish shouldn't technically be called "raw" because it contains cooked as well as uncooked seafood, it's still one of Farallon's big showstoppers. When the tiered, icy, seaweed-dripping platters are carried through the dining room by not one but two waiters, conversations stop and people turn and stare. It's an impressive and sexy dish that we love to send out to our VIPs. Once, when I actually sat down for dinner in the dining room to join in a friend's birthday celebration, my chef, George Francisco, was feeling creative and wanted to send me a really special version of the Indulgence. As I

ICED ATLANTIC and PACIFIC SHELLFISH INDULGENCE

caught sight of the waiters emerging from the kitchen with the tiered platters, I couldn't believe what I was seeing: The platters were glowing from within—a spectacular but eerie green and blue. George's young son had come home with some glow-in-the-dark plastic necklaces, and George had coiled them under the ice of each platter. As my anticipation and pride mounted, I watched the waiters approach my table—and then glide right by and place the phosphorescent seafood-laden platters on the table next to mine. Needless to say, George was a little upset with the new waiters, who had delivered my special Indulgence to the wrong table. You needn't to go to these lengths to create an impressive Indulgence platter of your own; it's a simple and beautiful dish that makes all guests feel special and indulged.

★ CHEF'S TIPS *I've selected a list of seafood to include here, but depending on your whim, budget, availability, and the season, you can mix and match whatever you want. Sometimes, in addition to the assorted shellfish, we put ceviche into a scallop shell, or if a customer requests it, we'll just serve all one kind of seafood, maybe with some housemade caviar. Whatever your choice, have some fun with it. You can easily increase the amounts to serve a crowd or decrease them for a romantic dinner à deux. | When buying and cooking shellfish like mussels or clams, you need to take into account those that don't open after cooking, or oysters that, when opened, smell "off." Discard these, as they're probably duds. We have allowed for this when we say 2 to 4 clams, 6 to 8 mussels, etc. | I never serve mussels raw. Raw clams are okay, but they can also be steamed, like the mussels, if you prefer.*

Makes 4 appetizer servings

2 tablespoons olive oil
2 cloves garlic, minced
3 shallots, minced
2 to 4 Manila or razor clams
6 to 8 mussels
2 cups dry white wine
1 teaspoon chopped fresh flat-leaf (Italian) parsley
Pinch of kosher salt
2 to 4 cockles (optional)
6 periwinkles (optional)

COCKTAIL SAUCE:
¼ cup ketchup
2 tablespoons fresh lemon juice
1 tablespoon fresh grated horseradish, or 1 teaspoon prepared horseradish
Kosher salt and freshly ground pepper to taste

LEMON VINAIGRETTE:
1 tablespoon fresh lemon juice
¼ cup extra-virgin olive oil
Kosher salt and freshly ground pepper to taste

HORSERADISH MIGNONETTE:
1 tablespoon grated fresh horseradish, or 1 teaspoon prepared horseradish
¼ cup Champagne vinegar
¼ cup Champagne or sparkling wine
Kosher salt and freshly ground pepper to taste

Crushed ice for serving
Seaweed for garnish (optional)
3 to 5 fresh oysters
½ ounce salmon or sturgeon caviar (optional)

4 large cooked, shelled shrimp, tails on
1 cooked rock or snow crab claw, or 2 cooked Dungeness crab claws, cracked
2 cooked lobster claws, cracked (optional)
2 cooked crayfish (optional)
4 lemon halves, wrapped in cheesecloth and tied with twine (optional), or 4 lemon wedges, seeded

continued

In a medium sauté pan or skillet, heat the olive oil over low heat and sauté the garlic and shallots until soft. Increase heat to high and add the clams. Cover and steam for 1 minute. Add the mussels and stir in the wine. Cover and cook for 2 minutes. Stir again, cover, and cook for 2 more minutes. Add the parsley and salt. Remove from heat. Using a slotted spoon, transfer the clams and mussels to a bowl. Discard any shellfish that have not opened. Refrigerate for up to 1 day.

Return the pan and liquid to medium heat and add the cockles, if using, stirring and cooking for 1 minute. Add the periwinkles if using, cover, and cook for 7 minutes. Remove the pan from heat and transfer the shellfish to a bowl. Discard the cooking liquid.

To make the cocktail sauce: Stir all the ingredients together. Cover and refrigerate for up to 1 day.

To make the lemon vinaigrette: In a small bowl, whisk the lemon juice with the olive oil. Season with salt and pepper. Set aside or refrigerate for up to 1 day.

To make the mignonette: In a small bowl, stir all the ingredients together. Set aside or refrigerate for up to 1 day.

To serve, toss the cooked mussels and clams in the lemon vinaigrette and set aside. Fill a small ramekin with the cocktail sauce and fill another with the horseradish mignonette. Fold 2 to 3 white napkins into squares and place them on a platter or large plate; this will help to absorb the ice as it melts. Mound crushed ice on top of the napkins and shape it into a fairly low, rounded shape. Make 2 indentations in the ice and firmly secure a ramekin in each. Drape the seaweed, if using, over the ice, leaving spaces to place the seafood. Shuck the oysters and nestle each one in a different place around the mound. Spoon small amounts of caviar, if using, into half of the oysters. Hook the shrimp, tail-side out, over the edges of the cocktail-sauce ramekin. Place the crab and lobster claws, if using, beside the ramekins so that they are sticking straight up, claws pointing skyward. Fill in any white spaces with the optional cockles, periwinkles, and crayfish until the dish looks as if it is full

to bursting. Serve with lemon halves or wedges, moist napkins, and long, thin seafood forks, or the smallest forks that you have.

IMPROVISATIONS *If you have a problem with raw seafood, you could serve all the ingredients of the Indulgence cooked. Either cook the oysters or omit them, and steam the clams as for the mussels. We sometimes add Maine-Diver Scallop Ceviche (page 34) and Oyster and Wild Salmon Tartare (page 36), served in small quantities on decorative scallop shells.*

ADVANCE PREP *Both of the vinaigrettes can be made 1 day in advance, as can the cocktail sauce. The shellfish can be cooked and chilled 1 day ahead. The oysters and clams should be opened just before serving, or they can be shucked 3 to 4 hours ahead and stored upright, nestled in rock salt, in the refrigerator.*

SIMPLIFYING *Serve fewer kinds of shellfish and only one of the dipping sauces. A simplified version of this dish is what we refer to as Oysters Farallon: oysters on the half shell served with a classic mignonette. Put the napkins and ice on a large platter, drape it with the seaweed if you have it, and place a dozen just-opened oysters on the ice. Place a small spoonful of any kind of caviar or fish roe you like on half of the oysters and serve with a Champagne mignonette: ¼ cup Champagne, ¼ cup Champagne vinegar, ¼ teaspoon minced shallot, kosher salt to taste, and lots of freshly ground pepper.*

WINE NOTE *The classic pairing for this cool, bountiful spread of raw and cooked shellfish is Muscadet, the utterly dry, extra crisp, and inexpensive white wine from France's northeast Atlantic coast. Champagne will make a splashier impression, and a good Chablis is also appropriate, but nothing beats Muscadet for echoing the sea-air freshness of just-harvested shellfish.*

The origins of buckwheat blini (Russian for pancakes) can be traced back to the Middle Ages in Russia. They were served everywhere, from vendors' carts to bourgeois homes, and on most occasions, from festivals to funerals. Most often the blini were accompanied with smoked fish, herring, hard-cooked eggs, sour cream, and (of course) caviar. (Vodka too, but that's another story.) Most modern Americans recognize

CAVIAR, SMOKED SALMON, *and* GRAVLAX *with* BUCKWHEAT BLINI *and* SOUR CREAM

blini as those little rafts for sour cream and caviar that are passed around at cocktail parties. But most Russians are familiar with blini that are more like American pancakes and served dripping with butter. In the interest of authenticity, as well as with a nod to our contemporary health consciousness, I've adapted a traditional recipe to make the pancakes large but light, and I serve them with all the trimmings—the best assortment of smoked and cured fish that the budget will allow. Oh, yeah, and caviar—preferably Russian.

★ *CHEF'S TIPS* *These blini use a combination of buckwheat and unbleached all-purpose flour, rather than all buckwheat, which makes blini that are too chewy, bitter, and heavy. The yeast batter is lightened with egg whites and cooked in an 8-inch nonstick pan that needs only a little butter. | We make large, thin blini, and then serve them as individually plated first courses. You can make your blini batter a little thicker and make smaller versions, serving 2 or 3 people.*

Makes 4 appetizer servings

BLINI BATTER:
½ teaspoon active dry yeast
½ cup warm (105° to 110°F) whole milk
1 large egg
1 teaspoon sugar
½ teaspoon kosher salt
⅔ cup unbleached all-purpose flour
⅔ cup buckwheat flour
1 cup cold whole milk
¼ cup clarified butter (page 237)

4 slices sliced smoked sturgeon
4 slices sliced smoked salmon
4 slices sliced home-cured salmon gravlax
 (page 241)

Sour cream or crème fraîche
2 ounces salmon caviar
½ bunch chives, thinly sliced

Preparation

To make the blini batter: Sprinkle the yeast over the warm milk and stir to dissolve. Separate the egg and put the yolk in a large bowl. Cover and refrigerate the egg white. Add the sugar, salt, ⅓ cup of the all-purpose flour, and ⅓ cup of the buckwheat flour to the yolk and whisk to blend. Add the yeast mixture and whisk until smooth. Cover with plastic and let rise in a warm place until doubled in volume, 1½ to 2 hours. Add the cold milk and remaining ⅓ cup all-purpose flour and ⅓ cup buckwheat flour. Whisk until smooth. If the batter seems too stiff (it should be like a medium-thick pancake batter), add a little more milk. Cover and let rise again for about 30 minutes. Meanwhile, remove the egg white from the refrigerator.

To cook the blini: Just before serving, beat the egg white until stiff peaks form. Gently fold into the blini batter. Heat an 8-inch nonstick crepe pan over medium-high heat until a drop of water dances over the surface without evaporating instantly. Add 1 teaspoon clarified butter to the pan, heat for a few seconds, then ladle in a scant ¼ cup batter and tilt to cover the bottom of the pan. Cook until bubbles begin to appear on the surface and the edges start to look a little dry, about 1 minute. Gently lift the pancake with a spatula to see if the underside is lightly brown. Flip the pancake over and cook for about 1 minute longer on

continued

the other side. Transfer to a 250°F oven to keep warm while making the other blini. You should have 6 to 8 nice blini.

To serve, place 1 of the best-looking blini on each of 4 warmed plates. Arrange 1 slice of each fish in a triangle on each plate. Drizzle with any remaining clarified butter. Drop a dollop or two of sour cream or crème fraîche into the center of the blini and top with caviar and chives.

IMPROVISATIONS *Vary the kinds of fish: Use whatever you like, smoked or cured. Obviously, caviar is an expensive luxury. If you don't have buckwheat flour, which can sometimes be hard to get, use the cornmeal blini recipe on page 238. Bite-sized blini make wonderful cocktail hors d'oeuvres.*

ADVANCE PREP *The cured fish can be sliced the day before, then carefully wrapped in waxed paper and plastic until ready to serve. The blini batter needs to be made the day it's cooked, but the blini themselves can be made 1 day ahead, covered with plastic wrap and refrigerated. Reheat, uncovered, in a preheated 350°F oven for 5 minutes, or until warm.*

SIMPLIFYING *The simplest way to serve this dish is to present a large platter of smoked fish with a platter of freshly made blini wrapped in a napkin. Provide bowls of sour cream or crème fraîche, chives, and caviar, and let your guests make their own appetizers.*

WINE NOTES *Put a bottle of vodka in the freezer, then pour the viscous liquid directly into small chilled glasses. It's a unique start to dinner, but traditionally Russian. The popular alternative is Champagne, which is also very nice, but vodka really enhances the flavors and textures.*

CAVIAR

In *With Bold Knife and Fork*, M. F. K. Fisher writes in her inimitable way of her passion for salty fish eggs: "...I seem doomed to live without actual pain or deprivation, but with undying hope, from my last taste of caviar to the next one." Heady stuff, but for those of us for whom caviar is an obsession, her statement rings true. At Farallon, from the very beginning, I was determined to overindulge my customers in caviar.

BUYING CAVIAR

When buying caviar, and by that I mean the kind that comes from sturgeon, keep one thing in mind: Price equals quality, and unlike other consumer purchases, good deals don't exist. There are some very good values from producers in the United States, but always buy from a reputable source and, if you're purchasing a fairly large quantity (say more than 8 ounces), don't be afraid to ask for a small sample. Fresh is best, but the vacuum-packed and pasteurized caviar that comes in refrigerated small jars can be quite acceptable. The main thing to look for is a fresh sea smell, nothing fishy at all, with eggs that are shiny and separate and are all the same or similar color. Here are the different terms you need to become familiar with when purchasing caviar:

BELUGA: Arguably the most desirable of all the caviars, with the largest eggs from the largest of the sturgeon species. The eggs can actually be pea-sized. The color of beluga eggs ranges from black to pewter-gray, and its flavor should be somewhat mild and buttery tasting.

OSETRA: The second largest of the sturgeons, with eggs that range from golden yellow to brownish-black in color and have a nuttier taste—more like brown butter. The sticker price of osetra qualifies it as a better value than beluga, and many connoisseurs prefer its taste.

SEVRUGA: This is the smallest of the sturgeons, and is recognizable by its tiny eggs, usually no bigger than a pinhead. The eggs range in color from dark gray to black, and because these sturgeon are the most plentiful, the cost of sevruga is the lowest of the three.

MALOSSOL: This is not an egg, but a term used to describe caviar that has been lightly salted, thereby making it even more highly prized, for the fresher the roe, the less salt it needs. Any one of the three kinds of sturgeon caviar may be designated as malossol.

STORING CAVIAR

If you've already mortgaged the house on the caviar for your dinner party, you need to seriously consider how you're going to store this very perishable and precious product. If you've bought it from a reputable dealer, it should be packed in ice. Keep it for a maximum of 5 days, on ice, in the coldest part of your refrigerator. At Farallon, we have a little refrigerator that is specifically designed just for caviar storage. Ideally, fresh caviar should be kept at a temperature of between 29° to 32°F, but lacking a thermometer to accurately read your own refrigerator's temperature, the safest bet is to just eat your caviar as soon as possible. Problem solved.

SERVING CAVIAR

Purists insist that the finest caviar should be served without adornment, using a mother-of-pearl spoon to get it to your mouth. At the restaurant, we serve our caviar with brioche toast points and wedges of lemon.

My favorite variety of shrimp is the spot prawn, native to our coastal waters from Alaska to Southern California. They're real lookers—a pretty pink-orange color, with black and white markings—and almost as sweet as lobster. One of their most attractive features, however, is that you can often find them sold live, particularly in Asian markets. Here in San Francisco, many of the Hong Kong–style

SPOT PRAWN SASHIMI *with* SAFFRON–WHITE TRUFFLE VINAIGRETTE *and* PRAWN ROE

restaurants have them swimming live in tanks. George, my chef de cuisine, loves the sweet prawns (*amai ebi*) on Japanese menus that are served raw, with the heads fried and served as a crispy edible garnish, and he suggested to me that he wanted to do a similar dish at Farallon. Aware that I was reluctant to put any more Asian-inspired dishes on the menu, he cleverly paired the prawns with a white truffle vinaigrette (also knowing that I'm a sucker for anything truffled). It's become one of my favorite ways to serve these tasty little crustaceans.

★ CHEF'S TIPS *As with all raw shellfish, the prawns should be impeccably fresh. Frozen prawns are an acceptable but inferior substitute. The roe on the females is delicious, but not necessary for this recipe. | The heads are edible after they been fried. Discard any heads that have black spots on them before cooking, as this is a sign of deterioration. | Although the recipe for the vinaigrette makes more than you'll need for this dish, it lasts in the refrigerator for a few days and can be used on other dishes.*

Makes 4 appetizer servings

12 fresh or frozen large spot prawns
  (5 to 7 ounces each)
4-inch piece daikon radish, peeled

SAFFRON-TRUFFLE VINAIGRETTE:
Reserved prawn shells and juice, above
4 shallots, chopped
2-inch piece fresh ginger, chopped
6 fresh shiso leaves, chopped
1 cup sake
½ cup water
2 teaspoons saffron threads
½ cup grapeseed or canola oil
¼ cup white truffle oil
1 tablespoon fresh lemon juice
Kosher salt to taste

Grapeseed, canola, or olive oil for frying
4 fresh shiso leaves for garnish
Reserved prawn roe, above, for garnish
  (optional)

Preparation

To prepare the prawns: Twist the heads off the prawns and reserve. Over a small bowl, peel each prawn, leaving the tail on. Reserve the shells and liquid in the bowl. Separate the roe, if any, and reserve. With a small, sharp knife, make a shallow incision along the back of each prawn, remove the vein, and lightly flatten the prawn. Rinse the prawns in cold water, drain, and pat dry. Refrigerate the heads and meat until ready to use.

To make the daikon garnish: Using a Japanese mandoline fitted with the fine julienne blade, slice the daikon. (You could also use a potato peeler or cheese planer to peel off thin layers of the daikon, then finely julienne these.) Rinse the daikon under cold running water and put it in a bowl of ice water. Refrigerate for at least 10 minutes to allow the daikon to crisp and curl.

To make the vinaigrette: In a small saucepan, combine the reserved prawn shells and juice, shallots, and ginger. Cook over medium-low heat for 4 to 5 minutes, stirring, until the shallots are translucent. Add the shiso leaves and stir. Add the sake and water and bring to a boil. Reduce to a simmer, add the saffron, and cook to reduce by about two-thirds, about 10 minutes. You should have ⅓ cup liquid.

Strain through a fine-mesh sieve, pressing on the solids with the back of a large spoon. Set the liquid aside to cool. Pour the cooled liquid into a blender. With the machine running, gradually add the grapeseed or canola oil, then the truffle oil. Add the lemon juice and salt. Set aside.

To fry the heads: Fill a large, heavy saucepan one-third full of oil and heat to 375°F. Fry the heads, in small batches, for about 5 minutes, or until lightly browned and crisp. Using a slotted spoon, transfer to paper towels to drain.

To serve, place a small mound of the daikon threads at the top of each plate. Lean a shiso leaf on one side and a fried head on the other. Spoon a large half-moon of vinaigrette at the bottom of the plate. Lean the spot prawns against the daikon, tails up and bodies splayed out in the vinaigrette. Scatter the roe, if using, over the bottom half of the plate.

IMPROVISATIONS *This vinaigrette can be used on all sorts of raw fish dishes. Even a prawn cocktail would be great with this dressing. If you want, you could make a Japanese-style salad using pea shoots dressed in a little lemon vinaigrette instead of the daikon, or a cucumber salad like the one on page 111. Flying fish roe (tobiko) is available in jars in many grocery stores and can be used, after a rinse, in place of the prawn roe. A little osetra caviar would look and taste beautiful in this dish.*

ADVANCE PREP *The vinaigrette can be made a day or two ahead and whisked to re–emulsify just before serving. The daikon can be julienned earlier in the day and refrigerated in its bowl of water.*

SIMPLIFYING *This unique dish would suffer from further simplification; however, the prawn heads could be eliminated.*

WINE NOTES *Many white wines would be appropriate here, but keep in mind the mild flavor of prawns. Champagne is a natural choice. Light and crisp, delicate and flavorful, it usually has a yeasty, nutty character that matches nicely with truffle oil. Leeuwin Estate Riesling from the Margaret River in western Australia would also be a good choice. Other excellent options would be a good bottle of Muscadet de Sèvre-et-Maine; a lighter bodied, unoaked white Bordeaux; or a Vouvray Sec.*

I recently read an article in a national trend-spotting magazine that declared ceviche was enjoying a renaissance in the stylish restaurants of a large city on the East Coast (hint: it's on an island). "Renaissance?" I enjoyed a chauvinistic chuckle, because here on the West Coast, where Latin American immigrants have been influencing the cuisine for centuries, ceviche was adopted long ago and has never gone

MAINE-DIVER SCALLOP CEVICHE *with* GREEN PEPPERCORNS, GRAPEFRUIT, *and* CHILI VINAIGRETTE

out of style. Ceviche (also spelled *seviche*) is a South and Central American preparation in which raw seafood is marinated in citrus juice, usually lime, then mixed with anything from chilies, herbs, and vegetables to onions, garlic, tomatoes, corn, and avocados. The marinating process tenderizes the proteins and turns them opaque, giving the finished dish a "cooked" appearance and texture. As in most rustic dishes with regional cultural influences, there are as many variations as there are cooks. Although the operative word in ceviche is *raw*, you'll sometimes find a ceviche that includes cooked or partially cooked seafood, such as lobster, crab, octopus, or squid. A close cousin of ceviche is escabeche, originally a Spanish dish, in which the seafood is heated in a pickling liquid. George's Sake-Pickled Salmon (page 46) is an Asian-inspired version of that dish.

★ CHEF'S TIP *I can't emphasize enough that for this dish and any other that employs raw seafood, your ingredients must be impeccably fresh. (See page 221 on buying and storing fish and shellfish.)*

Makes 4 appetizer servings

CHILI VINAIGRETTE:

2 tablespoons green peppercorns, drained, rinsed, and minced

2 tablespoons fresh grapefruit juice

1 tablespoon fresh lime juice

2 tablespoons fresh orange juice

¼ cup extra-virgin olive oil

½ small red bell pepper, seeded, deribbed, and cut into 1/16-inch dice

1 tablespoon minced jalapeno chili

2 teaspoons kosher salt

Freshly ground pepper to taste

8 ounces very fresh diver-harvested "dry-packed" scallops, rinsed and patted dry

2 bunches arugula, stemmed

2 pink grapefruits, peeled and sectioned (see page 236)

Kosher salt and freshly ground pepper to taste

Preparation

To make the vinaigrette: Whisk together all the ingredients and set aside, or refrigerate for up to 1 day.

To prepare the ceviche: Slice the scallops horizontally into 2 or 3 rounds, depending on their thickness, and put them in a medium bowl. Right before serving, toss the scallops with the vinaigrette. Set aside while you prepare the plates. If you like a more "cooked" seafood, marinate the scallops for up to 1 hour before serving.

To serve, fan the scallops equally at the bottom of 4 plates. Toss the arugula with the grapefruit segments, salt, and pepper. Place a small mound of salad in the middle of each plate. Drizzle the remaining dressing around and over the grapefruit.

IMPROVISATIONS *Ceviche can be made with many different kinds of fish—I especially like moderately lean and flavorful varieties like tuna and hamachi, or lean and mild ones, like tilefish, red snapper, and halibut. You can substitute any citrus segments for the grapefruit; orange, tangelo, or tangerine will work best because of their size. If you're doubling the recipe for the vinaigrette, try using 1 red and 1 green jalapeno for added color.*

ADVANCE PREP *The vinaigrette can be made and the grapefruit segments prepared 1 day ahead. Make sure you don't add the scallops to the vinaigrette too soon; more than 1 hour and they might "overcook."*

WINE NOTES *This is another appetizer that's great with a glass of bubbly wine. Taittinger Brut la Française is a beautiful example; it's elegant, yet fruity enough for the sauce. Many of these raw starters present the opportunity to try a bottle of sake. There are many styles and producers (some even vintage dated!) on the market now, all worth trying out with dishes like this one.*

Pick up a menu in any trendy restaurant today, and you most likely will come across tuna tartare. Tartares, and fish tartares in particular, have become almost ubiquitous, and that's unfortunate because they can be too much of a good thing. What next—tuna tartare pita pockets? But seriously, a tartare, properly prepared with unquestionably fresh ingredients, is a wonderful culinary example of less being more. I've been making tartares for most of my career, beginning in the late seventies at the Santa Fe

OYSTER and WILD SALMON TARTARE with ROASTED BEETS and CRISP GIANT CAPERS

Bar & Grill in Berkeley, California. Jeremiah Tower, in one of his many moments of culinary inspiration, came up with the idea of finely chopping raw salmon, tossing it with sesame oil, and serving it like an old favorite, steak tartare. At the Santa Fe, we served his salmon tartare, as well as one made with beef and ancho chili mayonnaise, which became one of our most popular appetizers. In the eighties at Stars, we always had some kind of tartare on the menu, but when we opened Farallon, I was reluctant to serve it because it had become so overdone. That is, until I came up with this variation: wild salmon paired with oysters in a combination that is so pristine it almost sparkles.

★ *CHEF'S TIPS* *The secret to a great tartare or, for that matter, any raw-fish preparation, is in the quality of the ingredients. Don't even think of using fish that is less than the freshest you can find—especially the oysters. Ask for a small, briny variety like Kumamotos, and watch out for anything too creamy or big. | Wild salmon has a clean, lean sea flavor that is enhanced by the equally clean taste of oysters. If you can't get wild salmon for this tartare, don't worry; farmed salmon is a fine substitute, although it tends to have a slightly more slippery, greasy feel in the mouth because of its higher fat content, and it can be difficult to cut. Emphasize fresh and firm to your fish guy.*

Makes 4 appetizer servings

8 ounces red beets, greens trimmed
   to 1-inch lengths
1 teaspoon olive oil
2 tablespoons water
3 sprigs thyme
Kosher salt and freshly ground pepper
   to taste
1 tablespoon fresh lemon juice

LEMON VINAIGRETTE:
1 tablespoon fresh lemon juice
3 tablespoons extra-virgin olive oil
Kosher salt and freshly ground pepper
   to taste

CRISP GIANT CAPERS:
½ cup caperberries or capote capers,
   drained
Olive oil for frying

8 ounces wild or farmed salmon fillet,
   skin and pin bones removed
8 oysters, shucked
Kosher salt and freshly ground pepper
   to taste
1 teaspoon extra-virgin olive oil

Preparation

To roast the beets: Preheat the oven to 400°F. Put the beets in a small, shallow baking dish and rub with the olive oil. Add the water and thyme and sprinkle with salt and pepper. Cover the dish with aluminum foil and roast for about 45 minutes, or until the beets are tender when pierced with a small knife. Uncover and let cool until still slightly warm. Peel the beets, removing the tops and tails as you go. Cut the beets into ¼-inch dice and toss in a small bowl with the lemon juice and a little more salt and pepper. Cover and set aside, or refrigerate for up to 1 day.

To make the lemon vinaigrette: In a small bowl, whisk the lemon juice together with the olive oil. Season with salt and pepper. Set aside, or refrigerate for up to 1 day.

To fry the caperberries or capers: Using a small knife, cut the caperberries lengthwise in quarters, but not all the way through to the stem. If you're using the smaller capote capers, you don't need to cut them, just drain, pat dry, and fry them whole. In a small skillet, heat about ½ inch olive oil over high heat until it shimmers. Add the caperberries and fry until they are crisp, the edges turn golden brown, and the "petals" open, about 3 minutes (less for capote capers). Using a slotted spoon, transfer to paper towels to drain for up to 8 hours. The leftover oil can be cooled, strained, and saved for another use.

To make the tartare: Not more than 1 hour before serving, finely dice the salmon and oysters (⅛- to ¼-inch dice) and mix together in a small bowl with 2 tablespoons lemon vinaigrette. Check for seasoning and add salt and pepper to taste. Cover and refrigerate until serving.

To serve, toss the beets with the extra-virgin olive oil. Place a 2½- or 3-inch ring mold in the middle of a dinner plate. Place one-fourth of the beets in the mold. Top with one-fourth of the tartare. With a spoon, pat the tartare down lightly to compact it, then carefully remove the ring mold. Rinse the mold to prevent the beets from staining the tartare and repeat with the other plates. If not using a ring mold, spoon the beets onto the plates in small mounds, then lightly pat the tartare into patties and place on top of the beets. Drizzle the remaining lemon vinaigrette around the tartare and beets, and strew the fried caperberries or capers around the plate.

IMPROVISATIONS As long as your ingredients are extremely fresh, you can make a tartare from almost any kind of fish or even meat, except of course chicken or pork. It's a perfect medium for improvisation. Sashimi-grade tuna would work, of course. Caviar folded into a fish tartare is incredible too, but be judicious when adding any additional salt to the dish.

ADVANCE PREP The beets can be cooked, peeled, and tossed with the lemon juice, covered, and refrigerated up to 1 day ahead. They can then be warmed slightly and tossed with the olive oil before serving. The caperberries or capers can be fried 8 hours ahead and left on the paper towels, uncovered, at room temperature until ready to use. The vinaigrette can be made 1 day ahead and refrigerated.

SIMPLIFYING Let's say you just hooked a salmon. Then you picked up some fresh oysters on the way home. I would do nothing more than dice the seafood, whisk up some vinaigrette, mix them together, and put a mound of the tartare on a thinly sliced bed of cucumbers or alongside a frisée salad tossed with a little of the vinaigrette. That's it. And if you're not okay with oysters, omit them, concentrating on really fresh fish.

WINE NOTES Choose a wine with racy acidity, lighter-bodied but concentrated, like the current crop of Sauvignon Blanc whites from the Loire Valley in France. The ripe citrus and green berry–melon flavors found in Sancerre or Pouilly-Fumé can refresh the palate, and the natural acid in the wine is a nice foil for the salty capers and lemony vinaigrette.

ONAGA CARPACCIO *with* CUCUMBER CONSOMMÉ, SALMON CAVIAR, *and* ENOKI MUSHROOMS

Consider this (literally) cool first course for the next dinner party when you want something easily executed but stunning. It's pretty, pale, and refreshingly light. Onaga is a gorgeous, highly prized red snapper caught in the tropical reefs off Hawaii. In this presentation, which we do frequently with other fish as well, thin alabaster medallions of fish are placed close together on sheets of plastic wrap and pounded out into a circle that resembles a crepe. They're served in the bottom of shallow soup bowls, ladled with a few intensely flavorful spoonfuls of pale green cucumber "consommé," and garnished with bright dollops of orange caviar.

★ *CHEF'S TIPS The cucumber "consommé" is really more like a cucumber water, but that description doesn't do it justice because it's an intensely flavorful preparation that's just the essence of the vegetable. Note that it must be made at least 2 hours in advance of serving. | This makes a great dish for serving to a crowd.*

Makes 4 appetizer servings

CUCUMBER CONSOMMÉ:
1 European (hothouse) cucumber (about
    12 ounces), peeled, seeded, and
    coarsely chopped
1 tablespoon kosher salt, plus salt to taste
1 tablespoon fresh lime juice or
    rice wine vinegar

8 ounces onaga (Hawaiian red snapper)
Enoki mushrooms and salmon caviar
    for garnish

Preparation

To make the consommé: Sprinkle the cucumber with the 1 tablespoon salt. Let sit for 5 to 10 minutes. Put in a blender and puree until very smooth. Pour into a fine-mesh sieve lined with damp cheesecloth and sitting snugly over a bowl. Refrigerate for 2 to 4 hours to let the juice drain. Discard the solids and reserve the cucumber water. Season with the lime juice or vinegar, and salt to taste.

To prepare the carpaccio: Using a very sharp knife, evenly slice the fish into ¼-inch-thick pieces. Lay out 4 pieces of plastic wrap, each a little larger than the dish or bowl you plan to serve the carpaccio in. Spray the plastic with a vegetable-oil cooking spray or coat with a few drops of oil. Place one-fourth of the slices on the first piece, in a rough circle, with the edges just touching. Lay another piece of plastic wrap over the top. With the flat back of a small sauté pan or with a mallet, gently pound the fish until it begins to spread and all the edges meet, without making any holes. Pound until very thin, but still within the edges of the plastic wrap.

To serve, chill 4 rimmed plates or shallow soup bowls. Take a sheet of carpaccio and remove the top piece of plastic. Turn the dish upside down over the layer of fish and, keeping both together, flip right-side up. Press the carpaccio into the bottom of the bowl and remove the second piece of plastic. Ladle ⅓ cup of the cucumber consommé into each bowl. Garnish by floating a few enoki mushrooms and a little salmon caviar on the surface.

IMPROVISATIONS *You could replace the onaga with any sashimi-quality tuna, particularly yellowtail hamachi, or even grouper. Ask your fishmonger what is freshest. Some finely sliced chives or very thinly sliced shiso leaves would look beautiful as an alternate garnish.*

ADVANCE PREP *The fish can be pounded out, wrapped with plastic, and stored in the refrigerator for up to 24 hours. The cucumber water should be used as soon as it has been extracted.*

SIMPLIFYING *This dish is already simplicity itself.*

WINE NOTES *Champagne or sparkling wine is the perfect match with this delicate appetizer. A light-bodied Sauvignon Blanc or Kabinett-level German Riesling is also a good match; you don't want anything too heavy. For something a little more exotic, track down a bottle of Lusco Albariño from Spain; it's light and floral, zesty, and slightly herb-scented, with not a trace of oak.*

One of the best parts of writing this book was that it gave me the opportunity to play around with some new ideas for dishes that I'd been thinking about for some time. I initially conceived this dish as a bass tartare sandwiched between crispy pieces of bass skin, then drizzled with a light vinaigrette. Well, it sounded like a good idea, but the bass skin never developed the brittle texture I envisioned (in fact,

BLACK BASS *and* SEA URCHIN TARTARE *in a* CRISP NORI SANDWICH *with* SHISO DRESSING

it was downright chewy), so we used toasted nori (dried seaweed) sheets instead and came up with a real winner. This is a perfect warm-weather first course: light, pretty, and easy. It's also a great hors d'oeuvre when made bite-sized.

★ *CHEF'S TIPS Fresh sea urchins are sold in boxes of 10 roes (see the Glossary, page 229). One option for this recipe uses the whole box. We sometimes use frozen uni for our vinaigrettes, but you must use fresh sea urchins for garnish. Look for a good caramel color, with well-formed roes and no melting or gray tinges. | Soybeans, or edamame, have become widely available in our supermarkets, I think because they're one of the tastiest beer snacks around. They're sold in the produce section, and all you need to do is pop the beans out of their pods and gulp them down. | Yuzu is a variety of citrus found in Japan. The zest and juice are used almost exclusively to perfume dishes with their highly floral aroma. Yuzu is difficult to find fresh, but you can buy bottles of the milky juice in Japanese supermarkets. An opened bottle will keep, tightly closed and refrigerated, for up to 1 year. | Pea shoots, as the name implies, are the tender stalks of the flowering pea plant. They have a light pea flavor and hold up well when tossed with vinaigrettes. They are commonly found in Asian markets.*

Makes 4 appetizer servings

SHISO VINAIGRETTE:
4 fresh shiso or cilantro leaves, chopped
⅓ teaspoon minced peeled fresh ginger
2 teaspoons yuzu juice or fresh
    lemon juice
⅓ cup grapeseed or canola oil
¼ teaspoon Asian sesame oil
Pinch of kosher salt

TARTARE:
1 tablespoon fresh lime juice
⅓ cup grapeseed or canola oil
Pinch of kosher salt
Freshly ground pepper to taste
8 ounces black bass fillets,
    cut into ¼-inch cubes
2 sea urchin roes, chopped

2 to 3 nori sheets

OPTIONAL GARNISHES:
½ cup pea shoots
8 sea urchin roes
12 to 16 edamame

Preparation

To make the vinaigrette: Combine all of the ingredients and blend, using a handheld mixer. Or, crush the leaves and ginger in a mortar, then whisk with the remaining ingredients. Cover and refrigerate for up to 1 day.

To make the tartare: In a small bowl, whisk the lime juice, oil, salt, and pepper together until combined. Add the black bass and sea urchin roe. Toss lightly and let sit for no more than 10 minutes.

To prepare the nori: Turn a gas flame on medium or preheat a broiler. Using tongs, toast the nori on one side by briefly waving it over the flame or holding it under the broiler just until it begins to shrivel and color a little. Remove from heat and cut into eight 4-inch squares.

To serve, mound a little of the marinated bass mixture on each plate and place a square of nori on top. Place a few pea shoots, if using, on top, then spoon a little more of the bass on top of that and set another square at a slightly different angle than the first. Cross 2 sea urchin roes, if using, on top of the stack. Drizzle the vinaigrette around each stack and place 3 or 4 edamame, if using, around the edge of each serving.

IMPROVISATIONS *You could replace the black bass with any very fresh, firm fish like yellowtail tuna, salmon, or Chilean sea bass.*

ADVANCE PREP *The vinaigrette can be made 1 day ahead. Make the tartare and assemble the dish just before serving.*

SIMPLIFYING *The tartare would make a nice addition to Iced Atlantic and Pacific Shellfish Indulgence (page 25). Serve simply in a scallop shell, or on a fried wonton as a passed hors d'oeuvre.*

WINE NOTES *This dish is one more opportunity to drink and enjoy Riesling. The subtle, sweet, briny bass and sea urchins, along with the floral shiso, point to a lighter-style Riesling. Also, try a Weissburgunder Pinot Blanc from Austria. Rudi Pichler and Heidi Schrock are both good names to look for.*

Salads and Such

The "such" here refers to the cold appetizers on our menu. As always, my approach to appetizers or first courses is that they should open the palate door but not close it: You want to tease and excite your taste buds, not overwhelm them. The recipes in this chapter run the gamut from easy to hard and light to rich, and three of them, the Maine Lobster Cobb Salad, Grilled Nantucket Scallops, and Summer Tomato Salad with Crisp Jumbo Shrimp, are fairly substantial dishes that can be served as luncheon or light dinner entrees. What the rest of the dishes in this chapter have in common, however, is that they can all be prepared either partially or entirely ahead of time, making them perfect for entertaining. The Warm Goat Cheese Galettes on Red Oakleaf and Belgian Endive Salad and the Grilled Nantucket Scallops with Apple and Endive Salad may be prepped ahead of time, though they require some last-minute cooking. One of the most versatile dishes, and I must confess probably my favorite, is George's Sake-Pickled Salmon. It's simply put together ahead of time, and can be served in tiny portions as cocktail food, or increased to serve a large number of people. On the other end of the scale is the Squab Breast Terrine. This dish, though not difficult, is time-consuming to prepare. The advantage is it must be made ahead and can serve 12 to 16 people.

While Farallon's menu invariably includes a riff on the ubiquitous mixed green salad, "Salads and Such" also always has some kind of seasonal salad or vegetable presentation. Included here are two of our most popular cold salads: Fuyu Persimmons and Autumn Greens with Candied Walnuts and Pomegranate Seeds, which makes a perfect beginning to a Thanksgiving menu, and Spring Asparagus and Wild Morel Salad with Borage Flowers, a simple and elegant way to show off spring's bounty. Both of these salads are also great served on platters for a large buffet.

George Francisco is Farallon's extremely talented chef de cuisine, and he's been with me since the restaurant opened. Before that, he was executive chef at the Miyako Hotel in San Francisco's Japantown, and going back a little further, we worked together at Stars. Through George, I've learned a great deal

GEORGE'S SAKE-PICKLED SALMON *with* WASABI CRÈME FRAÎCHE *and* HERB SALAD

about the complexities as well as the subtleties of Asian flavors, and this dish is only one of many on the Farallon menu that reflect his refined and restrained style of cooking. It's like an Asian escabeche in that the salmon is partially cooked in the hot pickling solution. This is one of the easiest recipes in this entire book and also one of the most popular appetizers on the menu at Farallon. Your guests will love it, and you won't believe how simple it is. It's also really versatile. My coauthor, Lisa Weiss, even served it with matzo as a first course at her Passover seder. To rave reviews, I might add.

★ *CHEF'S TIPS You can serve this pretty dish a number of ways: in a Martini glass as pictured or in a scallop shell on top of a bed of rock salt. The lobster seaweed used here can be found at your local fishmonger, or wherever fresh lobster can be purchased. | This recipe can be increased, but be careful with the pickling spices. You can double the quantity of salmon and the liquid without increasing the spices. | Be sure to use red onion here; it turns a beautiful, shocking pink in the pickling liquid. | To remove the pin bones (horizontal bones that are often not removed when a roundfish is filleted): Run your finger along the surface of the flesh to find any bones. Pull them out with tweezers or needlenose pliers.*

Makes 4 appetizer servings

SAKE-PICKLED SALMON:
1 tablespoon pickling spices
1 tablespoon Szechwan peppercorns
4 star anise pods
2 tablespoons minced fresh ginger
1 cup rice vinegar
½ cup sake
¼ cup sugar
1½ tablespoons kosher salt

½ cup thinly sliced red onion
12 ounces salmon fillets, skin and pin bones removed, cut into 1-inch cubes

WASABI CRÈME FRAÎCHE:
½ cup crème fraîche or sour cream
1 tablespoon wasabi powder
¼ teaspoon kosher salt

HERB SALAD:
Leaves from ½ bunch flat-leaf (Italian) parsley
Leaves from ½ bunch tarragon
½ bunch fresh chervil, stemmed
1 bunch fresh chives, cut into 1-inch lengths

Scallop shells and rock salt for serving (optional)
Seaweed for garnish (optional)

continued

To make the pickled salmon: Tie the pickling spices, peppercorns, star anise, and ginger into a cheesecloth square. Put the spice sachet in a medium saucepan and add the rice vinegar, sake, sugar, and salt. Bring the liquid to a boil. Add the onion, reduce heat, and simmer for 5 minutes. Remove and discard the sachet.

Put the salmon cubes in a small bowl. Pour the pickling liquid and onions over the salmon, making sure that it is covered by the liquid. If not, use a smaller bowl or add a little water to cover. Cover with plastic wrap and refrigerate for at least 2 hours or up to 10 hours. Stir gently once or twice to make sure that the fish is evenly covered with the liquid.

To make the crème fraîche: Stir all the ingredients together in a small bowl. Set aside, or cover and refrigerate for up to 2 days.

To make the salad: Toss all the herbs together in a small bowl. Refrigerate until ready to serve.

To serve, remove the salmon from its pickling liquid with a slotted spoon and drain on a kitchen towel. Place equal portions of salmon in each of 4 martini glasses, or alternatively, into scallop shells that are nestled into a bed of rock salt. Top with a dollop of the wasabi crème fraîche, then with some of the herb salad. Drape with a little seaweed, if using.

IMPROVISATIONS *Fish with a firm texture and a moderate-to-high fat content are best for pickling. Try this recipe with mackerel, cod, herring, or tuna. Sour cream easily replaces crème fraîche, and any combination of herbs may be used in the salad. Arugula would also be fine.*

ADVANCE PREP *This dish can be made as little as 2 hours in advance, but the fish really benefits from marinating in the pickling solution for at least 4 hours and can be made up to 10 hours ahead. The wasabi crème fraîche can be made 2 days ahead. The salad is best tossed just before serving.*

SIMPLIFYING *Eliminate the salad and the wasabi cream. Cut the fish into smaller cubes and serve it with flat bread or crackers as an hors d'oeuvre.*

WINE NOTES *The acidic pickling spices in this appetizer call for a wine that is also high in acid and fruit, even slightly off-dry. The richness of the salmon, however, suggests a rich wine as well. A classic dry or demi-sec Vouvray, like the 1996 Le Mont from Gaston Huet in France's Loire Valley, would be a lovely match. Or try a German Riesling, such as 1996 Spätlese Altenhoten from Ayler Kupp. Avoid wines that are too oaky or austere.*

SALAD *of* FUYU PERSIMMONS *and* AUTUMN GREENS *with* CANDIED WALNUTS, POMEGRANATE SEEDS, *and* SHERRY VINAIGRETTE

If you're looking for a salad to serve at a special fall dinner party, don't turn this page. As a matter of fact, this simple and beautiful salad would make a perfect beginning to a Thanksgiving meal. It has the tangy sweetness of persimmons, the crunch of candied walnuts, and the pop of pomegranate seeds. Not only is it beautiful, it's also easy, particularly if you've done the candied walnuts ahead of time. Watch out, though—the walnuts are addicting.

★ *CHEF'S TIP When pomegranates are in season, in the fall and winter, separate the seeds, pack them in an airtight container, freeze, and then use them within 3 months. You can sprinkle them over salads without defrosting. They'll lose a bit of their color and crispness in the freezer, but they will still be beautiful and flavorful.*

Makes 4 appetizer servings

CANDIED WALNUTS:

½ cup walnuts

3 tablespoons water

3 tablespoons sugar

¼ teaspoon ground allspice

Pinch of cayenne pepper

Kosher salt and freshly ground pepper
to taste

VINAIGRETTE:

1 tablespoon sherry vinegar

5 tablespoons walnut oil

1 teaspoon kosher salt

Freshly ground pepper to taste

1 teaspoon minced fresh thyme

2 firm Fuyu persimmons, cut into paper-
thin crosswise slices

6 cups mixed salad greens

Pomegranate seeds for garnish

Preparation

To make the candied walnuts: In a small sauté pan or skillet, combine all the ingredients. Bring to a boil and cook, occasionally swirling the pan, until the sugar dissolves, about 4 minutes. Continue to boil until the water has almost evaporated and the sugar thickens into a syrup and begins to turn golden. Immediately turn the mixture out onto a lightly oiled plate. Let cool and harden, then break the nuts into pieces. Set aside, or store in an airtight container for up to 1 week.

To serve, whisk all the vinaigrette ingredients together in a small bowl. On each of 4 salad plates, arrange a layer of slightly overlapping sliced persimmons. Toss the greens with the vinaigrette and place a small mound on top of the persimmons. Garnish with the broken pieces of candied walnuts and the pomegranate seeds.

IMPROVISATIONS *Pears and apples can be used in place of the persimmons. Instead of walnuts, try pecans or almonds.*

SIMPLIFYING *Cut the persimmons into wedges, toss them with the greens in a big bowl, and sprinkle with the pomegranate seeds and nuts. You could also use plain toasted walnuts or, just before serving, stir the walnuts in a pan with the allspice, salt, sugar, and a little butter until the sugar has melted and coated the nuts with the spices.*

WINE NOTES *The flavors in this salad are bright, fresh, and sweet, but balanced nicely by the sherry vinaigrette and bitter greens. Consider pairing this with an Alsace Riesling or Pinot Blanc: something dry and crisp, but fruity.*

As an executive chef, one of my bigger challenges lies not in managing food costs or dealing with the minutiae of running an efficient kitchen. It's in keeping the creative juices flowing. Returning customers are comforted to find their favorite dishes on the menu but also like to see new items as well. The people who become bored with our menu most quickly, however, are the same people who

WARM GOAT CHEESE GALETTES *on* RED OAKLEAF *and* BELGIAN ENDIVE SALAD *with* LAVENDER VINAIGRETTE

have to produce it. Night after night, our chefs and cooks are expected to produce a consistent product to serve to our guests, but like all innovative people, they need creative stimulation. This recipe is a simple example of how we like to tweak our dishes to keep them new. At one of our weekly chefs' meetings, we were trying to find an alternative to our ubiquitous but very popular warm crusted–goat cheese and mesclun salad. It was our pastry chef, Don Hall, who came up with this idea of baking a puff pastry shell stuffed with goat cheese and serving it on top of the greens. Someone else suggested the lavender vinaigrette, because lavender is a wonderful match with goat cheese. The dish turned out to be a winner: easy to prepare, elegant, and a nice twist on what's become a common salad.

★ CHEF'S TIP *I like to use a combination of goat cheeses, like Cypress Grove's chèvre and Bermuda Triangle Blue, mixed together, but you should feel free to use all one kind or any combination of soft goat and blue cheeses that you like.*

Makes 6 appetizer servings

1 sheet thawed frozen puff pastry
1 egg, whisked with 1 tablespoon water

LAVENDER VINAIGRETTE:
2 tablespoons Champagne vinegar
⅓ cup extra-virgin olive oil
Pinch of sugar
1 tablespoon dried lavender, ground in a spice grinder or mortar
Kosher salt and freshly ground pepper to taste

SALAD:
1 head long (Treviso) radicchio or round (Verona) radicchio, torn into bite-sized pieces
1 large or 2 small heads Belgian endive (about 6 ounces)
Leaves from 2 heads red oakleaf or common red lettuce, torn into bite-sized pieces

6 ounces goat cheese
Fresh chives, cut into ½-inch pieces, for garnish
Fresh lavender flowers, rinsed, or dried lavender, for garnish (optional)

Preparation

To start the galettes: Preheat the oven to 375°F. On a lightly floured surface, roll the puff pastry dough into a 12-inch square about ⅛ inch thick. Using a 4-inch round cutter, cut out six 4-inch rounds. Prick the rounds all over with a fork. Fold in ½ inch of the edges of each round, pleating as you go. Brush the rounds with the egg wash and place on a parchment paper–lined baking sheet. Bake the pastries until puffed and just barely golden, about 20 minutes. Remove from the oven and let sit for several minutes. Push down the center of the pastries to make an indentation large enough to put the cheese into later. The pastries can be prepared to this point, cooled, then stored in an airtight container for up to 1 day.

To make the vinaigrette: In a small bowl, whisk all the ingredients together.

To prepare the salad: Cut the radicchio and Belgian endive in half lengthwise and core them. Cut into ¼-inch shreds and put in a medium bowl. Add the lettuce. Cover with a damp towel until ready to serve.

continued

To finish and bake the galettes: Preheat the oven to 375°F. Crumble the goat cheese and sprinkle an equal amount into each galette. Bake the galettes until they are warmed through and the cheese has begun to soften, 5 to 7 minutes. Meanwhile, toss the endive, radicchio, and lettuce with a little of the vinaigrette. On each of 6 plates, place a mound of salad. Fluff the mixture up to create a little height and place a warm galette on top. It will sink down into the middle, leaving a circle of greens around it. Drizzle a little of the lavender vinaigrette on the galettes and around the salad. Garnish with the chives and optional lavender.

IMPROVISATIONS *This salad was created in the spirit of improvisation, and I encourage you to add to or change it to suit your own tastes. Try some different kinds of blue cheeses: a good Roquefort or Gorgonzola mixed with a little cream cheese, perhaps. You could add some cooked and chopped bacon or pancetta to the cheese mixture. Consider using herbes de Provence instead of lavender, or any fresh herb.*

ADVANCE PREP *The pastry for the galettes can be made and cooked 1 day ahead and filled with cheese just before serving, but the pastry will not be quite as flaky and nice the second day. The lavender vinaigrette is still delicious the next day—but watch for any browning of the lavender; if it does discolor, strain it and whisk in fresh lavender.*

SIMPLIFYING *Instead of making the galettes, cut ¾-inch-thick rounds from a log of goat cheese and coat them with chopped nuts, sesame seeds, or panko bread crumbs. Put them on a baking sheet and bake in a preheated 350°F oven until warmed through but still holding their shape, about 5 minutes. Serve on top of the greens.*

WINE NOTES *Goat cheese and Sauvignon Blanc are a terrific pairing. The regions of Sancerre and Pouilly-Fumé in the Loire Valley produce wines made from this grape that are unabashedly citric, herbaceous, and sometimes minerally. Californian versions tend more towards figs and melon. New Zealand and South Africa both produce styles like those of the Loire. The Casa Blanca Valley in Chile has a variety that has purity of fruit, bright acid, and lovely floral-herbal aromas and flavors.*

Nothing heralds the arrival of spring more than asparagus—except maybe fresh morel mushrooms. At least twice a week for the last seven years, Connie Green, "the mushroom lady," has made the 1½-hour journey to San Francisco from her home in the Napa Valley to deliver freshly foraged wild mushrooms. From California to Alaska, her foragers roam by day and by night, combing through forests and orchards, gravel and ash, searching for elusive wild fungi: chanterelles, porcini, black trumpets, and morels. In early April, all of us in the Farallon kitchen eagerly look forward to Connie's arrival with the first morels of the season. We put them in scallop risottos and lobster gratins, stuff large ones with seafood mousse, and pair them in salads with another springtime favorite, asparagus. The combination here

SPRING ASPARAGUS *and* WILD MOREL SALAD *with* BORAGE FLOWERS

of grassy asparagus with the earthy and nutty morel is a taste match that's unsurpassed. The flavor of each ingredient is enhanced and heightened by the other. This dish makes an elegant first course for a formal spring dinner or can be served on a large platter for a casual buffet.

★ CHEF'S TIPS *For my taste, fat asparagus spears taste better, and it's also easier to control their cooking—there's nothing worse than mushy, overcooked asparagus. Look for plump stalks at least ½ inch and preferably 1 inch in diameter, with tightly closed buds, a sign of freshness. If you're lucky enough to find them, white or purple asparagus are an exceptional treat. | Most cookbooks recommend that you snap off the woody asparagus ends, which will naturally break at the perfect spot. This is a good tip, but it doesn't work with fat asparagus. The fat spears tend to break closer to the precious tips. Instead, cut the asparagus at the point where the green fades to white. | Cleaning fresh morels can be a pain. Some are really clean, others are so gritty as to be inedible, while still others can be wormy; it depends on any number of variables, like the season, where they come from, and the forager. Forget what you've heard about not washing mushrooms; there's nothing worse than ruining a beautiful and expensive dish with gritty morels. Fill a large bowl with enough cold water that the morels can float. Add the morels and soak for 10 minutes. Lift the mushrooms from the water, discarding the dirt and grit at the bottom of the bowl. Spin in a salad washer, to get out the excess water. You may need to repeat the procedure for particularly dirty ones, but only for a few minutes the second time. You can also, as added insurance, spray water into the morel caps with a faucet hose. Squeeze gently and lay the drained morels out on kitchen towels; refrigerate, uncovered, until ready to use, up to 1 day ahead. | Borage flowers, in season from spring into summer, are used here mainly as a garnish. The pretty little star-shaped flowers of the borage plant have little taste; the leaves taste faintly of cucumbers, but they're unpleasantly prickly. Pick off the brown petals under the blue petals, as they give a bitter taste.*

Makes 4 appetizer servings

1 pound large asparagus spears,
  tough white ends cut off
2 tablespoons olive oil
12 ounces fresh morels, cleaned
  (see Chef's Tips)
1 teaspoon minced fresh thyme
1 tablespoon Madeira, dry sherry,
  or chicken stock
Kosher salt and freshly ground pepper
  to taste

MOREL VINAIGRETTE:
Half of sautéed morels, above
⅓ cup grapeseed, canola, or olive oil
2 tablespoons sherry vinegar
1 tablespoon fresh lemon juice
Kosher salt and freshly ground pepper
  to taste
⅓ cup hazelnut oil

2 tablespoons lemon-infused olive oil
  (page 242) or extra-virgin olive oil
  for tossing
Borage flowers or other edible flowers,
  like chive blossoms or nasturtiums,
  for garnish

continued

To cook the asparagus: Peel the bottom half of the asparagus. Fill a large sauté pan or skillet two-thirds full with lightly salted water and bring to a rolling boil. Drop the asparagus spears into the water and cook until tender, 4 to 8 minutes, depending on the thickness of the spears. Check for doneness by piercing the spears with a small knife. Drain the spears and drop into a bowl of ice water to stop the cooking. Remove after 3 minutes and pat dry on kitchen towels. Set aside.

To cook the morels: Heat a large sauté pan or skillet over high heat. Add 1 tablespoon olive oil, heat for a few seconds, then add half of the morels and sauté until beginning to turn golden, 4 to 5 minutes. Transfer to a medium bowl, add the remaining 1 tablespoon olive oil to the pan, then sauté the remaining mushrooms. Stir in the thyme and remove from heat. Add the Madeira, sherry, or stock. Stir and season with salt and pepper. Add to the bowl with the other mushrooms.

To make the vinaigrette: In a blender or food processor, puree the sautéed mushrooms until smooth, adding a little of the grapeseed, canola, or olive oil as needed to puree. With the machine running, add the vinegar, lemon juice, salt, and pepper. Gradually pour in the remaining grapeseed, canola, or olive oil and the hazelnut oil to make an emulsified sauce. Set aside, or cover and refrigerate for up to 1 day.

To serve, toss the asparagus in the lemon-infused oil or extra-virgin olive oil. Place on a platter or plates, tips facing the same direction. Drizzle the morel vinaigrette around, top with the remaining sautéed mushrooms, and garnish with flowers.

IMPROVISATIONS *In late spring or autumn, when morels are not in season, use porcini (cèpes), if you can find them. Toss the asparagus with cherry tomato halves instead of the flowers.*

ADVANCE PREP *The asparagus can be cooked 3 to 4 hours ahead and heated slightly in olive oil before serving. The vinaigrette can be made 1 day ahead, refrigerated, and brought to room temperature before serving.*

SIMPLIFYING *Serve all of the sautéed morels on top of asparagus, dressed with a simple lemon vinaigrette (page 247).*

WINE NOTES *This salad was served with Forefathers Sauvignon Blanc from New Zealand as part of the prix fixe menu at Farallon, and it was a hit. That version had sliced Sweet 100 tomatoes on top, along with the vinaigrette. Another recommendation is a Côtes-du-Rhône Blanc or a white wine from the hills of Provence.*

All the tastes of a New England summer barbecue are in this popular entree salad, served for lunch at Farallon. Our lobster Cobb was inspired by the original salad, created at the famous Brown Derby in Hollywood. Of course, many great restaurant dishes have been born out of necessity, but the Cobb

MAINE LOBSTER COBB SALAD *with* SWEET CORN, HARD-COOKED EGGS, BACON, *and* SMOKED-TOMATO VINAIGRETTE

salad is legendary. It's said that in 1926, the Brown Derby's owner, Bob Cobb, searching the walk-in refrigerator for leftovers, gathered together a salad of chicken, avocado, watercress, bacon, hard-cooked eggs, tomatoes, and Roquefort cheese, chopped them all up, then tossed them with French dressing. Syd Grauman was so enamored of the dish that he told all his friends about it, and another Hollywood star was born. Bradford Barker, Farallon's lunch chef and a native New Englander, was inspired by the legendary Cobb to create a contemporary version that includes Maine lobster, corn, and frisée, with a smoked-tomato vinaigrette.

★ CHEF'S TIPS *Adding smoked rather than roasted tomatoes to the vinaigrette takes this salad to another taste level. The smoking takes less than 30 minutes, but you need either an outdoor or stovetop smoker. Slow-roasting is an alternative that gives a depth of flavor even to poor-quality, off-season tomatoes. | Another, more elegant, way to serve this dish is to slice, rather than chop, the ingredients and present it as a composed salad, which would be good for a more formal luncheon.*

Makes 4 entree salads

SMOKED-TOMATO VINAIGRETTE:
8 smoked tomato halves (page 247) or
    slow-roasted tomato halves (page 247)
3 tablespoons fresh lemon juice
⅓ cup extra-virgin olive oil
Kosher salt and freshly ground pepper
    to taste

8 strips smoked bacon, cut into ½-inch
    crosswise strips
2 lobsters (about 1½ pounds each)
    cooked and shelled (see page 233),
    claws reserved for garnish, or
    6 to 8 ounces cooked lobster meat

1½ cups fresh corn kernels, blanched
    for 1 minute (about 2 ears)
4 hard-cooked eggs, yolks sieved and
    whites finely chopped
1 small red onion, finely diced
1 large avocado (preferably Hass),
    peeled, pitted, and cut into ½-inch dice
½ bunch fresh chives, finely chopped
¼ cup fresh lemon juice
½ cup extra-virgin olive oil
Leaves from 1 bunch frisée lettuce
1 head long (Treviso) radicchio or
    round (Verona) radicchio, cored and
    thinly sliced

Preparation

To make the vinaigrette: Combine the tomatoes, lemon juice, and olive oil in a blender and puree until emulsified, about 20 seconds. Season with salt and pepper. Set aside, or cover and refrigerate for up to 2 days.

In a small sauté pan or skillet, fry the bacon strips until slightly crunchy and the fat has started to render. Using a slotted spoon, transfer to paper towels until ready to use.

Cut the lobster meat into ½-inch pieces. In a large bowl, combine the cut-up lobster, bacon, corn, eggs, red onion, avocado, and chives. Whisk the lemon juice and olive oil together, and toss with the lobster mixture.

To serve, toss the frisée and radicchio together and divide among the plates. Mound on some of the lobster mixture. Whisk the vinaigrette and drizzle it around the salads, placing an extra spoonful on top. Garnish each salad with a lobster claw, if using, and serve.

IMPROVISATIONS *Chicken, prawns, crab, even salmon could be used in place of lobster. The original Cobb included Roquefort cheese, but I wouldn't add cheese if you use fish or shellfish in the salad.*

ADVANCE PREP *The tomato vinaigrette can be made as much as 2 days in advance. Except for the avocado, which should be diced and added just before serving, all the salad ingredients can be cooked and diced ahead and stored in the refrigerator for up to 24 hours.*

SIMPLIFYING *Use cooked lobster meat instead of preparing your own. If you don't have time to either smoke or roast your tomatoes, just make the vinaigrette with peeled, seeded, and chopped tomatoes. The dish will still be delicious.*

WINE NOTES *Salads are notorious for being difficult to pair with wines because of the acidity of vinaigrettes, but they needn't be. Just remember to choose a wine with enough of its own acidity to stand up to the dressing. This salad would be delightful with a crisp, barrel-fermented Sauvignon Blanc from California. A white Burgundy like Mâconnais or Pouilly-Fuissé is a great foil for the natural sweetness of the lobster. If a red wine is called for, try one of the lighter-bodied Zinfandels from California. They're very versatile and will work with the tomatoes and vinaigrette.*

The pleasures of this dish are in its familiarity as well as its finesse. Who doesn't love fried shrimp? Or sweet, ripe, juicy tomatoes with fragrant basil? When I was a kid, one of my favorite restaurant dishes was fried shrimp with cocktail sauce. It was (and still is) a great combination that I could rarely get enough of. As I and my palate grew, however, my taste for fried shrimp and cocktail sauce was forgotten. One of Farallon's first menus contained a sophisticated first-course salad of sliced garden-fresh

SUMMER TOMATO SALAD *with* CRISP JUMBO SHRIMP *and* SWEET BASIL

heirloom tomatoes topped with a lobster beignet: a kind of savory doughnut. Something about that dish appealed to me, but it always seemed to fall a little short of my expectations. One day, Farallon's lunch chef, Bradford Barker, fried some batter-coated shrimp and used them instead of the beignets. The moment I took a bite of that dish I immediately tasted the fried shrimp of my childhood. Maybe it's simply the combination of tomato and shrimp, but there's also something about having the sweet and tart flavors and crunchy and soft textures all in your mouth at the same time. Try this dish on your kids as well as your most sophisticated friends.

★ CHEF'S TIPS *This is one of the few times where I think a batter enhances the final fried dish. Too often, fried foods taste mostly of dough and grease. The coating we use on these shrimp actually does what it is supposed to do: contribute a flavorful, crunchy, greaseless shell that preserves the sweet, moist meat inside. And if all these qualities were not enough to make these shrimp attractive, the fact that they can be prepared ahead just adds to their appeal. This coating doesn't seem to ever get soggy. | I've specified 3 jumbo shrimp per serving here for 4 first-course servings. But I love this dish so much that I could eat all 4 servings by myself. Increase the proportions to suit the appetites of your guests, as well as the occasion. It makes a great summer luncheon salad or casual supper. | Fleur de Sel, or "flower of the salt," is an expensive and sublime specialty salt from France that we like to sprinkle on fresh vine-ripened tomatoes or foie gras.*

Makes 4 appetizer servings

BASIL VINAIGRETTE:
2 tablespoons balsamic vinegar
¼ cup basil-infused oil (page 241)
Kosher salt and freshly ground pepper
   to taste
2 tablespoons minced fresh basil

FRIED BASIL:
Peanut or vegetable oil for deep-frying
20 fresh basil leaves

CRISP JUMBO SHRIMP:
12 jumbo shrimp, shelled (tails left on)
   and deveined
Kosher salt and freshly ground pepper
   to taste

½ cup rice flour
1 cup buttermilk
1 to 2 cups cornmeal, depending on size
   of prawns
Peanut or vegetable oil for deep-frying

8 ripe heirloom tomatoes, in a mixture
   of colors, sliced ¼ inch thick
½ teaspoon Fleur de Sel or kosher salt

To make the vinaigrette: In a small bowl, whisk all the ingredients together. Set aside, or cover and refrigerate for up to 1 day.

To fry the basil: In a deep, heavy pot or deep fryer, heat 3 inches of oil to 375°F. Carefully fry the whole basil leaves in small batches of about 6 to 8 leaves at a time (stand back, as the oil will splatter) until crisp but still green, about 10 seconds. Using a slotted spoon, transfer to paper towels to drain. Keep the oil hot for frying the shrimp.

To fry the shrimp: Toss the shrimp in a medium bowl with the salt and pepper. Put the rice flour, buttermilk, and cornmeal in 3 separate shallow bowls. Coat the shrimp first in the rice flour, then the buttermilk, and finally the corn-meal, shaking them off between each stage to remove any excess. Deep-fry the shrimp in 2 or 3 batches, until golden, about 2 minutes. Using a slotted spoon or wire-mesh skim-mer, transfer the shrimp to paper towels to drain.

To serve, arrange the tomatoes on each of the plates, alternating the colors. Sprinkle the tomatoes with a little salt. Place the shrimp on each plate, balanced with their tails up, and drizzle a little of the vinaigrette around and over the shrimp. Garnish with the fried basil leaves.

IMPROVISATIONS *You could omit the basil oil in the vinaigrette and just use a very good extra-virgin olive oil instead. The real key to this dish is the contrast of the fried shellfish with the cool, sweet, and acidic tomatoes. Try any kind of fried seafood, like soft-shell crabs, calamari, scallops, or even pieces of cod or rockfish. Go ahead and experiment with the fried fish, but please, please, don't make this dish with anything other than beautiful, ripe, and in-season tomatoes—that is, from August through October.*

ADVANCE PREP *This is an ideal first course for a dinner party, because all of the components can be prepared in advance. The tomatoes can be sliced and arranged on plates or a platter, covered with plastic wrap, and kept at room temperature. The shrimp can be breaded and stored in the refrigerator on a wire rack for 3 to 4 hours before frying, or fried and served at room temperature, or fried and then heated in a preheated 375°F oven for 10 minutes. The vinaigrette can be made 1 day ahead. Be careful not to keep the shrimp (or any seafood) at room temperature for too long, to avoid any accumulation of bacteria (see page 223).*

SIMPLIFYING *The only thing I can think of that would be simpler would be to toss poached shrimp with a little of the basil vinaigrette and omit the fried basil. Beautiful garden-fresh tomatoes really need no adornment, but . . . oh, those fried shrimp.*

WINE NOTES *Sauvignon Blanc is a good match, but this recipe calls for something a bit fruitier. Try one from the Marlborough region in New Zealand; their wines are more readily available than ever and are not unlike those from the Loire Valley in France in a ripe year.*

As a chef, I've always loved the art of charcuterie. At Stars, in our perennially busy kitchen, I'd try to find any excuse to go off alone into the basement to make some duck sausage, or maybe some foie gras terrines. At that time, duck leg confit was one of the most popular items on Stars' menu, and it seemed like we always wound up with a surplus of duck breasts. We found various uses for them: We'd

DUCK BREAST PROSCIUTTO *with* SUMMER MELON, FIG COMPOTE, *and* LEMON VERBENA GRANITA

sauté them whole as an entree, or we would roast them and add them to a salad. Sometimes we would smoke them. But always, there seemed to be more than we could use, and one day, I thought of curing the duck breasts like a prosciutto ham. Through trial and error, I came up with a recipe that we're still using at Farallon. Don Hall, Farallon's creative pastry chef and former line cook, played around with some savory granitas and came up with this unique one infused with lemon verbena. The components of this dish—salty prosciutto, sweet melon, and tart lemon granita—add up to an incredible explosion of taste and texture.

★ CHEF'S TIPS *Of course, you don't need to make your own duck prosciutto—recently I've seen it for sale in some upscale delis. There are also plenty of other substitutes, like Italian prosciutto and my own personal favorite, serrano ham. | You'll probably end up with more fig compote (it's more like a syrup, actually) than you'll need for this recipe. The good news is that it keeps for up to a month in the refrigerator, and you'll be able to find all kinds of uses for it—try it on toast in the morning. | The use of verjus, or verjuice, dates back to the Middle Ages. It is made from the juice of unripe grapes; generally white varieties. We use white grape verjus in sauces and vinaigrettes because it's slightly less acidic than either vinegar or lemon juice, with a hint of grape.*

Makes 4 appetizer servings

FIG COMPOTE:
1 cup ruby port
½ cup sugar
7 to 8 fresh or dried figs, halved

LEMON VERBENA GRANITA:
½ cup white verjus, or ¼ cup fresh lemon juice mixed with ¼ cup water
2 cups water
½ cup sugar
6 to 8 fresh lemon verbena leaves, or 2 stalks lemongrass, white part only, thinly sliced
Pinch of kosher salt

About 1 pound very thinly sliced homemade duck prosciutto (page 240), serrano ham, or Italian prosciutto
2 cups finely diced cantaloupe (about ½ melon)
4 to 8 sprigs watercress for garnish

continued

To make the fig compote: In a small saucepan, combine all the ingredients. Bring to a boil, reduce heat to a simmer, and cook to reduce to about ½ cup. Remove from heat and let cool for 10 minutes. Puree in a blender or food processor, then push through a medium-mesh sieve with the back of a large spoon. Set aside, or cover and refrigerate for up to 1 month. Reheat just before serving.

To make the granita: Combine all the ingredients in a small nonreactive saucepan and cook over medium heat, swirling occasionally, until the sugar dissolves, about 5 minutes. Remove from heat and let sit for 15 minutes. Strain into a stainless-steel or glass flat-bottomed dish and let cool completely. Transfer to the freezer. Scrape thoroughly with a fork every 20 minutes or so until frozen, to break up the ice crystals and give it a granular texture. The freezing time will vary, depending on the size of your pan and the temperature of your freezer. Transfer to another container, cover, and freeze for up to 5 days. Make sure to fluff up the granules with a fork just before serving.

To serve, lay 4 slices of prosciutto, slightly overlapping, on each of the salad or dinner plates. Place a 2½- or 3-inch ring mold on top of the prosciutto and fill with a ½-inch layer of granita. With a spoon, pat the granita down lightly to compact it. Top with a layer of diced cantaloupe, lightly tamping it down, then carefully remove the ring mold. If you don't have a ring mold, carefully arrange a mound of the granita with the melon on top. Spoon a little of the warm fig compote around and over the dish and garnish with a sprig or two of watercress.

IMPROVISATIONS *Any sweet, ripe, melon can be used in place of the canteloupe. If figs are not in season, you might want to try fresh or dried cherries. And if you are lucky enough to have access to rose geranium, try that with the dish (about 2 tablespoons of the flowers instead of the verbena).*

ADVANCE PREP *The compote can be sealed and refrigerated for up to 1 month. The granita tastes best when just frozen, but will last for up to 5 days in the freezer. The melon can be cut and stored in the refrigerator, covered, for up to 24 hours.*

SIMPLIFYING *Fresh figs or cherries can be quartered and strewn around the plate in place of the fig compote. And you could buy a good-quality lemon or melon sorbet instead of making your own.*

WINE NOTES *One of the servers at Farallon suggested to Peter Palmer, our sommelier, that he try the 1997 Thomas Fogarty Gewürztraminer, which we were pouring by the glass, with this dish. What a match it was! Try a Pinot Gris or Riesling as well, especially ones from Alsace, Germany, or particularly Leeuwin Estate in Australia. You want a wine that is high in acid and has a lot of fruit, but be careful that it isn't too sweet on the palate or it will overwhelm the dish.*

I created this dish for a multicourse banquet held at Farallon for the New Zealand Venison Council. They wanted every course to contain venison, and it presented me with some interesting challenges (dessert is another story). As I was planning the menu, one of my very first thoughts was to include a tartare of venison—what better way to highlight the meat's unique flavor than by serving it raw? Well, more quickly than I could believe, I got an "ix-nay on the artare-tay" from the coordinator of the event. Traditionally, raw venison is a strict no-no in New Zealand. Okay, I could deal with that. I decided

CHARRED RARE VENISON TARTARE *with* CELERY ROOT *and*
CHERVIL SALAD, BLACK TRUFFLE COULIS, *and* PORT GASTRIQUE

to quickly sear the exterior of the venison, as you would for tuna, leaving a beautifully medium-rare interior, just skirting the "no raw deer" issue. I can't even describe how they raved about this dish, and it was such a success that we're still serving it for special occasions. While I generally avoid fussy and overly manipulated presentations, this is one dish that works for me. If you're planning a dinner party and want to wow your guests with a stunning presentation, try this first course. In spite of the lengthy ingredient list, it's quite easy to prepare, and most of the components can be made ahead of time. Also, farm-raised venison is commonly available today, from specialty butchers and by mail order.

★ *CHEF'S TIPS Relating to my little anecdote about raw venison—don't even think of doing this dish with anything but farm-raised venison from a reputable source. Save the wild venison for well-cooked preparations. | Farm-raised venison has an incredibly fine taste and texture as well as some nutritional points in its favor. It's lower in fat, calories, and cholesterol than beef, and the loin, in particular, is similar in nutritional content to salmon. | The gastrique is a sweet-tart syrup that in France is traditionally served with duck. At the restaurant, we make large quantities of it at a time, because while not difficult, it requires some time and quite a few ingredients. The great thing is that it seems to keep forever. If you make extra, store the leftover syrup to serve drizzled over ice cream or grilled figs. For the truffle coulis, you'll have more than you need for this recipe, but it keeps for a long time and has many uses. Try it on scrambled eggs, mix a little into some ground beef, or stir it into a vinaigrette. It's great stuff.*

Makes 4 appetizer servings

½ teaspoon juniper berries
3 tablespoons olive oil
1 teaspoon minced fresh thyme
1 teaspoon balsamic vinegar
Kosher salt and freshly ground pepper
    to taste
12 ounces farm-raised venison fillets

PORT GASTRIQUE:
2 shallots, minced
2 or 3 thyme sprigs
3 dried juniper berries, lightly crushed
1 clove garlic, lightly crushed
2 thin slices fresh ginger
¼ cup fresh orange juice
⅔ cup ruby port
½ cup Merlot or other dry red wine
½ cup Madeira
⅓ cup sherry vinegar
½ cup sugar
Pinch of ground mace or allspice
2 bay leaves
Kosher salt and freshly ground pepper
    to taste

CELERY ROOT SALAD:
Juice of 1 lemon
1 celery root
1 teaspoon Champagne vinegar
1 tablespoon hazelnut or walnut oil
1 teaspoon minced fresh thyme
2 tablespoons chopped fresh chervil
Kosher salt and freshly ground pepper
    to taste

BLACK TRUFFLE COULIS:
One 3½-ounce can black truffle peelings
    with juice, or 2½ ounces black truffle
    peelings with juice plus ½ to 1 ounce
    shaved fresh or frozen black truffle

2 tablespoons water
½ teaspoon chopped fresh thyme
1 teaspoon sherry or Champagne vinegar
⅓ cup grapeseed or canola oil
1 tablespoon white truffle oil
Kosher salt and freshly ground pepper
    to taste

8 to 10 quail eggs
Kosher salt and freshly ground pepper
    to taste
4 slices brioche (page 237) or white
    bread, lightly toasted, crusts removed
    (optional)
⅓ cup fresh chervil sprigs for garnish

continued

To marinate the venison: Using a mortar and pestle, crush the juniper berries to a fine paste. In a small bowl, whisk 1 tablespoon of the olive oil with the thyme, balsamic vinegar, juniper paste, salt, and pepper. Put the venison fillets in a self-sealing plastic bag with the marinade. Remove as much air as possible from the bag as you close it, then turn the meat in the bag until it's well coated with the marinade. Refrigerate for 8 hours or preferably overnight.

To make the gastrique: Combine all the ingredients in a medium saucepan, bring to a boil, reduce heat, and simmer until thickened and reduced to about ⅓ cup. Avoid reducing it too much, or the sugars will burn and make the gastrique bitter. Set aside to cool.

To cook the venison: In a large sauté pan or skillet, heat the remaining 2 tablespoons olive oil over high heat until the surface shimmers. Sear the fillets until nicely browned all over, 1 to 2 minutes on each side. Remove from the pan and let rest for about 15 minutes.

To make the salad: Add the lemon juice to a bowl of water. Peel and julienne the celery root, adding it to the lemon water as you go. In another bowl, whisk together the vinegar, hazelnut or walnut oil, thyme, chervil, salt, and pepper. Drain the celery root and put it in a medium bowl. Pour the vinaigrette over the celery root and toss to combine thoroughly. Cover and refrigerate for up to 1 day.

To make the coulis: Puree all the ingredients in a blender until thickened and emulsified. Cover and set aside.

To cook the quail eggs: Immerse the quail eggs in a small saucepan of boiling water for 2½ minutes. Using a slotted spoon, transfer the eggs to a bowl of ice water to stop the cooking. Peel, cut in half, and set aside. (You'll only need 6 eggs for the recipe, but because of the difficulty in peeling them, I've suggested a few extra for backup.)

To serve, cut the venison into ¼-inch dice and put it in a bowl with any juices that were released onto the cutting surface. Rewarm the gastrique over low heat. Mix the venison with a little of the gastrique and season with salt and pepper. In the middle of each dinner plate, place a toast, if using. Top with mounds of the venison tartare. Place 3 alternating mounds of celery root and truffle coulis around the tartare, and a quail egg half, yolk-side up, on each of the coulis dollops. Sprinkle each egg with a little salt and pepper. Drizzle the gastrique around the plates and garnish with chervil sprigs on each of the celery root mounds.

IMPROVISATIONS *You can use beef loin, veal, lamb, or tuna, in this "tartare." Any kind of herb can stand in for the chervil.*

ADVANCE PREP *The venison needs 8 hours to marinate. It can be cooked early in the day you plan to serve it. You can wrap it in plastic and refrigerate it for up to 1 day. If you refrigerate it, let the venison come to room temperature before you prepare it. Don't cut it into pieces until right before serving, 1 hour ahead at the most, or it may turn an unappetizing gray, losing its beautiful red, rare color. The truffle coulis keeps, covered in the refrigerator, for at least 1 month. The salad and vinaigrette may be prepared, covered separately, and refrigerated for up to 1 day.*

SIMPLIFYING *Serve the venison on a piece of grilled bread or toast, with the celery root salad alongside.*

WINE NOTES *A classic, dry rosé would be perfect: delicate but flavorful, a great color combo with the rare meat, earthy enough to match those truffles, but with enough fruit to stand up to the natural sweetness of the dish and the gastrique. Some European rosés can be quite austere, so you may want to try the subtle but fruity Robert Sinskey Vin Gris of Pinot Noir from the Napa Valley.*

TRUFFLES

Colette said, "If I can't have too many truffles, I'll do without truffles." Well, for me, I'll take one over none any day, although if given a choice, I'll always opt for more. In fact, it's a common joke in the Farallon kitchen that if you want to create a new dish that will get the chef's approval, make sure it contains some truffles. So intense is my desire for these underground fungi that for years I was afraid that there was something perverse about it, and me. But in January of 1999 I was invited by Ken Hom to go on a truffle hunt with a small group of chefs in Quercy, the region slightly southeast of Périgord, arguably the most famous truffle-producing area of the world. It was on this extraordinary trip that I realized that I'm not alone in my passion for truffles: during the months roughly from November to March, thousands of French citizens become intoxicated with the black diamonds and indulge themselves to a point that would make most Americans shake their heads in disbelief. As guests of the Pébeyres, the largest truffle-producing family in France, we were fêted, as only the French know how to do, morning, noon, and night, with meals featuring truffles in every course. On the average, I think we consumed a pound per person in truffles—daily—and while a couple of my friends were waning after so much indulgence, I kept going strong. My capacity for truffles appears to have no limits.

BUYING AND STORING TRUFFLES

Truffles are the fruit of a fungus, like mushrooms, but grow three to twelve inches underground in a complicated symbiotic relationship with host trees, primarily oak (their favorite), hazelnut, beechnut, birch, and chestnut.

While at least seventy kinds of truffles are found in temperate regions all over the world, only a handful have any culinary interest, and the two best known and most highly prized come from Europe. The soils of Italy, Spain, and France are all hospitable to the *tuber melanosporum*, also known generically as the Périgord black winter truffle, perhaps the most famous truffle of all. Italians will argue, with some merit I might add, that their own white truffle from Alba in the Piedmont region, the *tuber magnatum*, is the more desirable of the two. There are also the *aestivum*, or black summer truffles, which are black on the outside and white on the inside, and although they're considerably cheaper than winter truffles, they're definitely inferior, both in flavor and aroma.

About thirty years ago, the French devised a way to cultivate black truffles by inoculating saplings with melanosporum spores and then planting them in areas that had proven to be hospitable, and now 30 percent of the French truffle harvests are from truffle "farms." A few enterprising Americans have

begun to harvest truffles from inoculated trees planted in Oregon, Texas, and North Carolina, and they are of quite good quality.

Whole truffles can be purchased fresh, preserved in cans and jars, or flash frozen. The season for fresh black truffles runs from about November to March and from October to December for white. Fresh truffles should be firm but not hard, and have no sponginess or blemishes. Whole preserved truffles in cans and jars are available year-round and can be quite good, but make sure that you buy the ones that are labeled *surchoix*, or "first-cooked," which means that they've only undergone one cooking process, done when they were sterilized in their containers. Frozen truffles are acceptable, and we even freeze our own at the restaurant when the season for fresh comes to an end. Truffles are also marketed in other forms, all of which have their uses: canned truffle peelings, infused truffle oil (both white and black), truffle juice, truffle paste, and truffle butter. See page 249 for a list of suppliers.

Try this, you'll like it. And don't be scared off by the crayfish vinaigrette, which sounds like it might be hard to make but isn't. I'll give you a few suggestions for other vinaigrettes to use in this dish, but first I want to talk about scallops, a personal favorite of mine. While scallops are native to both American coasts and the Gulf of Mexico, I prefer the scallops harvested in the North Atlantic—those cold waters seem to produce a sweeter scallop. But not only are scallops incredibly meaty and succulent,

GRILLED NANTUCKET SCALLOPS *with* APPLE *and* ENDIVE SALAD *and* CRAYFISH VINAIGRETTE

they're a cook's dream: They're quick and easy to prepare, they are usually already shelled, and people who normally shy away from eating shellfish seem to like them. This dish pairs autumn-harvested Nantucket scallops with a crisp apple salad, a natural complement.

★ *CHEF'S TIPS On menus today, it's increasingly common to see terms such as "dry-packed," "day-boat," or "diver" scallops. These refer to scallops that haven't been injected with preservatives to help retard moisture loss and that have been brought in on a boat that's been at sea for only a few hours. This kind of scallop will be more ivory than white in color, maybe with a tinge of peach. They shouldn't look like they've been stamped out of a cookie cutter; real scallops, like everything in nature, vary in size and shape. Look to see if they're sitting in water, which indicates that they may have been frozen and defrosted, or that they were injected with preservatives. Water-injected scallops never cook properly, because when heated they release their moisture and shrink to nothing. | When sautéing scallops, to get a good crust, make sure your pan is hot before you add the oil, and that you've patted the scallops dry with paper towels (see Improvisations below). If you've bought scallops with injected water, forget the browning—it will never happen and you'll need to find a different fish purveyor next time. | When either sautéing or grilling scallops (as well as any other dense, firm fish), remove them from the heat just before they're opaque throughout. The residual heat will complete the cooking.*

Makes 4 appetizer servings

1 pound "dry-packed" scallops, rinsed and patted dry (from 3 to 5 per person, depending on the size of the scallops)
2 tablespoons olive oil
1 teaspoon chopped fresh thyme
Kosher salt and freshly ground pepper to taste

CRAYFISH VINAIGRETTE:
¼ cup crayfish essence (page 245)
Juice of ½ lemon
2 tablespoons grapeseed or canola oil
½ teaspoon chopped fresh tarragon

Juice of 1 lemon
1 unpeeled, tart, crisp apple, such as Braeburn, Fuji, or Jonathan, cored and quartered
3 heads Belgian endive, cored and cut lengthwise into julienne
1 bunch arugula, stemmed

To marinate and cook the scallops: In a medium bowl, toss the scallops with the olive oil, thyme, salt, and pepper. Cover and refrigerate for 30 minutes. Meanwhile, soak 4 wooden skewers in warm water.

To make the vinaigrette: Whisk all the ingredients together in a small bowl. Set aside, or refrigerate for up to 1 day.

Add the lemon juice to a bowl of water. Using a mandoline or a very sharp knife, thinly slice the apple quarters. Drop the slices in lemon water as you go to prevent the apples from turning brown. The apples can stay in the lemon water for up to 30 minutes.

Light a gas or charcoal grill, or heat a ridged grill pan over high heat. Thread the scallops equally onto the skewers. Grill over high heat for 2 to 3 minutes on each side, or until golden brown on the outside and almost opaque throughout. Let the scallops sit for a few minutes off heat to finish cooking while preparing the plates.

To serve, drain the apples and pat them dry with paper towels. In a medium bowl, toss the apples with the endive, arugula, and vinaigrette. Divide the salad among the plates. Either place 1 skewer on each plate, or remove the scallops from the skewers and place individual portions of the scallops on the salads. Spoon any remaining vinaigrette around.

IMPROVISATIONS *To sauté the scallops, in a large sauté pan or skillet, heat 1 tablespoon grapeseed, vegetable, or olive oil over high heat until it shimmers. Add the scallops and sauté on each side for about 2 minutes, or until golden brown on the outside and almost opaque throughout. Shrimp or lobster would work well here instead of scallops, and Asian pears could substitute for the apples. Lobster essence could be used in place of crayfish essence in the vinaigrette. You could make the vinaigrette with all sherry vinegar, or sherry vinegar combined with apple juice and a little chopped fresh mint. To get really sexy, stir in a few drops of truffle oil.*

ADVANCE PREP *The scallops may be cooked a couple of hours ahead of time—they taste just as good at room temperature, or even chilled, although I prefer the contrast of warm scallops with the cool salad. The apples can be sliced 30 minutes ahead and kept in their bowl of lemon water, but don't drain them and toss the salad until serving time. The vinaigrette can be made up to 1 day in advance.*

SIMPLIFYING *The crayfish vinaigrette, though delicious with the scallops, is certainly optional; instead, use any vinaigrette you like—preferably one with a little sweetness to complement the apples.*

WINE NOTES *A Chardonnay with good balance and natural acidity, one that tones down oak and alcohol levels, is the wine to drink with this scallop dish. American producers include Iron Horse in the Russian River Valley, Hendry and Forman in the Napa Valley, Domaine Drouhin in Oregon, and Au Bon Climat and Sanford on the Central coast. A somewhat exotic option would be Viognier, a wine originally made in the Rhône Valley of France that is becoming popular in California. Try the Alban Estate Vineyards or Qupé Wine Cellars, two of the best in California.*

Here's a dish that makes a spectacular presentation and will make you look like an old pro in the kitchen, though I have to warn you that it's not one you can whip up on a moment's notice. Quite the contrary: terrines are the kind of dishes that chefs like to create when they want to show off their culinary muscles, and they can tend toward decorative excess: Visualize a large hotel or a cruise ship grand buffet, laden with elaborate chaud-froids and terrines. Regrettably, too, terrines and pâtés can

SQUAB BREAST TERRINE *with* SHIITAKE DUXELLES, SEARED FOIE GRAS, BRAISED LEEKS, *and* BROKEN BEET VINAIGRETTE

sometimes function as catchalls for kitchen discards, full of overcooked vegetables and bits of leftover meat. But many contemporary chefs have taken a fresh approach to making terrines, viewing them as another new culinary territory to be explored and combining impeccably fresh ingredients in inventive ways. We've played around with a lot of various terrines at Farallon, but this one of squab, leeks, shiitake mushrooms, and foie gras has endured and been refined to the point that it's stunning in its simplicity. It may not be quick, but if you do some advance preparation it's not difficult to assemble, and I can't think of a more sophisticated first course for a special-occasion dinner.

★ CHEF'S TIPS *Duxelles is a classic French preparation of minced mushrooms and shallots, cooked in butter until a dry paste is formed. | We tested this recipe with a 6-cup Le Creuset terrine mold, easily found in gourmet shops nationwide. | A simple and very contemporary way to garnish a plate is to use a "broken" vinaigrette, one that's not completely emulsified and separates into beads of color when spooned onto a plate.*

Makes one 6-cup terrine; serves 12 as a first course

BROKEN BEET VINAIGRETTE:
6 beets
2 tablespoons olive oil
1½ cups water
¼ cup sugar
2 tablespoons Champagne vinegar
1 cup extra-virgin olive oil
Kosher salt and freshly ground pepper
    to taste

2 whole squab breasts, skinned, boned,
    and halved
1 teaspoon minced fresh thyme
6 tablespoons Cognac
Kosher salt and freshly ground pepper
    to taste
2 tablespoons canola oil
Three 2-ounce slices fresh foie gras

SHIITAKE DUXELLES:
3 tablespoons unsalted butter
3 tablespoons grapeseed, canola, or
    olive oil
12 shallots, thinly sliced
12 ounces shiitake mushrooms, stemmed
    and sliced
1 teaspoon minced fresh thyme
1 cup Madeira
Kosher salt and freshly ground pepper
    to taste

BRAISED LEEKS:
4 cups chicken stock (page 243)
Kosher salt and freshly ground pepper
    to taste
4 large leeks, white and light green parts
    only, rinsed

2 envelopes plain gelatin
Mâche or frisée leaves, or herb sprigs
2 tablespoons Lemon Vinaigrette
    (page 247)

Preparation

To make the beet vinaigrette: Preheat the oven to 400°F. Put the beets in a small, shallow baking dish and rub with the 2 tablespoons olive oil. Add 1 cup of the water and cover the dish with aluminum foil. Roast until tender and easily pierced with a small knife, about 45 minutes. Uncover and let cool. Peel the beets and cut into coarse chunks. In a blender or food processor, puree the beets with the remaining ½ cup water until liquefied, adding more water as necessary. Push through a fine-mesh sieve with the back of a spoon. You should have about 1 cup liquid. In a small saucepan, combine the beet juice and sugar. Bring to a simmer and cook to reduce by half. Remove from heat and let cool. Add the vinegar, extra-virgin olive oil, salt, and pepper. Whisk lightly and set aside, or refrigerate for up to 1 day.

To marinate and cook the squab breasts: Sprinkle the squab breasts with the thyme and 3 tablespoons of the Cognac. Set aside at room temperature for 30 minutes to 1 hour. Season them generously with salt and pepper. In a small sauté pan or skillet over high heat, heat the canola oil and cook the squab breasts, skin-side down, for 4 to 6

continued

minutes. Flip over and cook until browned on the outside and medium to medium rare on the inside, 4 to 6 minutes. Remove and cool, then refrigerate until ready to assemble the terrine.

To cook the foie gras: Season the foie gras with salt and pepper. In a small sauté pan or skillet over high heat, quickly sear the foie gras for about 2 minutes each side, or until browned. Add the remaining 3 tablespoons Cognac, being careful not to splatter. Let simmer for 1 minute, then remove from heat. Using a spatula, transfer the foie gras to a plate. Immediately put it in the freezer for 10 minutes to stop the cooking. Transfer to the refrigerator until ready to assemble the terrine.

To make the duxelles: In a medium sauté pan or skillet, melt the butter with the oil over medium-low heat and sauté the shallots until translucent, about 4 minutes. Add the shiitakes and thyme and cook until soft, about 10 minutes. Add the Madeira and cook to reduce until almost dry. Remove from heat and set aside to cool with the liquid. In a food processor, pulse the cooled mushrooms until they're finely minced but not pureed. Transfer to a medium bowl and add the salt and pepper. Set aside.

To braise the leeks: In a medium saucepan, bring the chicken stock to a simmer, season with salt and pepper, and cook the leeks until soft, about 20 minutes. Using a slotted spatula or tongs, transfer the leeks to a plate. Strain and reserve the cooking liquid. While the leeks are warm, carefully remove 2 or 3 of the outer leaves of each one and discard. Reserve the white cores of the leeks (now about the diameter of a dime) for the inside of terrine.

To assemble the terrine: Measure out the reserved leek stock into a medium stainless bowl; you should have about 4 cups. Set the bowl over a pan of gently simmering water. Add the gelatin and stir gently to dissolve. Spray a 6-cup terrine mold with a vegetable-oil cooking spray. Lay 1 or 2 pieces of plastic wrap in the mold and press it flush against the mold with about 2 inches of overhang on either side. Spray the plastic with the cooking spray. In a separate bowl, add enough of the leek and gelatin mixture to the duxelles to make a thick paste, leaving at least 1 cup of the leek liquid for sealing the terrine later; keep this reserved liquid warm over the simmering water.

Spread 1 cup of the duxelles in a smooth layer in the bottom of the mold. Lay the whole leeks over the duxelles, reaching from end to end in 2 rows. Spoon 1 cup of the duxelles on top of the leeks and spread it smoothly, making sure that the mixture can drip down through the cracks. Lay the foie gras in unbroken lengths along the duxelles. Spoon 1 cup duxelles on top and down the sides of the foie gras and smooth it out. Lay the squab breasts in one layer in the terrine, with the wide ends of the breast facing in opposite directions and overlapping slightly at the ends so that each slice of terrine will have some breast in it. Pour the last of the leek-gelatin mixture in a layer on top and down the sides of the squab breast to seal it. Refrigerate, uncovered, overnight.

To serve, dip the mold into a pan of hot water for 30 seconds. Using the plastic wrap as handles, carefully lift out the terrine and transfer to a flat surface. (If the terrine doesn't easily slide out of the mold, dip it in the hot water again for 15 to 30 seconds.) Dip a very sharp slicing knife in hot water, dry it, and using a slow sawing motion, cut the terrine into 1-inch-thick slices and place one on each plate. Toss the greens with the lemon vinaigrette and mound over one corner of the terrine. Drizzle around a little beet vinaigrette.

IMPROVISATIONS *You could substitute duck breasts for squab, although the squab is just the right size for the terrine. A duck breast would have to be cut down to fit the terrine mold properly.*

ADVANCE PREP *The beet vinaigrette yields a little more than needed for the recipe and can be made up to 1 day ahead; use it on salads or other dishes as desired. The terrine will keep for up to 4 days in the refrigerator.*

SIMPLIFYING *Terrines are a little daunting and may take some practice, but the different components are easy in themselves, and making them ahead is the best part.*

WINE NOTES *This starter is definitely a step up in richness and opulence, so turn up the volume on the wine served with it. For whites, try a rich, exotic Pinot Gris from Alsace or an estate-bottled Roussanne like Alban Vineyards' from California. An older white Burgundy, from a softer vintage like '94 or '97, would also be delicious. If you're looking for red, try a softer and lighter-bodied Pinot Noir, a Sangiovese, or a Grenache.*

I'm really proud of this dish, which has become somewhat of a Farallon signature. It's a stunning presentation, and although I'm not known for architectural food, there's a reason for its architecture. When I was designing our first menus, I was inspired to create something for Farallon that resembled a dish of the incredible (and now retired) Swiss chef and restaurateur, Fredy Girardet. Girardet served a beautiful sliced terrine: mosaic chunks of fresh seafood bound by an intensely flavored fish gelée, or aspic. | The dilemma I encountered when creating this dish was to make a terrine that wouldn't fall apart when sliced. My solution was to serve individual terrines, eliminating the necessity of cutting slices and allowing me to add just enough gelatin to suspend the seafood in the consommé. Next, I needed to

SEAFOOD PYRAMID *with* SHELLFISH GELÉE, JULIENNED LEEK SALAD, *and* SAFFRON ESSENCE

find molds for the terrines; the only ones available at the time were standard small timbales. George Francisco, Farallon's chef de cuisine, happened to come in with several new molds a metal-working friend had made, the pyramid being one of them. It turned out to be the perfect shape: graceful, beautiful, and not one that everyone else was using at the time (now they're available from several mail-order sources). Finally, I began to play with the ingredients and flavors of the pyramid; here I was inspired by the classic Provençal bouillabaisse, hence the saffron and leeks with the seafood. This is not an easy dish to put together—far from it—but if you're up for the culinary challenge and you like aspic, set aside some time and go for it.

★ *CHEF'S TIPS Because of all the flavors in this dish, I poach the shellfish in water rather than the more traditional court bouillon. | Saffron, like other spices, benefits from a light toasting before use. Place it in a small pan and toast in a preheated 350°F oven for 5 minutes, then gently grind with the back of a spoon. | Pyramids are by no means the only molds to use here. Feel free to use larger timbales, ramekins, or custard cups—anything except open-ended ring molds. Any 6-ounce mold you choose must be sealed so that the liquid aspic doesn't leak out. Even the pyramids I use have a small hole at the apex that requires plugging with a paste made of flour and water. | If you are using pyramids, we've worked out a technique for filling them and plugging them at the same time. The tricky part is to keep them upright and level while they chill and firm up in the refrigerator. Here's what you'll need for 4 pyramids: 1 empty egg carton, a paste made from 1 cup flour mixed with ¾ cup water, and vegetable-oil cooking spray or a paper towel dipped in vegetable oil. When you're ready to assemble the pyramids, make your paste, stirring until the paste is like a thick Elmer's Glue, adding a little more flour or water as needed to reach the right consistency. Pour or spoon the paste into 4 egg carton cups, hopscotching diagonally down the carton. Spray the molds with vegetable-oil cooking spray and place the apex end in the paste. Place a baking sheet evenly over all of the pyramids and press lightly to level them.*

Makes 6 appetizer servings

4 ounces medium to large sea or small bay scallops, preferably "dry-packed"

4 ounces prawns, cooked, peeled, and deveined

SHELLFISH GELÉE:

4 cups shellfish consommé (page 238), clear fish stock (page 243), or tomato (page 247) or cucumber (page 38) consommé

2 ½ envelopes plain gelatin

¼ teaspoon saffron threads, lightly toasted (see Chef's Tips)

1 teaspoon kosher salt, or to taste

4 ounces chilled cooked lobster meat

1 teaspoon chopped fresh tarragon or chives

SAFFRON ESSENCE:

⅓ cup shellfish stock (page 244) or good quality store bought fish stock

¼ teaspoon saffron threads, lightly toasted (see Chef's Tips)

2 teaspoons Champagne vinegar or white wine vinegar

Kosher salt and freshly ground pepper to taste

⅔ cup grapeseed or canola oil

LEEK SALAD:

1 large leek, white part only, halved crosswise and lengthwise

1 teaspoon white truffle oil

Kosher salt and freshly ground pepper to taste

Salmon or sturgeon caviar for garnish (optional)

continued

To poach the seafood: In a medium saucepan of salted simmering water, poach the scallops for 1 to 3 minutes, or until opaque throughout. Using a slotted spoon, transfer to a plate. Poach the prawns for 1 minute, or until just pink. Transfer to the plate with the scallops. Refrigerate until thoroughly chilled, about 30 minutes.

To make the gelée: Put the consommé in a double boiler over simmering water. Sprinkle the gelatin into the consommé and stir to dissolve. Stir in the saffron threads and salt. Keep the gelée warm until ready to use; if it gets cold, it will start to set up.

To assemble the molds or pyramids: Seal the pyramid molds, if using (see Chef's Tips). Cut the lobster into attractive bite-sized pieces. Cut the prawns and scallops in half, or leave whole if they're small, and toss with the chopped tarragon. Spray the inside of six 6-ounce ramekins or sealed pyramid molds with vegetable-oil cooking spray or rub with a paper towel dipped in vegetable oil. Begin layering the lobster, scallops, and prawns in the molds, with some on the sides and some in the middle, thinking of how they will look when unmolded. Pour in the warm gelée to within ½ to ¼ inch from the top of the molds. Let set up for 10 minutes, then carefully transfer the egg carton, if using pyramid molds, or the ramekins to the refrigerator. Let the molds chill, uncovered, for at least 2 hours or up to 24 hours before serving.

To make the saffron essence: In a small saucepan, combine the shellfish stock and saffron and heat over low heat until just below the boiling point. Remove from heat and let the saffron steep in the hot liquid. Transfer to a blender or food processor. Add the vinegar, salt, and pepper. With the machine running, gradually add the oil to make an emulsified sauce. Set aside, or let cool, cover, and refrigerate for up to 1 day.

To make the leek salad: In a small bowl, toss the leeks with the truffle oil, salt, and pepper.

To serve, pool a little of the saffron essence in the center of each plate. Remove the pyramid gelée from the molds by dipping each into a bowl of hot water for 30 seconds and inserting a small, thin-bladed knife between the gelée and mold on one side. Wiggle the knife a bit to break the seal and carefully slide it along the edges to pop the mold into one hand. Place a mold in the center of the saffron essence on each plate. Garnish each plate with 3 small mounds of leeks and a few grains of caviar, if using, on top of each of the leek mounds.

IMPROVISATIONS *The seafood I've specified here is only a guide. Use whatever you'd like: all lobster or prawns, or even salmon or crab. You'll need a total of 12 ounces of cooked meat. If you don't like saffron, try a light tomato consommé (page 247) or a cucumber consommé (page 38), and use a simple lemon vinaigrette (page 247) for the leek salad and around the plate.*

ADVANCE PREP *There are several steps to creating this dish, none terribly difficult, but to make it easier on yourself, stretch your preparations out over a few days. First, make the shellfish stock and consommé, which can be refrigerated for up to 2 days or frozen for up to 3 months. You'll need to make at least 1 gallon, because the clarification technique will not work on smaller quantities. The gelée can be made when you're ready to prepare the molds, but the finished molds can be refrigerated for up to 24 hours before serving. The vinaigrette and seafood can all be made and refrigerated up to 1 day in advance.*

SIMPLIFYING *This is another one of the dishes in this book for which there are not many shortcuts; the suggestions under Improvisations, above, will make the dish less difficult.*

WINE NOTES *If you're starting with this dish, the meal is probably an occasion. To kick off the evening in style, open a bottle of vintage tête-de-cuvée Champagne like Bollinger Grande Année, Dom Perignon, or Pommery Cuvée Louise.*

Warm Appetizers

Of all the courses, warm appetizers are my favorites. I like to think of them as vignettes of the main course: smaller, less complex, but more intensely flavorful portions that stimulate and soothe the appetite yet leave it wanting more (although at the restaurant, people will order two or even three a la carte appetizers and skip right to dessert). Where hors d'oeuvres are simply meant to be flirty little enticements, first
courses are expected be more than that; after all, they're the opening act and set the tone for the entire meal. As part of a multicourse menu, a first course should not muddy or fatigue the palate. You'll find that most of the dishes in this chapter have at most, two or three major flavor components. But I also like to indulge my guests at the beginning of the meal with luxurious ingredients like foie gras and lobster, and many of my first courses are quite rich, so small portions are in order. The Crab Imperial Gratin with Corn, Potatoes, Tarragon Crème Fraîche, and Lemon Zest, though we often serve it in three-bite portions as an opener, is really more of a luncheon dish.

Everyone loves soup, whether a simple broth or a meal-in-a-bowl, so this chapter begins with that most traditional of all first courses and the perfect choice if you want to serve something that can be made ahead. At Farallon, we've made hundreds of kinds of soups, and I've chosen five that represent our basics, from a light and unusual Maine Lobster and Matsutake Mushrooms in a Chrysanthemum Consommé, to a rich Black Mussel Bisque with Seafood Quenelles and Chive Oil. There's a quick and comforting Oyster Stew with Ancho Chili Butter, and an intense Asparagus Soup with Salt Cod, a basic vegetable soup that can be varied according to the season. The Lobster Minestrone, and the Lobster and Fava Bean Ragout (though not really a soup), are both rich dishes that make stunning openers to formal meals but could be increased and served as entrees. Besides soups, gratins make perfect do-ahead first courses. The Champagne-Baked Oysters with Braised Leeks and Truffle Cream and the Curried Mussel Glaçage with Wilted Hearts of Romaine are simple and similar recipes using an egg-enriched whipped-cream sauce that can be prepped in advance of a dinner party and cooked moments before serving.

If you want to see your guests smile when you bring out the first course, give them something fried. The guilt that's associated with fried food is assuaged if it's served in discreet portions, and anything called *crisp* on our warm appetizer menu seems to fly out of the kitchen. The Giant Tempura Prawns with Scallop Mousse would be a wonderful contrast of taste and texture to a simple main course like the Farallon Hot Pot. The Crispy Saffron-Marinated Frog's Legs makes not only a terrific first course, combining the delicate tempura legs with a salad, but the frog's legs can also be served without the salad as a passed hors d'oeuvre.

When I'm planning banquet menus where wines are featured, I often need to turn to a few tried-and-true favorites that I know are wine friendly and easy to serve to large groups. The Sautéed Fillet of Rouget with Brandade fits those criteria, as does the Peeky-Toe Crab with Truffled Mashed Potatoes, a Farallon signature dish that looks spectacular (particularly if you can get some sea urchin shells) but can be made ahead and assembled before serving.

BLACK MUSSEL BISQUE *with* SEAFOOD QUENELLES *and* CHIVE OIL

Twenty years ago, bisques were served at all the most elegant restaurants, while today they're an endangered culinary species. I'm not sure why they've fallen out of favor, but I think it has something to do with the perception that a bisque is a supremely rich preparation. A proper bisque, however, should taste mostly of seafood, not cream or butter—cream should only be added as a final flourish, if at all. When I make a bisque, whether with lobster, crab, mussels or oysters, I cook the shellfish first, remove the meat, and reserve the liquid (and the shells, if I'm using lobster or crab). Then I make a classic velouté using flour, butter, and fish stock and add that to a soup base of onions, celery, carrots, and fennel. The vegetable base is then cooked with the reserved shellfish and the whole thing is pureed, giving texture and body to the soup. I add only a touch of cream as a final enrichment, and if you're watching your fat intake, you could eliminate the cream altogether. This soup is so intensely flavored, you won't miss it. Like any soup, it can, and probably should, be made in advance.

★ CHEF'S TIP *For this bisque, any fresh mussel variety will do, with one word of caution: Skip the "green-lip" mussels from New Zealand. They're big and beautiful, but they can be flavorless, depending on the season.*

Makes 4 appetizer servings

MUSSELS:

2 tablespoons olive oil

2 shallots, coarsely chopped

2 sprigs thyme

3 pounds black mussels, scrubbed and debearded

1 cup Champagne or dry white wine

VELOUTÉ BASE:

4 tablespoons unsalted butter

1 cup coarsely chopped onion

1 cup coarsely chopped fennel

4 tarragon stems (reserve leaves for soup)

4 thyme stems (reserve leaves for soup)

½ cup all-purpose flour

2 cups fish stock (page 243) or clam juice

Kosher salt and freshly ground pepper to taste

SOUP BASE:

1 tablespoon olive oil

2 shallots, coarsely chopped

3 cloves garlic, coarsely chopped

½ cup coarsely chopped onion

½ cup coarsely chopped fennel

Reserved fresh tarragon and thyme leaves, above

1 cup Champagne or dry white wine

Reserved mussels, above

About 1½ cups fish stock (page 243) or clam juice

1 cup water

Velouté Base, above

QUENELLES:

4 ounces shrimp, shelled and deveined

4 ounces scallops

2 tablespoons heavy cream

1 large egg white

1 tablespoon coarsely chopped fresh tarragon

2 teaspoons fresh lemon juice

Kosher salt and freshly ground pepper to taste

Pinch of cayenne pepper

Heavy cream or half-and-half for garnish (optional)

Chive-infused oil (page 241), or chopped fresh chives for garnish

Preparation

To cook the mussels: In a large stockpot, heat the olive oil over medium heat and sauté the shallots and thyme until the shallots are soft but not colored, about 5 minutes. Increase heat to high and add the mussels. Add the wine, cover, and steam the mussels for about 3 minutes, shaking the pan once or twice. Remove from heat and let sit for 5 minutes, or until most of the shells have opened. Using a slotted spoon, transfer the mussels to a bowl, leaving the liquid in the pan. Let the mussels cool. Remove the meat from the shells, discarding any mussels that haven't opened. Reserve the mussel meat to add to the soup. Pour the mussel cooking liquid into a glass measuring cup and let sit to allow the solids to settle to the bottom.

To make the velouté base: In a medium saucepan, melt the butter over medium-low heat. Add the chopped onion, fennel, and tarragon and thyme stems. Cook, stirring occasionally, until the vegetables have softened but not colored, about 4 minutes. Add the flour and stir the mixture for 3 to 4 minutes. Remove from heat and gradually whisk in ½ cup of the stock or clam juice until smooth. Gradually whisk the remaining 1½ cups stock or clam juice and season with salt and pepper. Return the saucepan to low heat and simmer, stirring frequently with a wooden spoon to prevent scorching on the bottom. After 15 to 20 minutes, the velouté base will become quite thick and have a velvety texture and silky sheen. Remove from heat. Strain the base through

continued

a medium-mesh sieve into a bowl or measuring cup, using the back of the spoon to press the solids through the sieve. Set aside and let cool slightly. Press a piece of plastic wrap directly onto the surface of the velouté to prevent a skin from forming. Set aside, or cover and refrigerate for up to 1 day.

To make the soup base: In a large saucepan, heat the olive oil over medium heat and sauté the shallots, garlic, onion, fennel, tarragon, and thyme until the vegetables are soft but not colored. Add ½ cup of the Champagne or white wine and the reserved mussels. Add enough fish stock or clam juice to the reserved mussel cooking liquid to equal 2 cups of liquid and carefully pour into the soup base, discarding the sediment in the bottom of the measuring cup. Add the water and velouté. Whisk to combine. Cook over low heat for 15 minutes to let the flavors marry, stirring occasionally to prevent scorching on the bottom of the pan. Remove the soup from heat and let cool for 15 minutes. Puree in a blender or food processor. Strain through a fine-mesh sieve, pressing on the solids with the back of a large spoon. The soup can be cooled, covered, and refrigerated at this point for up to 2 days.

To make the shellfish mousse for the quenelles: The mousse will hold together better if all the ingredients are as cold as possible, so make sure all your ingredients come directly from the refrigerator. Put the work bowl and blade of a food processor in the freezer for at least 15 minutes as added insurance. Remove the bowl and blade from the freezer. In the food processor, combine the shrimp and scallops and process until they're coarsely chopped. Add the cream and egg white and pulse on and off for about 10 seconds. Add the tarragon, lemon juice, salt, pepper, and cayenne and process for about 20 seconds more, scraping down the sides of the bowl if necessary, until the mixture forms a smooth, sticky paste that is somewhat firm and holds its shape. If the mixture is too firm, it tends to become rubbery and too loose and your quenelles will fall apart in the water. If you're unsure of the consistency, first try forming one and cooking it in a small saucepan of barely simmering water. Scrape the mixture into a clean container, cover, and refrigerate until you're ready to form and poach the quenelles.

To form and poach the quenelles: Bring a medium saucepan of salted water to a boil and reduce heat to a low simmer. (Rapidly boiling water can cause the quenelles to disintegrate.) Using 2 wet soup spoons, pick up a heaping spoonful of mousse in one spoon and transfer the mixture from one spoon to the other, smoothing and shaping as you go to form a rounded oval. In small batches, gently drop the quenelles in the water and cook until they float to the surface, about 5 minutes, depending on their size. Using a slotted spoon, transfer the quenelles to a bowl of cold water to stop their cooking. Serve now, or refrigerate the quenelles in their bowl of water or drain, place on a plate, and cover with plastic wrap for up to 3 days. Reheat in the soup or in a saucepan of simmering water for a few minutes.

To serve, heat the soup and add the remaining ½ cup Champagne or wine. Taste and adjust the seasoning. Stir in the optional cream or half-and-half. Ladle the soup into warmed shallow bowls. Put 2 warm quenelles in each bowl and dot the surface of the soup with the chive oil.

IMPROVISATION At the restaurant we often make this bisque with oysters instead of mussels. At home, you can use two 10-ounce jars of shucked oysters. Add the oysters with their liquor to the soup base instead of the reserved mussels.

ADVANCE PREP The velouté can be made 1 day before you make the soup and kept refrigerated. The soup can be made, short of the cream addition, up to 2 days in advance and refrigerated. Just before serving, bring the soup to a low simmer and add the cream, more Champagne, salt, and pepper. You can form and poach the quenelles, place on a plate, and cover with plastic, or keep them in their bowl of water. Refrigerate for up to 3 days.

SIMPLIFYING The quenelles may be deleted. While the velouté contributes a subtle and sublime texture, there's a much easier way to thicken this soup. Instead of the velouté, add 1 cup of stale bread cubes and 1 cup of water to the soup base just after adding the fish stock and mussel liquid.

WINE NOTES Delicate, rich soups like this one are good with sparkling wines. They're not only great wines to start a meal with, but also incredibly versatile at the table. Try a Champagne like Bollinger Special Cuvée, or Jacques Selosse, both from houses that still use barrel fermentation for the base wine. They have a rich, creamy style that's perfect with this soup.

ASPARAGUS SOUP *with* SALT COD

There's asparagus soup and then there's asparagus soup, and no doubt about it, this is the real deal. Here, I've borrowed from the Chinese technique of stir-frying—where green vegetables are flash-cooked to intensify their flavors before the liquid is added. I use water rather than stock because I want the soup to taste like fresh asparagus, not chicken stock or cream. The use of salt cod as a garnish may seem odd but serves to contrast and accentuate the flavor of the soup. As it often happens, I discovered this terrific combination quite by accident. Right after we opened, I was experimenting with making salt cod on the same day that we were serving asparagus soup. I'd been testing and tasting the salt cod recipe for days. Just as I poured myself a bowl of soup for dinner I decided to toss in some of the salt cod and boy, were my taste buds pleasantly ambushed! The taste of the salty cod with the grassy asparagus was an unexpected and sexy combination.

★ *CHEF'S TIPS Of course I'm partial to the salt cod recipe in this book (see page 242), but purchased salt cod is perfectly fine since it's simply used as a garnish here. If you do use commercial salt cod, be aware that quality varies. Whichever you use, just be sure you don't oversoak the cod and remove all the flavor. It should retain a nice hit of salt. | This could be considered a master recipe for vegetable soup (see Improvisations, below).*

Makes 6 to 8 appetizer servings

1½ pounds asparagus
3 tablespoons unsalted butter
1 large yellow onion, diced
2 stalks celery, diced
1 large leek, white part only, rinsed and diced
4 cups water

1 cup tightly packed fresh spinach leaves
Kosher salt and freshly ground pepper to taste
1 tablespoon fresh lemon juice
One 4-ounce piece 24-hour salt cod (page 242), or commercially prepared salt cod, soaked

Preparation

Break off and discard the woody stems from the asparagus. Cut the tips from the spears about 1 inch from the top and set aside. Cut the stalks into ½-inch pieces. You should have about 4 cups of stalk pieces. Blanch the tips in salted boiling water until tender but still a vibrant green, 3 to 4 minutes. Run the tips under cold running water and drain. If they are very large, slice them in half lengthwise.

In a large saucepan, melt the butter over medium heat. Add the diced onion, celery, and leek. Reduce heat to low and cook, stirring occasionally, until softened but not browned, about 5 minutes. Add the asparagus stalks, increase heat to medium-high, and cook, stirring constantly, for 1 minute. Add the water, reduce heat to a simmer, partially cover, and cook until the asparagus is tender, 20 to 30 minutes. Remove from heat and stir in the spinach, then let the soup cool for 10 minutes.

In a blender or food processor, puree the soup in batches. Strain the soup through a medium-mesh sieve and discard the solids. Add the salt, pepper, and lemon juice. If the soup seems too thick, add a little extra water. It should be a bit thicker than heavy cream.

To serve, ladle the hot soup into warmed shallow soup bowls. Garnish with flakes of salt cod and the reserved asparagus tips.

continued

IMPROVISATIONS *Broccoli would make a nice substitute for the asparagus in the fall and winter, and English peas in season are a delicious alternative. You can, if you want, add just a touch of cream or, as the Italians would do, a little extra-virgin olive oil at the end—it depends on your taste preference.*

ADVANCE PREP *This soup is just as delicious prepared ahead. Be sure to let it cool down before you refrigerate it so that it doesn't lower your refrigerator temperature to unsafe levels. Covered, the soup will last up to 2 days. The salt cod will need to soak for at least 4 or up to 36 hours, depending on its saltiness.*

SIMPLIFYING *This fresh-tasting asparagus soup can stand alone with no adornment. Just serve it without the salt cod. If you prefer a thicker, country-style soup, eliminate the straining process or pour the soup through a large-mesh sieve.*

WINE NOTES *A full-bodied Champagne or sparkling wine is a delicate choice for this elegant starter. Either one would be dry and slightly acidic with the asparagus, yet creamy and round with the salt cod. And let's face it, Champagne turns everyday events and simple meals into celebrations.*

CRAB IMPERIAL GRATIN *with* CORN, POTATOES, TARRAGON CRÈME FRAÎCHE, *and* LEMON ZEST

Comfortingly retro, this dish makes me think of the kind of deviled crab casserole you might have found on the menu at an elegant lady's luncheon in the fifties, though it's been lightened, of course, for our more contemporary palates. It's a simple combination of fresh crab, corn, and potatoes, bound lightly with crème fraîche and subtly accented with fresh tarragon and lemon. Right before serving, it's run under the broiler to crisp the bread-crumb topping. We serve this dish as an appetizer at lunch, and though delicate and not as rich as you might think, it's quite filling. I've noticed that many Farallon regulars like to order it as a lunch entree with a salad on the side. In smaller portions it makes a terrific first course because it's a cinch to put together ahead of time.

★ *CHEF'S TIPS This is a filling dish. To serve it as a first or appetizer course, divide it into 6 ramekin portions. | We serve the crab in 4-by-1-inch round gratins. Four-ounce ramekins would also work, or large scallop shells would make a beautiful presentation.*

Makes 4 luncheon entrees

3 medium red potatoes, peeled and cut into ¼-inch dice

8 ounces fresh lump crabmeat, preferably Dungeness, picked over for shells

1½ tablespoons unsalted butter

½ cup fresh or frozen corn kernels

½ cup crème fraîche

1 tablespoon grated lemon zest

1 teaspoon chopped fresh tarragon

½ to 1 teaspoon white truffle oil or olive oil

Kosher salt and freshly ground pepper to taste

BREAD CRUMB TOPPING:

1 tablespoon unsalted butter

½ cup dried bread crumbs (page 240)

½ teaspoon chopped fresh thyme, or ¼ teaspoon dried thyme

Kosher salt and freshly ground pepper to taste

White truffle oil or extra-virgin olive oil for drizzling

4 sprigs tarragon or thyme for garnish

Preparation

Butter four 4-inch-diameter shallow baking dishes or 4-ounce individual ramekins or scallop shells and set aside. Cook the diced potatoes in salted boiling water until barely tender, about 5 minutes. Drain. Put the crabmeat in a medium bowl and set aside. In a small sauté pan or skillet, melt the butter over low heat, add the corn kernels, and cook until soft, about 3 minutes. Remove and add to the crabmeat. Add the potatoes, crème fraîche, lemon zest, tarragon, oil, salt, and pepper to the crab, and stir thoroughly to combine. Set aside, or cover and refrigerate for up to 1 day.

To prepare the topping: In a small sauté pan or skillet, melt the butter over medium heat. Add the bread crumbs and thyme, and stir until the crumbs are golden and crunchy, 2 to 3 minutes. Season with salt and pepper. Set aside, or let cool and store in an airtight container for up to 1 day.

To serve, preheat the oven to 400°F. Spoon the crab mixture equally into the prepared baking dishes and top evenly with the bread crumbs. Put the dishes or shells on a baking sheet and drizzle with a little truffle oil or olive oil. Bake in the top third of the preheated oven until golden and bubbling, about 10 minutes. Carefully place each hot gratin on a plate lined with a folded napkin. Garnish with tarragon sprigs and serve immediately.

continued

IMPROVISATIONS *Shrimp, lobster, or cooked and flaked salmon would be good substitutes for the crab. Instead of corn, many other combinations would work, such as mushrooms, artichokes, and fresh peas. Vary the herbs to suit your taste with basil, thyme, or chives.*

ADVANCE PREP *The crab mixture and topping can be made 1 day ahead. The gratins can be made 1 day ahead, cooled, then covered with plastic and refrigerated. They can also be frozen for up to 1 week, then broiled or baked just before serving.*

SIMPLIFYING *The only two frozen vegetables that I find acceptable are corn and peas, and frozen corn is perfectly acceptable here.*

WINE NOTES *California Sauvignon Blanc, barrel fermented in new oak, can end up tasting almost like Chardonnay: too ripe and woody. But white Bordeaux, which is Sauvignon Blanc with varying amounts of Semillon, for reasons of soil and climate comes out tasting unlike anything else.*

OYSTER STEW *with* ANCHO CHILI BUTTER

I offer this recipe as proof that not all restaurant cooking is complicated, and in fact, some of the best dishes are often the simplest. We served this oyster "stew" at the Santa Fe Bar & Grill in Berkeley for years and it was a perennial favorite. In a break with tradition, we seasoned ours with ancho chili butter instead of the more typical Worcestershire and Tabasco. When we serve this at Farallon and guests ask for the recipe, they are always amazed at how few ingredients are included. It's really nothing more than fresh-shucked oysters cooked in a warm cream bath. The Grand Central Oyster Bar & Grill serves such a wonderful version of this classic dish that every time I visit New York City I make a point to break from my itinerary so I can sit at the counter and have a bowl of their oyster stew.

★ *CHEF'S TIPS It's important not to overcook the oysters; they should be just warmed through, so make sure you add them and their liquid just at the moment the cream comes to a gentle simmer. | Toasting dried chilies before rehydrating them gives them an added depth of flavor, but be careful not to scorch or burn them or they'll taste bitter. They can also be toasted in a preheated 350°F oven for 2 to 3 minutes.*

Makes 4 appetizer servings

ANCHO CHILI PUREE:

5 dried ancho chilies, stemmed and
   seeded
1 teaspoon fresh lime juice
¼ cup grapeseed, canola, or olive oil
Kosher salt to taste

ANCHO CHILI BUTTER:

2 tablespoons unsalted butter, softened
2 tablespoons ancho chili puree, above
1 teaspoon fresh lime juice
Kosher salt to taste

STEW:

2 cups heavy cream
2 cups half-and-half
24 medium oysters, shucked, liquor
   strained and reserved
Kosher salt and freshly ground pepper
   to taste

2 tablespoons minced fresh chives
   for garnish

Preparation

To make the ancho chili puree: In a small dry sauté pan or skillet, toast the chilies over medium heat for 2 to 3 minutes. Transfer to a bowl and pour in boiling water to cover, weighting down the chilies to keep them submerged, if necessary. Let stand for 30 minutes, or until the chilies are completely soft. Drain and transfer to a blender or food processor. Add the lime juice and oil and puree. Season with salt. Strain through a fine-mesh sieve and set aside 2 tablespoons of the puree for the butter. Cover and refrigerate the remaining puree for up to 2 weeks.

To make the chili butter: In a small bowl, cream the butter, chili puree, lime juice, and salt together until fully incorporated. Scrape into a small bowl and refrigerate for at least 15 minutes or up to 2 weeks.

To make the stew: In a large saucepan, combine the cream and half-and-half. Bring to just below a gentle simmer over low heat. Add the oysters and the reserved liquor and turn off the heat. Season with salt and pepper.

To serve, warm the soup bowls and ladle the stew into warmed soup bowls and place 1 teaspoon of ancho chili butter in the center of each and garnish with chives. Serve piping hot.

IMPROVISATIONS *Mussels work well here in place of oysters. The ancho chili puree can be made with a puree of spicier, smokier canned chipotle chilies in adobo sauce mixed with an equal amount of crème fraîche. Garnish with sliced green onions or float fresh tarragon leaves on top.*

ADVANCE PREP *The recipe for ancho chili puree makes about 1 cup—much more than you'll need for the stew—but both the puree and the butter will keep for up to 2 weeks in the refrigerator or up to 6 months frozen, and can be used in other ways. Try on eggs, grilled fish, or chicken, or use a little of the puree to flavor a salad dressing.*

SIMPLIFYING *Eliminate the chili puree if you wish and go classical with Worcestershire and Tabasco, or just sprinkle the stew with snipped fresh chives or green onions.*

WINE NOTES *Once again, this is a delicate and rich but ever-so-spicy starter that would be perfect with a glass of bubbly. Choose a style that is rich and broad on the palate, like Bollinger Grand Année, Jacques Lassalle, or Roederer L'Ermitage from California. If you're feeling flush, go for Krug Grande Cuvée.*

LOBSTER MINESTRONE

Minestrone is one of those recipes that invites improvisation. Thick or thin; with beans or without; made with beef broth, chicken, or water—everyone has a favorite method. The Italians, who invented it, all have their regional versions and are quick to argue over whose is better (although it's rare to find two Italians who will agree on anything). But one thing most people will agree on is that minestrone should contain vegetables, and this one does—lots of them—floating in a flavorful but delicate lobster broth with pieces of freshly cooked lobster meat. It makes a terrific starter at a formal dinner but would be just as appropriate for a casual family dinner.

★ *CHEF'S TIPS This soup seems more difficult to make than it really is, but it's important to start from the beginning and make the lobster stock, otherwise it's just another vegetable soup garnished with lobster. Besides, if you're going to go to the trouble of cooking lobsters, you might as well make the stock as well. Shortcuts just don't work here, because all the flavor is in the rich broth. And don't skim the stock; that's where all the color is. | Fresh herbs, particularly tarragon, give this soup an intense aroma that's intoxicating.*

Makes 8 first-course or 4 entree servings

Two 1½-pound lobsters

LOBSTER STOCK:
¼ cup olive oil
Reserved shells from lobsters, above
2 cups coarsely chopped carrots
2 cups coarsely chopped celery
2 cups coarsely chopped onion
4 pounds fennel bulbs, trimmed and coarsely chopped, reserve fronds for garnish
2 tomatoes, halved
2½ quarts water
2 bay leaves
3 sprigs thyme
1 cup dry white wine
Reserved liquid from lobsters, above

3 pounds fava beans, shelled
1 cup finely diced onion
1 cup finely diced fennel
1 cup finely diced carrot
1 cup finely diced celery
5 ounces shiitake mushrooms, stemmed and thinly sliced
1 cup cooked white beans
1 tablespoon chopped fresh tarragon, blanched
Kosher salt and freshly ground pepper to taste

Lemon-infused oil for garnish (page 241), optional
Reserved fronds from 1 fennel bulb, minced

Preparation

To cook and clean the lobsters: Bring a large pan of heavily salted water to a boil. Drop the lobsters in and cook for 5 minutes, then plunge them into a large bowl of ice water. Refrigerate them for 30 minutes. To clean the lobsters, set out 3 medium bowls. Begin by pulling the legs from each lobster over the first bowl to catch all the liquid, then twist off the tails and head. Discard the white feathery gills and lungs and the brown-green mud sac. Using a nutcracker or small sauté pan, crack the tail and claws and remove the meat. Put all the shells in the second bowl and the meat in the third. Refrigerate the meat and liquid until ready to use.

To make the lobster stock: In a large stockpot over medium-high heat, heat the olive oil. Toss in the reserved lobster shells. Using a wooden spoon, stir and pound the shells while cooking, for about 5 minutes. Add all the vegetables and cook for 5 minutes more, stirring. Add the water and herbs. Bring to a gentle simmer and cook for 15 to 20 minutes. Do not skim the stock. Add the white wine and reserved lobster liquid and simmer for 20 minutes. Remove from heat, strain, and set aside.

To blanch and peel the fava beans: Drop the beans in a large pot of salted boiling water. Cook for 1 to 2 minutes, then plunge them into ice water to stop the cooking. Drain and cool. Break the skin of each bean with your thumbnail at the stem end and slide the bean out. Use immediately or store the beans in a self-sealing plastic bag in the refrigerator for up to 4 days.

In a large saucepan, bring the lobster stock to a simmer, add all the diced vegetables, and cook until tender, 5 to 7 minutes. Add the shiitakes, fava beans, lobster meat, white beans, and tarragon and cook for 5 minutes to heat through.

To serve, ladle the minestrone into warmed shallow soup bowls, drizzle with the lemon-infused oil, if using, and garnish with minced fennel fronds.

IMPROVISATIONS *Use whatever vegetables strike your fancy, as long as they're fresh and in season. You could use prawns or crab in place of the lobster. Instead of the lemon-infused oil, use grated lemon zest and drizzle with extra-virgin olive oil.*

ADVANCE PREP *The lobster can be cooked and the stock made 1 day ahead. All the chopping can be done 1 day ahead as well. The soup should be made just before serving.*

SIMPLIFYING *In place of fava beans, you could use shelled soybeans (edamame). Drizzle the soup with a purchased lemon-infused oil, if using.*

WINE NOTES *Taittinger from Champagne and Domaine Carneros from California are delicate, feminine styles of bubbly that will complement this unique soup in a grand fashion. If you prefer a still wine, keep it light-bodied and unoaked.*

WARM APPETIZERS 91

Many years ago, Jeremiah Tower introduced me to a little Japanese restaurant called Kabuto in the Richmond District of San Francisco. I started going there often and later found out that, coincidentally, so did George, my chef de cuisine, and many other cooks as well. The chef's name is Sachio Kojima, and on our many late-night, after-work meals there, he loved to serve us many new and exotic

MAINE LOBSTER *and* MATSUTAKE MUSHROOMS *in a* CHRYSANTHEMUM CONSOMMÉ

foods, knowing how receptive and eager we were. On one occasion, he served us cod-semen sushi, which George immediately loved and thought would make a great canapé. Let me go on record as saying that that was one ingredient that has never made an appearance on a Farallon menu. But Sachio has often inspired us, and this is George's and my tribute to him.

★ *CHEF'S TIPS At the restaurant, we make a special presentation of this dish. A bowl with the leaves, lobster, and mushrooms already arranged inside is taken to the table, with the broth in a separate Japanese teapot. The waiters pour the soup in front of the customers so that they can appreciate every nuance of aroma. | This mushroom consommé is probably the easiest type of clarification to achieve. There is no "raft" of protein needed, merely clean ingredients and the mysterious clarifying action of soy sauce. The matsutake mushrooms and chrysanthemum leaves are costly and highly seasonal ingredients, yet they make this dish something to look forward to once a year. I've included some substitutions, but try to get the real things, as they're really special. | For a lighter colored stock, remove the gills of the portobello mushrooms.*

Makes 6 appetizer servings

MUSHROOM CONSOMMÉ:	2 portobello mushrooms, stemmed and coarsely chopped	Claws and tail meat of 3 cooked and cleaned lobsters (see page 233)
1 tablespoon grapeseed or canola oil	4 cups chicken stock (page 243)	1 matsutake mushroom, or 4 shiitake mushrooms
12 shallots, thinly sliced	4 cups fish stock (page 243)	
3-inch knob fresh ginger, thinly sliced	4 cups water	6 fresh chrysanthemum leaves, stemmed
1 whole stalk lemongrass, lightly smashed and cut crosswise into 4 pieces	¼ cup soy sauce	1 lemon, ends trimmed, cut into 6 wedges
3 pounds cremini mushrooms, coarsely chopped	¼ cup fish sauce (optional)	

To make the consommé: Heat the oil in a large stockpot over medium-low heat and sauté the shallots, ginger, and lemongrass. Add the mushrooms and cook until softened but not browned, about 10 minutes. Add the stocks and water and bring to a boil. Reduce heat to a simmer and cook to reduce by half, about 1½ hours. Strain the stock through a fine-mesh sieve lined with a double layer of cheesecloth, gently pushing on the solids with the back of a large spoon to extract as much liquid as possible. Discard the solids. Let cool, then add the soy sauce and fish sauce, if using. Taste and adjust the seasoning. Serve now, or let cool, cover, and refrigerate for up to 2 days. Reheat before serving.

To serve, cut the lobster tails in half lengthwise. Cut each tail half on the diagonal into 4 or 5 sections and arrange in the bowls with 1 claw each. Using a mandoline or sharp knife, carefully shave the matsutake or shiitake mushrooms into paper-thin slices and arrange in the bowls. Cut the chrysanthemum leaves into fine julienne and distribute among the bowls. At the last moment, or at the table, pour the very hot broth over and serve with a lemon wedge sitting on the rim of the bowl.

IMPROVISATIONS The chrysanthemum leaves can be substituted with with cilantro sprigs and a little bit of finely sliced lemon zest. The mushroom consommé makes a terrific soup by itself, or with any number of other combinations, such as oyster and enoki mushrooms, baby bok choy and lotus root, or finely julienned carrots, leeks, and asparagus tips with a dollop of truffled crème fraîche for garnish.

ADVANCE PREP You can make the consommé up to 2 days ahead and reheat it. The lobster can be sliced earlier in the day. The mushrooms should be shaved shortly before serving.

WINE NOTES This is a delicate, perfumed dish that could easily be overpowered by the wrong beverage. A very delicate Champagne or a crisp, unwooded Oregon Pinot Gris, which is floral and scented with tangerines, would be a good match. Even a delicate Vin Gris would be terrific.

CHAMPAGNE-BAKED OYSTERS *with* BRAISED LEEKS *and* TRUFFLE CREAM

This is a sexy first course: sweet, earthy, briny, and voluptuous. If there's an oyster lover you're trying to seduce, begin a meal with this dish and you may not even get around to the entree. Really, though, the great part is that it's a cinch to pull off. The only trick is shucking the oysters, particularly if you're a novice shucker, but many fish purveyors will shuck them for you. Though this dish is called Champagne-Baked Oysters, only 1 tablespoon of Champagne is used to bake the oysters, leaving the rest of the bottle to be drunk at the table.

★ *CHEF'S TIPS In the ideal world, you would have a 2-ounce fresh black truffle to make this dish. But it can also be made using just 1 teaspoon of white truffle oil. | If you have them, black or dark-colored plates that contrast with the white salt look particularly stunning for this dish. | For a really special occasion, garnish the dish with caviar.*

Makes 4 appetizer servings

12 fresh oysters, shucked, liquor and
  bottom shells reserved separately
  (see page 236)
4 to 6 cups rock salt

BRAISED LEEKS:
1 large or 2 medium leeks, white part
  only, halved lengthwise
1 tablespoon unsalted butter
½ teaspoon chopped fresh thyme
Kosher salt and freshly ground pepper
  to taste

TRUFFLE GLAÇAGE:
½ cup heavy cream
1 tablespoon Champagne
1 egg yolk
Reserved oyster liquor, above
1 teaspoon chopped fresh black truffle
  or white truffle oil
Kosher salt and freshly ground pepper
  to taste

3 tablespoons finely julienned fresh black
  truffle, or lightly toasted nori (see
  page 40) for garnish, optional

Preparation

To prepare the oysters: Rinse, scrub, and dry the reserved oyster shell bottoms. Using a large gratin dish or broiler-pan bottom, pour in 2 cups of rock salt and pat into a thick layer. Nestle the shucked oyster-shell bottoms firmly in the salt and set aside. Divide the remaining rock salt between each of the 4 serving plates and set aside while you make the dish.

To prepare the leeks: Cut them crosswise into thin half-circles. Rinse in a colander and dry well. In a small sauté pan or skillet, melt the butter over medium-low heat, add the leeks, and cook until soft but not colored, about 5 minutes. Add the thyme, salt, and pepper and cook for 1 minute. Remove from heat and set aside.

To make the glaçage: In a deep bowl, beat the cream until soft peaks form. In a small bowl, whisk the Champagne, egg yolk, reserved oyster liquor, and truffle or truffle oil together. Add to the whipped cream and beat again until the cream begins to hold firm peaks. Season with salt and pepper. Refrigerate for up to 6 hours.

To serve, preheat the broiler. Put a little of the sautéed leeks in the bottom of each shell and place a shucked oyster on top of each serving of the leek mixture. Spoon on enough glaçage to cover the oysters. Place the prepared shells under the broiler 4 to 5 inches from the heat source until the glaçage is speckled golden and brown, about 30 seconds. Remove the oysters from the broiler, carefully lift them out of the salt, and arrange 3 in the bed of rock salt on each plate. Garnish with the truffle or nori, if using.

continued

IMPROVISATIONS *If you're in the mood for something less fancy, sautéed spinach would make a good combination with the oysters. You could replace the Champagne with the same still white wine that you might choose to drink with the dish. Garnish simply with fresh chives.*

ADVANCE PREP *The dish can be made up to the point just before covering the oysters with the glaçage and placing them on the rock salt. Refrigerate for up to 1 hour before serving, but be sure to cool the leek mixture first so that the heat from the leeks doesn't begin to cook the oysters. The glaçage can be refrigerated for up to 6 hours before serving and rewhisked just before serving.*

SIMPLIFYING *The beauty of this dish lies in its simplicity and there's not much you could do to make it easier, but please don't use oysters from a jar. If you're pressed for time, have your fishmonger shuck the oysters for you.*

WINE NOTES *Champagne is the natural choice for this dish, not only because it is used in the recipe but because it is also one of the great food and wine pairings. The second-best foil to the creamy oysters would be a Riesling, another of the most glorious white wines in the world. This dish presents the perfect opportunity to try some good German and Alsatian Rieslings. They combine a purity of fruit and depth of flavor with an acidity that makes them very refreshing, even if there is a bit of residual sugar.*

Many years ago in the South of France, Richard Olney took a small group of friends, who had not quite recovered from their hangovers, for a late lunch at a small family-owned bistro on the water's edge near Bandol. I don't remember much else of that day except for the bistro owner proudly emerging from the tiny kitchen onto the outdoor patio with an enormous platter of assorted *fruits de mer:* lobsters, clams, mussels, and oysters, all freshly steamed or shucked and in their opened shells. He crossed

CURRIED MUSSEL GLAÇAGE *with* WILTED HEARTS *of* ROMAINE

the patio to the open hearth, ladled a thick, pale sauce over the shellfish, placed the platter near the fire, and within minutes it again appeared at our table, bubbling and golden brown. The sauce turned out to be a combination of hollandaise, velouté, and whipped cream—it was heaven. Of course, those were the halcyon days when I was blissfully ignorant of calories or cholesterol, but I still like to glaze shellfish with egg-enriched cream sauces. This little first course is a mere shadow of that wonderful meal in France, but the flavors are all still there, and the sauce has been lightened considerably.

★ *CHEF'S TIPS A classic "royal glaçage" is both a technique and sauce, whereby equal parts of hollandaise, whipped cream, and velouté are folded together, spooned over meat, fish, or vegetables, then glazed under a broiler. It's a wonderful technique that we use frequently at Farallon (see Champagne-Baked Oysters, page 94), but we omit any velouté and hollandaise and enrich the whipped cream with egg yolks instead. | We serve this dish in individual oval gratins, but it can be served from a large, shallow baking dish as well. | Always inspect mussels before cooking them. Live mussels have tightly closed shells or, if open, they will close when tapped. Mussels average about 12 to the pound, and for this dish you'll need 5 or 6 mussels per person. Buy extra in case you have to discard some.*

Makes 4 appetizer servings

1 tablespoon olive oil

1 shallot, minced

2 cloves garlic, minced

½ bunch thyme sprigs

2 to 3 pounds black mussels, scrubbed and debearded

¼ cup dry white wine

Kosher salt and freshly ground pepper to taste

4 heads of romaine, large outer leaves removed and stems trimmed but left on

GLAÇAGE:

1½ cups heavy cream

2 egg yolks

2 tablespoons reserved mussel liquid, above

⅛ teaspoon curry powder

Kosher salt and freshly ground pepper to taste

Preparation

Heat the olive oil in a medium sauté pan or skillet over low heat and cook the shallot, garlic, and thyme in the olive oil until the shallot and garlic are soft, about 3 minutes. Increase heat to high and add the mussels. Add the white wine, salt, and pepper. Cover immediately and cook, shaking the pan occasionally, until most of the mussels have opened, 4 to 7 minutes. Discard any mussels that haven't opened. Let the mussels cool in their liquid. Remove and discard the shells, and set the mussels aside. Strain the liquid through a fine-mesh sieve and reserve.

Bring a medium saucepan of lightly salted water to a boil. Using tongs, blanch each of the romaine hearts in the water for 30 seconds. Transfer to a bowl of ice water. Remove after 1 minute and squeeze gently to remove the water. Lay the hearts on a towel and slice off the stems. Wrap in the towel and set aside at room temperature for up to 2 hours.

continued

To make the glaçage: In a deep bowl, beat the cream until soft peaks form. In a small bowl, whisk the egg yolks, reserved mussel liquid, and the curry powder together just to combine. Add to the whipped cream and beat until the cream holds firm peaks. Season with salt and pepper.

To serve, preheat the broiler. Place 1 wilted romaine heart on each of 4 individual gratins or ovenproof dishes, top with 5 or 6 mussels, and spoon 3 tablespoons of the glaçage over the mussels. Broil about 5 inches from the heat source until heated through and golden brown, 1 to 2 minutes. Place each hot dish on a plate lined with a folded napkin and serve immediately.

IMPROVISATIONS *I prefer Prince Edward Island mussels for their exquisite flavor and size, but any kind will work in this recipe, as will clams or oysters. Clams need to be steamed, but oysters could be shucked raw onto the romaine. Strain the juices of either and substitute for the mussel liquid. Also instead of mussels, you could use lobster medallions or crabmeat. Pale green heads of curly endive would make a good substitute for the romaine, but use them only if you like their bitter taste. You might omit the curry powder entirely, although it adds a subtle complexity of flavor to the glaçage. At the restaurant, we sometimes serve this dish on a bed of beluga lentils.*

SIMPLIFYING *This is such an easy first course that it's difficult to think of a way to make it simpler, but you could purchase cooked mussels in their shells and use Champagne or white wine in place of the mussel-steaming liquid. The mussels are also great served without the braised romaine.*

ADVANCE PREP *The mussels can be steamed 1 day ahead and the liquid and the mussels refrigerated overnight. Let sit at room temperature for about 45 minutes before continuing with the recipe. The romaine may be blanched up to 2 hours before serving, and the glaçage can be made up to 6 hours before serving.*

WINE NOTES *This rich and somewhat spicy dish needs a wine that is fruity, rich, and exotic too. Pinot Gris comes to mind. Etude Wines in the Napa Valley is producing Pinot Gris in the Alsatian way: fruity, unoaked, and tropical, with bright acids. Riesling and Muscat are also worth trying, as is a ripe rosé that's not too dry. Several Californian wineries make good rosés of Pinot Noir and Pinot Meunier, perfect served slightly chilled. Either a Chardonnay or white Burgundy, fruity and simple, without too much oak to clash with the complex curry flavors, would work. Sauvignon Blanc has a great affinity for crab, and California Sauvignon from Honig, Spottswoode, Matanzas Creek, Robert Mondavi, Cain Vineyards, and others are making Sauvignons that are true to the variety.*

This is a dish of beautiful contrasting flavors and textures. The oysters are sweet and briny, the celery root is crisp and earthy, and the gnocchi are light and voluptuous. And the caviar—food doesn't get sexier than this. It's hands down one of our more popular first courses, and it's not unusual for our guests to request it as an entree. Even your most "oyster-challenged" guests will love it. Dan Weiss, a friend of mine who is both oyster- *and* caviar-challenged, eats this with gusto.

★ CHEF'S TIPS *We make pounds of potato gnocchi every day at Farallon, and Farallon's talented lunch chef, Bradford Barker, is our "gnocchi maven." We all think that his gnocchi are the best in the world. Reducing a recipe that requires 16 pounds of potatoes, 8 pounds of flour, and 40 egg yolks into a manageable amount*

POTATO GNOCCHI *with* CELERY ROOT, POACHED OYSTERS, *and* BLACK CAVIAR

for a home kitchen, however, requires a bit of experimentation and research. We came up with a few tips that you'll find helpful: Baking potatoes (called russet or Idaho) are dry, fluffy, and starchy and make the lightest gnocchi. | You can either boil or bake the potatoes, but whichever method you choose, the main thing to keep in mind is that you want them to dry out as much as possible after cooking so that they absorb as little flour as possible. Less flour means lighter gnocchi. Passing the potatoes through a food mill or ricer also helps to fluff up the potatoes and steam them dry more quickly. But it is important that they still be warm when you start to work the gnocchi dough. | To avoid adding too much flour in the initial mixing of the dough, hold back ¼ cup in the beginning. Also, avoid kneading too much, which strengthens the gluten in the flour and results in tough gnocchi. If you are new to gnocchi making, try testing a few in a small saucepan of boiling water before you roll out and cut all the dough. | Once you have rolled out and cut all the gnocchi, you can feel free to liberally flour them, because any extra flour will not be absorbed and will float off in the cooking water. | At Farallon, we don't put the characteristic ridges on our gnocchi because it's one more labor-intensive step and we think they hold the sauce just fine without them. | This dish is bit of a juggling act when it comes to serving, but it's actually not as difficult as it sounds. Here's what needs to happen almost simultaneously: The gnocchi have to be cooked and tossed with the warm sauce; the celery root needs to be cooked; and the oysters need to be poached in the warm sauce. Keep in mind that you should also have the warmed shallow soup bowls ready to go.

Makes 4 appetizer servings

GNOCCHI:
1¼ pounds (about 2 large) unpeeled russet potatoes, scrubbed
2 egg yolks
1 teaspoon kosher salt
¼ teaspoon freshly ground pepper
1 cup unbleached all-purpose flour

BUTTER SAUCE:
1 tablespoon unsalted butter
2 shallots, minced
¼ cup dry white wine
1 cup fish stock (page 243)
1 bay leaf
4 sprigs thyme, or ½ teaspoon dried thyme, crumbled
1 cup (2 sticks) cold unsalted butter, cut into tablespoon-sized pieces
Kosher salt and freshly ground pepper to taste

Juice of ½ lemon
1 celery root (about 12 ounces)
20 oysters, shucked, liquor reserved
1 to 2 ounces good-quality black caviar for garnish

Preparation

To make the gnocchi: Cut the potatoes into quarters and place in a medium saucepan with salted water to cover. Bring to a boil, reduce heat to a lively simmer, and cook until tender when pierced with a knife, about 40 minutes. Drain and let cool to the touch. Remove the peels. Place the potatoes on a baking sheet and dry out in a preheated 250°F oven for about 20 minutes. Alternatively, the potatoes may be baked in a preheated 375°F oven for about 45 minutes. Scoop the flesh out of the baked potatoes (reserving the skins for another use) and dry the flesh as for the boiled potatoes.

Pass the still-warm potatoes through a ricer or food mill fitted with a medium-hole disk onto a clean cutting board. In small bowl, whisk the egg yolks, salt, and pepper together. Add the egg mixture to the potatoes and knead

continued

until the dough just begins to come together. Knead in ¾ cup of the flour for about 2 minutes. If the dough seems too sticky and unworkable, add the ¼ cup remaining flour. Even more flour can be added, but be careful not to knead for more than about 4 minutes or to let the dough become too dry. The dough is ready as soon as it is soft, malleable, and still a little sticky. Liberally flour the work surface and break off a quarter of the dough at a time, covering the remainder with a damp cloth to keep it from drying out. Roll the dough into a log about ¾ inch in diameter. Cut the log into ½-inch pieces with a knife or the edge of a fork.

To test, bring a large pot of salted water to a boil (a pot that is wider than it is deep is best). Drop in a couple of the gnocchi, reduce heat to a simmer, and cook until the gnocchi are floating on the surface, 4 to 5 minutes. You may need to gently nudge them with a wooden spoon to make them rise. Using a large skimmer or slotted spoon, transfer to a bowl. If the gnocchi fall apart in the water, knead a little more flour into the dough. If they hold up well, cut the rest of the gnocchi. Sprinkle the gnocchi with flour and set aside while you make the sauce. Reserve the same pot and water for cooking the gnocchi.

To make the sauce: In a 6-cup saucepan, melt the butter over medium heat and add the shallots. Sauté for 2 to 3 minutes, then add the wine, stock, bay leaf, and thyme. Bring to a boil and cook to reduce the liquid by half. Reduce heat to very low and whisk in the cold butter 1 piece at a time, until it is completely incorporated, to make an emulsified sauce. Strain the sauce through a fine-mesh sieve. Season with salt and pepper. Keep the sauce in a warm place until ready to serve, up to 4 hours. Whisk occasionally if it begins to separate.

To cook the gnocchi: Bring the reserved pot of water to a boil, add the gnocchi in batches, reduce heat to a simmer, and cook until they float to the surface. As they're cooked, transfer each batch to a bowl and gently toss with a large spoonful of the sauce to coat. Set aside in a warm place.

To prepare and cook the celery root: Fill a medium bowl with water and add the lemon juice. Peel the celery root, cut it into ⅜-inch dice, and drop it into the lemon water. Cook now or set aside for up to 24 hours. Bring a small saucepan of water to a boil and blanch the celery root for about 2 minutes, or until tender. Drain and set aside while preparing the rest of the dish.

To poach the oysters: Whisk the remaining warm sauce and place all of it in a small saucepan over very low heat. Add the oysters and gently poach until they plump and the edges curl, 2 to 3 minutes. Using a slotted spoon, transfer the oysters to a warm plate and use immediately.

In a medium bowl, gently toss the gnocchi and celery root together with the oyster poaching sauce and evenly divide among the warmed plates. Place the reserved oysters on top and garnish each with a little caviar. Serve immediately. (If there is any caviar left over, save it for the cook.)

IMPROVISATIONS Clams or mussels are excellent in place of the oysters. If you prefer not to use shellfish, try salmon or sea bass, cut into small chunks. Fennel, small turnips, or even diced and parboiled yellow-fleshed potatoes would make good substitutes for the celery root.

ADVANCE PREP If you're not cooking the gnocchi right away, they can be kept tightly covered in the refrigerator for up to 8 hours or frozen. Freeze them on a baking sheet, then transfer them to self-sealing bags. They'll keep in the freezer for up to 2 days. Drop frozen gnocchi into simmering water. Check for doneness, because they may take a bit longer to cook than the fresh. The sauce may be carefully held for as long as 4 hours if kept barely warm and whisked occasionally. The oysters, however, should be used immediately. The celery root can be cut and left in the acidulated water for up to 24 hours. It can also be cooked, drained, and reheated with a few tablespoons of the warm sauce just before serving.

SIMPLIFYING While we think our ethereal gnocchi are the best part of this dish, the combinations of flavors makes this dish worth trying even with purchased gnocchi. If you do choose to buy gnocchi, you can have this on the table in less than 30 minutes. But make sure you don't skimp on the caviar.

WINE NOTES Oysters and Chablis can be even better than oysters and Champagne! This is a pretty rich first course, so choose a ripe vintage like 1992. An Italian white also might be tasty, perhaps a 1997 Gini Soave from the Veneto. And for something totally different, check out the '97 Gruner Veltliner from Willi Brundlemeyer in Austria: crisp but full, like a cross between Riesling and Sauvignon Blanc.

Foie gras can be intimidating for the home chef: It's exotic, expensive, hard to find, and not for the cholesterol-shy. But put these concerns aside, because it's a once-in-a-while-extravagance that is really worth the effort and expense. If you've only had foie gras in a restaurant, conquer your fears and try this recipe in your own kitchen. Foie gras makes a luxurious first course, and if you're organized, you can serve 10 people an impressive dish in under 5 minutes.

SEARED FOIE GRAS *with* APPLE GALETTES, WATERCRESS, *and* CALVADOS SYRUP

★ *CHEF'S TIPS Keep in mind when cooking fresh foie gras that it is almost pure fat. It's not like cooking a steak. If you overcook it, you'll end up with some very expensive melted fat (which you can save and use for another dish). Read the recipe a couple of times to make it clear. Start with a good-quality, heavy sauté pan or skillet. Heat until hot but not super hot, a couple of minutes. Don't add any fat—the foie gras has plenty. Add a ½- to ¾-inch piece of foie gras and sear for 2 minutes on each side for a caramelized exterior and a meltingly tender, rare interior. Set aside in a warm place until ready to serve. | A-grade foie gras lobes usually weigh about 1 pound each, but you will only need half of that for this recipe. You might want to make some foie gras butter (page 241) with the rest. Foie gras also freezes, well wrapped, for up to 6 months. | As more home cooks are using foie gras, the demand has increased and so has the supply. Some American suppliers will ship fresh duck foie gras overnight (see page 249), but ask your local purveyors first.*

Makes 4 appetizer servings

CALVADOS SYRUP:
¾ cup Calvados or Cognac
¼ cup sugar
2 tablespoons fresh orange juice
2 tablespoons apple cider vinegar
2 shallots, minced
2 teaspoons minced peeled fresh ginger
½ teaspoon ground allspice

APPLE GALETTES:
2 tablespoons olive oil
4 large apples, preferably Granny Smith, peeled, cored, and cut into thin slices
1 tablespoon minced fresh thyme
Kosher salt and freshly ground pepper to taste

6 ounces fresh grade-A duck foie gras (see page 106)
Kosher salt and freshly ground pepper to taste
Watercress sprigs for garnish

Preparation

To prepare the syrup: In a small saucepan, combine all the syrup ingredients and simmer over low heat for 20 minutes. Strain through a fine-mesh sieve set over a bowl, pressing the solids through with the back of a large spoon, and return to the saucepan. Increase heat to medium-low and cook until the syrup is reduced to ¼ cup, about 10 minutes. Set aside and keep warm until serving, or cover and refrigerate for up to 4 days.

To make the galettes: Preheat the oven to 425°F. Brush four 4-inch tartlet molds with the olive oil. Arrange the apple slices in concentric circles, like a tart, to about ¾ inch above the top edge of the molds. (The galettes will shrink as they cool.) Sprinkle with the thyme, salt, and pepper and pour over any remaining oil. Put the molds on a baking sheet and bake until the galettes are golden brown and tender when pierced with a small knife, about 20 minutes. If the galettes are tender before they've colored, run them under a broiler for a minute or two to brown them. Remove from the oven and let cool.

continued

To cook the foie gras: Heat a knife under hot running water. Wipe the knife dry and, holding it at a slight 45-degree angle, cut the lobe of foie gras into four ½-inch-thick slices. Season both sides of each slice with salt and pepper. Heat a medium sauté pan or skillet over high heat and sear the slices of foie gras until golden and slightly caramelized, about 2 minutes on each side. Using a slotted spatula, transfer the foie gras to a plate lined with paper towels. Set aside in a warm place for up to 1 hour before serving.

To serve, reheat the galettes if necessary. Unmold them and place one on each of 4 warmed plates. Place a slice of warm foie gras on top of each galette and drizzle the Calvados syrup around. Garnish with a small sprig of watercress.

IMPROVISATIONS *There's no substitute for foie gras, but you could use pears in place of apples in the galettes, and any peppery or bitter greens could substitute for the watercress.*

ADVANCE PREP *The foie gras can be cooked as much as 1 hour in advance and kept in a warm place, such as near a pilot light (be careful that it doesn't get too hot),*

but it cannot be reheated. The apple galettes may be made up to 8 hours ahead and reheated in a preheated 375°F oven for 7 to 10 minutes. The Calvados syrup will keep for up to 4 days in a sealed container in the refrigerator.

SIMPLIFYING *You could sauté the apple slices rather than baking them as galettes, and you could deglaze the foie gras pan with Calvados or Cognac, rather than making the syrup: Place the same pan used to cook the foie gras over medium heat and add 2 tablespoons of the Calvados or Cognac, stirring to scrape up the browned bits from the bottom of the pan.*

WINE NOTES *The classic wine pairing with naturally rich and sweet foie gras is a naturally rich and sweet wine. It's a battle of decadence: a kind of "more is better" school of thought. Almost any late-harvest wine will work here: Sauternes, Vouvray, Muscat, ice wine—but my recommendation would be a Grand Cru Pinot Gris from a producer like Zind-Humbrecht or Domaine Weinbach. It has less residual sugar than the wines mentioned above, but lots of rich, viscous tropical fruit, honey, orange blossom, spice, and smoke. You get the picture.*

FOIE GRAS

Foie gras, pronounced *fwah-grah*, is the French name for *fatty liver*, hardly a term that conjures up all the royal and romantic lore with which it's been associated for thousands of years. Foie gras, the stuff of a gastronome's dream—sublime, decadent, and without compare in the world of food—is the liver of a goose or duck that has been force fed a rich diet that causes its liver to store fat and grow in size. Historians have found hieroglyphs in Egyptian tombs dating from 2500 B.C. depicting farmers feeding geese with balls of grain. But it was the French who elevated the production of fattened goose and duck liver to an art form.

To this day, the French love their foie gras and per capita, consume more of it than people of any other nation.

Americans, however, are only recent converts to foie gras, within the last fifteen years. Because U.S. law prohibited the importation of raw meat products until 1998, the only kind of foie gras available in the United States was the stuff that was cooked and packed into tins. Only well-heeled travelers to France were familiar with the pleasures of fresh foie gras. But in the mid-eighties, some enterprising duck farmers in New York and Northern California realized that there was a market here for fresh duck foie gras among European chefs who had been smuggling it in from other countries, mostly for their own consumption. Today, the only foie gras produced in the United States comes from ducks, because not only are ducks less temperamental than geese, they're less prone to disease.

BUYING AND CLEANING FRESH FOIE GRAS

Fresh foie gras, though somewhat difficult to find outside of upscale gourmet stores or butchers, can be easily purchased from mail-order suppliers and delivered fresh to your door. Livers are graded according to quality. This grading is not regulated in the United States as it is in Europe, but producers are generally consistent. Grade A is firm, round, and pale pink/beige in color. It contains the least amount of veins and blemishes and ranges from 1 to 3 pounds. One whole grade-A lobe of about 1½ pounds will yield 5 to 6 thick slices for cooking. Grade B is used for terrines and pâtés. More cleaning is needed and this foie is generally softer and smaller in size. Grade C is used in sauces, roulades, torchons, and compound butters, where flavor is more important than visual impact.

Fresh foie gras is highly perishable, so keep it well chilled in the coldest part of your refrigerator. Each lobe comes vacuum packed, so it's a good idea to rinse and pat it dry. Store it wrapped tightly in plastic, because it quickly starts to break down and discolor. Use it within a couple of days after opening. Storing the whole foie gras immersed in milk is a traditional French technique said to soften the liver and

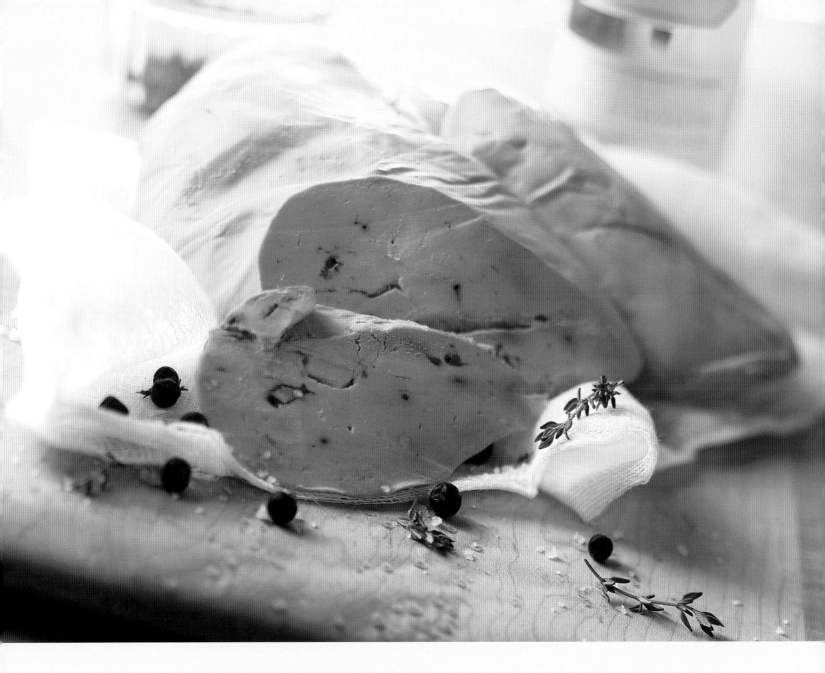

whiten any blemishes, but these days the livers are of such a high quality that most people skip this step.

When preparing whole foie gras for slicing (for searing or roasting), keep the liver chilled. Remove any veins or loose fat between the large and small lobes and, using a paring knife, trim off any blemishes. Cut out any large veins or membranes; any smaller veins will disappear with high heat. Store with parchment paper placed over any cut surfaces to avoid oxidization, and wrap tightly.

To clean the liver for a terrine, have the liver at room temperature. Use the tip of a sharp paring knife, needle-nose pliers, or your fingers to pull out the red veins, starting with the central vein and working outwards, and taking out as many as seems practical without breaking the liver into too many pieces. Wipe the blood away and clean the paring knife as you go, using a damp kitchen towel. Keep any scraps of liver for foie gras butter or for finishing sauces.

The whole liver or scraps will keep frozen for up to 6 months but will only be good for sauces, as the texture tends to break down and become mealy.

The dilemma I encountered when it came time to write the recipe for this lobster ragout represents the larger struggle I had in writing this book: how to write recipes that accurately reflect the dishes that we serve at Farallon, and at the same time make them accessible to the home cook. In this case, I think the dish evolved into something even better: equally as impressive, but not as technically difficult as the original. In the version we serve at the restaurant, giant beef bones are soaked for 24 hours, then blanched and the marrow removed. We poach the marrow and then include it in a lobster ragout

LOBSTER *and* FAVA BEAN RAGOUT *with* ROASTED BONE MARROW, POACHED GARLIC, *and* TARRAGON

that's put back into their sculptural white bones. It's a striking presentation, with complex flavors and textures. During our testing, I decided that it would be easier to just broil the marrow in their bones and put the bones in the bowls to serve as little cradles for the marrow. Well, not only did the broiling add flavor to the marrow, I served the ragout with the broiled bones, which gave the dish a rustic look that made much more sense in the context of a home meal. Taking it one step further, we realized that what the dish could also use was some toasts on which to spread the succulent marrow, and just like that, our complicated dish became much more simple.

★ *CHEF'S TIPS Shelling fava beans is labor-intensive, but their taste is incomparable and worth the effort. Once the beans are removed from their large pods, they're briefly blanched for about 1 minute and then popped out of their thin skins. | Many people buy beef bones for soup or for their dogs without realizing what they're missing: bone marrow. Bone marrow is a rich, creamy food that, when used sparingly, contributes a unique flavor and unctuous texture to a dish. For this recipe, ask your butcher for beef marrow bones, cut from the thick leg bones, and ask to have them halved lengthwise and then cut crosswise into 2- to 3-inch pieces. This will leave you with the marrow exposed the length of the bone. The marrow will look better if it is soaked overnight in cold water; this draws out the blood and gives it a clean, white color. At a minimum, you can soak the marrow for 1 hour or so; it just won't be as white. | Be very careful when eating from inside the marrow bone; scoop gently because there are sharp splinters lurking underneath the soft marrow.*

Makes 4 appetizer servings

POACHED GARLIC:

2 cups water

12 garlic cloves, stem ends trimmed

3 pounds fava beans, shelled

FAVA BEAN PUREE:

1 cup water

½ cup skinned fava beans, above

1 shallot, minced

Kosher salt and freshly ground pepper to taste

BONE MARROW:

Four 2- to 3-inch-long pieces marrow bone , 7 to 8 ounces each, split lengthwise

Kosher salt and freshly ground pepper to taste

LOBSTER AND FAVA BEAN RAGOUT:

½ cup fish stock (page 243), shellfish stock (page 244), or clam juice

Sliced poached garlic, above

1 cup skinned fava beans, above

1 tablespoon blanched, chopped fresh tarragon

Meat from 2 cooked lobsters (see page 233), cut into bite-sized pieces

Kosher salt and freshly ground pepper to taste

12 slices baguette, brushed with olive oil and lightly toasted

continued

To poach the garlic: In a small saucepan, bring the water to a boil and add the garlic cloves. Reduce heat to a simmer and cook the garlic until tender, 10 to 15 minutes. Drain the garlic and let cool. Slice thinly lengthwise and set aside, or refrigerate for up to 1 day.

To blanch and peel the fava beans: Drop the beans in a large pot of salted boiling water. Cook for 1 to 2 minutes, then plunge them into ice water to stop the cooking. Drain and cool. Break the skin of each bean with your thumbnail at the stem end and slide the bean out. Use immediately or store the beans in a self-sealing plastic bag in the refrigerator for up to 1 day.

To make the fava bean puree: In a small saucepan, combine the water, ½ cup fava beans, the shallot, salt, and pepper. Simmer until the beans are soft, about 10 minutes. Let cool briefly. While still warm, puree all the ingredients in a blender or food processor to a smooth paste, scraping down the sides, adding additional warm water, if necessary, to make a thick sauce. Set aside in a warm place. The puree will thicken as it sits, so thin with a little warm water if necessary before serving.

To prepare and cook the bone marrow: Soak the marrow bones in lightly salted water for at least 1 hour or preferably overnight. Remove the bones, discard the water, and pat the bones dry. About 15 minutes before serving, preheat the broiler. Place the bones, marrow-side up, on a baking sheet or broiler pan and season with plenty of salt and pepper. Broil about 5 inches from the heat source until lightly browned, 4 to 5 minutes. Keep an eye on them, because they tend to cook very quickly, and the marrow, because it is very fatty, can melt away. You can tell the marrow is cooked when the hard white interior becomes an almost a clear, pearl-gray color. Remove from the oven, cover, and set aside.

To make the ragout: In a medium sauté pan or skillet, bring the stock or clam juice to a low simmer. Add the sliced garlic, 1 cup fava beans, the tarragon, and lobster. Warm just enough to heat through, 2 to 3 minutes. Season with salt and pepper.

To serve, ladle a pool of warm ragout in the center of warmed shallow soup bowls, making sure that there are equal portions of lobster and fava beans in each bowl. Drizzle the warm fava bean puree around and lean a roasted marrow bone at an angle on top. Serve with small spoons to scoop out the marrow. Place the croutons in the bowls or serve them alongside, and encourage your guests to spread the marrow on the croutons.

IMPROVISATIONS *You could use fresh peas or lima beans here instead of the fava beans. Shelled edamame (soybeans) make a surprisingly good substitute for favas. Depending on the season, you could add a little mint or basil instead of the tarragon. Consider increasing the amounts of lobster to make this a main course—it's a special dish, worthy of entree status.*

SIMPLIFYING *You could buy 12 ounces cooked lobster and warm the meat in the poaching liquid for serving. Use fresh lima beans, peas, or edamame in place of fava beans. Soak the marrow for only 1 hour if time is limited.*

ADVANCE PREP *The fava puree tends to get brown when made too far ahead, so it should be made the day of serving. The fava beans can be shelled and peeled up to 2 days in advance. The lobster may be cooked and the garlic poached 1 day ahead. The marrow, toast, and ragout should be made just before serving.*

WINE NOTES *This sumptuous, warm appetizer has Chardonnay written all over it: the New World versions of California and Australia, or a classic lesser white Burgundy like St. Aubin, Savigny-les-Beaune. You want a wine that is rich and balanced, naturally sweet but not too oaky, and light enough to leave room for something fuller with the main course.*

Whether you call them shrimp or prawns, they're the world's most popular shellfish. The terms are used interchangeably, prawns being from fresh water and slightly longer in the body and legs than their salt-water cousins. Generally the term *prawn* is used for any large shrimp, but for this first course we use the giant Asian prawns that are about 2 or 3 to the pound and then serve only one per person—they're

GIANT TEMPURA PRAWNS *with* SCALLOP MOUSSE, CUCUMBER SALAD, *and* CHILI PONZU

that big. If you shut your eyes, you would swear that they're lobster, they're that sweet. The prawns are stuffed with a scallop mousse, then wrapped in sheets of nori and fried in a light tempura batter. Nori, the dried seaweed that's most commonly used in sushi, provides a subtle sea flavor and helps to encase the prawns in a crisp protective shell when fried. Contrasting with the crackling prawns is a refreshing sweet and tangy cucumber "noodle" salad and spicy-hot chili ponzu. This is a full-flavored dish, perfect for making a big impression on your guests.

★ CHEF'S TIPS *The key to the emulsification of a mousse is to have all your ingredients very cold. As an added insurance, refrigerate your food processor bowl and blade for 15 minutes before mixing. | See the Chef's Tips on page 114 for information on making and cooking with tempura batter. | Nori is dried seaweed, formed and cut into sheets about 8 inches square. Its most common use is for wrapping sushi rolls.*

Makes 4 appetizer servings

SCALLOP MOUSSE:

4 ounces scallops

1 large egg white

1 tablespoon heavy cream

½ tablespoon chopped fresh tarragon

1 tablespoon fresh lemon juice

Pinch of kosher salt and freshly ground pepper to taste

PONZU DIPPING SAUCE:

¼ cup soy sauce

1 tablespoon fresh lemon juice

1 tablespoon fresh lime juice

1 tablespoon sugar

1 teaspoon minced fresh ginger

1 green onion, sliced, including some green parts

1 teaspoon red pepper flakes or chili oil

CUCUMBER SALAD:

1 large English cucumber, peeled and halved crosswise

Kosher salt for sprinkling

1½ tablespoons rice wine vinegar

Pinch of sugar

6 fresh mint leaves, chopped, or 2 green onions, thinly sliced, including some green parts

½ teaspoon black sesame seeds (optional)

4 jumbo (2 to 4 count) Asian prawns, shelled, tails on

Kosher salt and freshly ground pepper to taste

2 sheets nori

TEMPURA BATTER:

⅓ cup rice flour

⅓ cup unbleached all-purpose flour

⅓ cup cornstarch

1 teaspoon baking soda mixed with 1 cup cold water, or 1 cup cold soda water

Kosher salt and freshly ground pepper to taste

Peanut or vegetable oil for deep frying

continued

To make the scallop mousse: Refrigerate a small food processor bowl and blade for 15 minutes. Remove from the refrigerator and puree the scallops with the egg white for 30 seconds. Scrape down the sides of the container with a small rubber spatula. Add the remaining ingredients and process for 1 minute. Refrigerate the mousse for up to 1 day.

To make the ponzu dipping sauce: In a small saucepan, whisk all the ingredients except for the pepper flakes or chili oil together and bring to a boil over high heat. Continue to boil until reduced by half. Stir in the pepper flakes or chili oil. Let cool to room temperature, then strain and discard the solids. The dipping sauce may be covered and refrigerated for up to 2 days.

To make the cucumber salad: Using a mandoline fitted with the fine-julienne blade, slice the cucumber lengthwise, turning it after each couple of passes, so that you end up slicing it all around evenly, leaving the interior seeds. Alternatively, use a vegetable peeler or cheese planer to peel off thin layers of the cucumber, then finely julienne these. Put in a colander over a bowl and sprinkle with salt. Let sit for 10 minutes to drain, pressing down gently on the cucumber with the back of a large spoon to extract as much juice as possible. Pat the cucumber dry on a kitchen towel and discard the liquid. In a separate small bowl, combine all the remaining ingredients, then toss in the cucumber. Refrigerator for up to 4 hours before serving.

To assemble the prawns: Make an incision down the back of each prawn and remove the black vein. Season the prawns with salt and pepper. Open up the back and smooth in 1 tablespoon or so of scallop mousse. Place a sheet of nori on the work counter and cut it in half. Place the prawn across the bottom of the nori sheet so that the tail and ends stick out slightly over the edges (you may have to trim the nori slightly to fit, depending on the size of your prawns). Roll the prawn up in the nori loosely; the dried seaweed has a tendency to stick to the prawn and will split if it's wrapped too tightly. Moisten the end and press to seal closed.

To make the tempura batter: In a large bowl, whisk the dry ingredients together. Gradually stir in the baking soda mixture or soda water to make a lumpy batter. Stir in the salt and pepper.

To cook the prawns: Fill a deep, heavy pot or deep fryer one-third full with oil and heat to 350°F or until surface shimmers. Hold a prawn by the tail and dip it into the tempura batter, letting the excess drip off. Add the prawn

to the hot oil and cook until golden brown, 5 to 6 minutes. Using a slotted spoon, transfer the prawn to paper towels to drain. Repeat with the remaining prawns, making sure the oil has returned to 350°F before you add each one.

To serve, mound a little of the cucumber salad on a plate slightly off center. Place the prawn, tail-side up, leaning against the salad. Drizzle the ponzu glaze in a zigzag or spiral pattern over the dish. Serve immediately.

IMPROVISATIONS *This is a filling first course, but if you want to take it a step further to entree size, add a scoop of fluffy steamed Japanese (short grain) or jasmine rice and a little more of the ponzu glaze. Real noodles, as opposed to the cucumber "noodles," would be good too. Any large (jumbo or colossal) shrimp would work in this recipe in place of the prawns. The combination of the nori and tempura can be used on vegetables as well; try wrapping and frying jumbo asparagus to serve as an appetizer.*

ADVANCE PREP *The scallop mousse can be made 1 day ahead and kept well chilled. The ponzu sauce can be covered and refrigerated for up to 3 weeks and brought to room temperature for serving. The tempura batter should be made at the last minute, but you can mix the dry ingredients ahead and then stir in the water just before you fry. The fried prawns can be held in a low oven for up to 30 minutes. The cucumber salad can be made up to 4 hours ahead and kept in the refrigerator. The assembly of the prawns, mousse, and nori should be done within 2 hours of frying.*

SIMPLIFYING *The scallop mousse could be omitted altogether; try just wrapping the prawns in nori and rolling them in either rice flour or bonito flakes (see page 152) before frying. Thinly slice the cucumbers instead of cutting them into noodles.*

WINE NOTES *Many grapes and styles will complement this succulent but full-flavored dish. Chardonnay and white Burgundy are naturals. Full-bodied, ripe Sauvignon Blanc, Riesling (naturally), Roussanne, some of the Rhône-style wines from France and California, or a Semillon from Australia—all are worth finding and trying.*

One of my first sous-chefs at Farallon, Johnny Alamilla, nicknamed this dish "Legs with Eggs" because the mustard seeds looked like frog's eggs. But considering that frog's legs tend to be a tough sell, I doubt that this name would have helped increase our diners' demand for this terrific dish. Frog's legs are somewhat similar in taste and texture to chicken, but fresh, meaty ones can even be compared to

CRISPY SAFFRON-MARINATED FROG'S LEGS *with* MUSTARD SEED VINEGAR, TARRAGON PUREE, *and* HERB SALAD

lobster. In this dish, the legs are marinated in a saffron-steeped water, then fried in a light tempura batter. Frog's legs go well with full flavors, and we like to finish this dish with a mustard-seed vinegar and tarragon puree that form a kind of separated vinaigrette on the plate. But the tempura-style frog's legs are so good that they can be served alone. The seven-year-old son of one of my cooks recently gave them a supreme compliment when he told me that they were better than Kentucky Fried Chicken.

★ CHEF'S TIPS *Fresh frog's legs can be found in many seafood markets in the southern coastal states and in areas of the country where there are large Asian communities. Many butchers and fish purveyors can order frozen ones for you, and they're quite acceptable. | To get a light, delicate tempura coating, don't overmix the batter, which causes it to become heavy; there should be visible lumps of flour after mixing. Fry only a few legs at a time; it's important for the oil to recover quickly and maintain its temperature. | The combination of the oil-based tarragon puree and the acidic mustard seeds cause the vinaigrette to separate and blend on the plate in an attractive pattern. We use this technique a lot; try it with other oils and vinegars. Oils that have color, like the tarragon puree we use here, look best.*

Makes 4 appetizer servings

1 pound fresh or thawed frozen
    frog's legs
1 teaspoon saffron threads
½ cup hot water

MUSTARD SEED VINEGAR:
½ cup yellow mustard seeds
1 cup Champagne vinegar
½ cup water

TARRAGON PUREE:
Leaves from 4 bunches tarragon
6 tablespoons water
1 ice cube
1 cup grapeseed, canola, or olive oil
Pinch of kosher salt

TEMPURA BATTER:
⅓ cup rice flour
⅓ cup unbleached all-purpose flour
⅓ cup cornstarch
1 teaspoon baking soda mixed with 1 cup
    cold water, or 1 cup cold soda water
Kosher salt and freshly ground pepper
    to taste

Peanut or canola oil for deep-frying
Kosher salt to taste

¼ cup ½-inch pieces fresh chives
¼ cup fresh tarragon leaves
¼ cup fresh flat-leaf (Italian) parsley
    leaves
¼ cup fresh chervil sprigs
Lemon Vinaigrette (page 25)

If using fresh frog's legs, cut off the feet and backbone with a sharp knife. Steep the saffron in the hot water for 10 minutes. Let cool, then mix with the frog's legs and marinate in the refrigerator for at least 20 minutes or up to 1 day.

To make the vinegar: In a small sauté pan or skillet, combine the mustard seeds, vinegar, and water and simmer over medium-low heat until the liquid is almost reduced, stirring frequently. When finished, the seeds should be swollen. Set aside.

To make the tarragon puree: Bring a medium saucepan of water to a boil. Put the tarragon leaves in a medium-mesh sieve and immerse in the water for 4 seconds. Transfer the sieve to a bowl of ice water. After 10 seconds, remove the tarragon, squeeze dry, and put in a blender with the water and ice cube. Blend on high, then gradually add the oil and salt. Set aside, or refrigerate in an airtight container for up to 1 day.

To make the batter: In a large bowl, whisk the flours and cornstarch together. Gradually stir in the baking soda mixture or soda water until just blended, with some lumps. Stir in the salt and pepper.

To fry the frog's legs: Fill a deep, heavy pot or deep fryer one-third full with oil and heat to 350°F, or until the surface shimmers. Remove the frog's legs from the marinade, drain, and pat dry on paper towels. Working in small batches, dip the legs in the batter, carefully lower them into the hot oil, and fry until lightly browned and crispy, 2 to 3 minutes. Using a slotted spoon or wire-mesh skimmer, transfer the legs to paper towels to drain. Season with salt.

To serve, dress the herbs with the vinaigrette and place a mound on each plate. Place the frog's legs over the top of the salad and drizzle the tarragon puree around the plate. Place small clusters of the mustard seeds on the tarragon puree.

IMPROVISATIONS If you like the sound of this dish but can't get past your aversion to frog's legs, consider using chicken wings, chicken tenders, or goujonnettes of sole or any other white-fleshed fish. (Goujonnettes are ½- to ¾-inch-wide and 3- to 4-inch-long strips cut from white fish fillets.) If you use chicken wings, remove the last joint and slice the skin between the other two sections so that the wings can be opened up lengthwise so they resemble frog's legs. Parsley oil would make a great substitute for the tarragon oil and is a classic with frog's legs in France. Use any fresh herbs you'd like for the herb salad; those listed here are only suggestions.

ADVANCE PREP The tarragon puree will keep in the refrigerator for 1 day, as will the frog's legs in the marinade. The mustard seed vinegar can be made a few hours ahead. Stir the dry ingredients for the tempura batter together early in the day, but don't add the water until you're ready to fry. The fresh herbs can be combined 1 day ahead, but not dressed with the vinaigrette until just before serving.

SIMPLIFYING Instead of making the tarragon puree and mustard seed vinegar, use a good-quality purchased infused oil and flavored vinegar. Rather than clean and pick all those herbs, any kind of delicate salad leaves will do.

WINE NOTES Cassis Blanc from the small fishing village east of Marseilles or a Chinon, the light-bodied Cabernet Franc from the Loire Valley, would both look and taste terrific with this dish. Serve them slightly cool to accentuate the herb-tinged, leafy, strawberry fruits of the wines.

Salt cod, or Spanish *bacalao* and Italian *baccalà*, is salted and dried Atlantic cod. While many Mediterranean cultures developed their own, very similar preparations for this preserved fish, the French *brandade de morue* is the most famous. In it, salt cod is soaked, poached until tender, and pureed into an emulsion with milk, cream, olive oil, and garlic. As salt cod became more expensive, however, potato was often added as an extender and also to tone down the strong flavor of fish and garlic. The word *brandade* is a derivative of a French Provençal word meaning "to stir." Our banquet chef,

SAUTÉED FILLET *of* ROUGET *with* BRANDADE, SWEET GARLIC PUREE, *and* BASIL OIL

Nathan Powers, who is a total fanatic about the stuff, takes the translation of the word literally, and is adamant about whisking it well to form a lighter-than-air emulsification. In this warm first course, Nathan underscores brandade's Provençal origins by pairing it with fresh basil, a mellow garlic puree, and rouget, or red mullet, the superstar of Mediterranean fish.

★ CHEF'S TIPS *Commercial salt cod, if using, varies wildly in quality and therefore soaking times and saltiness, so you might want to experiment by trying the brandade as an appetizer first, served with toasted croutons. Get to know how salty the brand is and how long you need to soak it, if only to get the hang of Nathan's technique. | While the brandade is not difficult to make, you do need to have all the components warming in a couple of saucepans before they're combined. | Brandade doesn't reheat well. If you do have some left over, you can make a great hors d'oeuvre by combining the brandade with mashed potatoes, forming it into small balls or cakes, coating them with flour, egg, and bread crumbs or cornmeal, and frying them until they're golden. | Always be sure to check for pin bones in any fish, even if it was already cleaned. These are the thin vertical backbones that run down the center of the fillet. To remove, put the fish, skin-side down, over the bottom of a curved bowl. It makes it easier to see and pull out any tiny bones with tweezers or needle-nose pliers. | The old-fashioned way of making brandade is by hand with a mortar and pestle, adding the oil and cream by droplets to form a mayonnaiselike emulsion. Try it if you have the time and the inclination; it gives an even smoother texture.*

Makes 4 appetizer servings

BRANDADE:
One 4-ounce piece commercial or
    homemade salt cod (see page 242)
¾ cup heavy cream
2 bay leaves
¼ cup dry white wine
3 sprigs thyme
6 tablespoons extra-virgin olive oil
1 garlic clove, crushed

GARLIC PUREE:
25 garlic cloves (from about 1 head)
1 cup heavy cream
2 to 3 teaspoons Cognac
1 tablespoon olive oil
Kosher salt and freshly ground pepper
    to taste

Eight 2- to 3-ounce rouget (red mullet)
    fillets, pin bones removed
    (see Chef's Tips)
1 tablespoon fresh thyme leaves
Kosher salt and freshly ground pepper
    to taste
20 large fresh basil leaves for garnish
3 cups vegetable or olive oil for frying
    the basil (optional)
Basil-infused oil for garnish (page 241)

continued

To prepare the brandade: Soak the salt cod in water to cover for 2 days, changing the water twice a day. (If using 24-Hour Salt Cod, soak for 4 hours.) Drain. Cut the salt cod into several pieces and put it in a small saucepan with the cream, bay leaves, wine, and thyme. Bring just to a bare simmer and cook for 10 minutes. Remove from heat. Discard the bay leaves and thyme sprigs, cover, and let sit for 10 minutes. Meanwhile, warm a heavy-duty mixing bowl by filling it with hot water. Drain and dry the bowl. Using a slotted spoon, transfer the cod to the bowl, reserving the poaching liquid. Using the paddle attachment, beat the cod for 5 minutes on medium-high speed to whip it into tiny flakes; you may have to add a little more cream to get the cod whipping. If necessary, cover the mixer and bowl with a kitchen towel to contain the splattering.

Strain the reserved poaching liquid into a small saucepan and set over low heat. In another small saucepan, combine the olive oil and garlic, bring to a simmer over low heat, and cook for 3 minutes. Discard the garlic and keep the oil warm over low heat. With the mixer running on low speed, gradually pour in one-third of the warm garlic oil. Increase the speed to high and beat until thoroughly mixed into the salt cod. Repeat the procedure with one-third of the warm cream, and continue alternating between the two liquids until the mixture has a loose, mashed-potato-like consistency. Pause occasionally to scrape down the sides of the bowl with a rubber spatula. Set the brandade aside in a warm place or over a pan of warm water for up to 3 hours.

To make the garlic puree: Put the garlic cloves in a small saucepan of water over high heat and bring to a boil. Drain, reserving the garlic. Repeat this procedure twice. Put the garlic in a small saucepan with the cream and 1 teaspoon of the Cognac. Bring to a simmer and cook for 5 minutes. Using a slotted spoon, transfer the garlic to the bowl of a food processor. Add 1 tablespoon of the cream mixture and the olive oil. Process until thoroughly pureed, scraping down the sides of the container as needed. Add 1 or 2 teaspoons Cognac, the salt and pepper. The puree should have a fairly thick consistency, like loose mashed potatoes. Keep warm over simmering water until ready to serve, or cover and refrigerate for up to 2 days ahead. Reheat gently on top of the stove.

To cook the rouget: Preheat the oven to 350°F. Sprinkle both sides of the rouget with the thyme, salt, and pepper.

Put the rouget fillets skin-side up in an oven proof, nonstick pan or skillet and bake for 5 minutes. Remove from the pan and set aside while you prepare the plates.

To fry the basil leaves (optional): Fill a medium, heavy saucepan one-third full with oil and heat over high heat to 350°F or until the oil is shimmering. Drop the basil leaves in and let cook until dark green and crispy, about 30 seconds. Using a slotted spoon, transfer the basil leaves to paper towels to drain and sprinkle lightly with salt. Set aside. To store, place in an airtight container for up to 2 days. Cool and reserve the oil for another use.

To serve, place a small pool of warm garlic puree followed by a generous mound of brandade in the center of each of 4 warmed plates. Wrap 2 fillets, skin-side out, around each of the mounds. Drizzle the basil oil around and garnish with the fried or fresh basil leaves.

IMPROVISATIONS *Try some filleted fresh sardines (double the quantity used) in place of the rouget, or similar small fillets.*

ADVANCE PREP *The garlic puree will keep, refrigerated in a covered container, for up to 2 days. Reheat just before serving. The brandade does not reheat well but can be kept warm for up to 3 hours. The fried basil may be stored in an airtight container for up to 2 days.*

SIMPLIFYING *Don't fry the basil leaves. Use a good-quality commercial basil oil available in many markets and specialty stores.*

WINE NOTES *Rouget with brandade is a natural with the wine of the tiny fishing village of Cassis, just east of Marseilles. These Marsanne-based wines are best drunk within the first few years after the vintage. Clos Sainte-Magdelaine is one of the best of the appellation: fresh and stony, with a dry honey-floral character and medium body. Check out the wines of a good Soave producer as well; they are no longer the insipid, trendy wines of the 1970s. The 1998 Gini La Frosca is a good choice: old vines, hillside vineyard, barrel fermentation (in old oak, not new), and low yields make for a classic white wine from Italy's Veneto region.*

At Farallon's opening, this starter was the one that most captured everyone's attention, media and customers alike. At first, I think they were captivated by the presentation: a beautiful purple-hued sea urchin shell on top of a bed of rock salt, surrounded by tendrils of seaweed and garnished with glistening orange beads of salmon caviar. But it was the taste that made them fall in love, for this dish is not just a pretty face. Inside the shell are awesomely rich, truffled mashed potatoes, fresh peeky-toe crab from Maine, and a sauce made from fresh Santa Barbara sea urchins. For me, the appeal of this dish is

PEEKY-TOE CRAB *with* TRUFFLED MASHED POTATOES *and* SEA URCHIN SAUCE

in its incredible blend of flavors. In one bite you get the taste of sea—sweet crab and briny sea urchin—with earthy truffles. It's such a simple but astounding combination that it's repeated often on our menus; truffles show up with all kinds of shellfish—lobster and scallops are perhaps an even better match than crab. This dish has been so popular that it's now considered one of our signatures.

★ CHEF'S TIPS *The sauce of hauntingly sweet and briny sea urchin takes this dish over the top, but we've also served it with a crayfish-essence sauce; completely different, but just as good. It was a toss-up as to which recipe might appeal to the home cook: Crayfish are fairly easy to find, at least frozen, but making an essence adds another step to the recipe. A fresh sea urchin roe is simply chopped and added to the sauce at the last minute, but these are not always easy to come by outside Japanese or large coastal seafood markets. I've decided to give you both alternatives and let you choose. | Sea urchins resemble little round porcupines, and it's the meat, or roe, inside that's edible. Often you'll find the roe referred to as uni, tongues, or coral. Fresh whole sea urchins are highly perishable, but the meat is sold in little wooden boxes at Japanese markets. | If you do come across fresh sea urchins, it's an easy task to clean them and remove their coral, with the added bonus of having shells to use for presentation. Otherwise, serve the dish in pretty glass bowls, ramekins, or individual gratin dishes—it will still look great. | I'm aware that fresh crab can be ridiculously expensive, but this first course stretches 8 ounces of crab to serve 4 people. I conceived it as a four-bite little "hello," but it's an incredibly rich dish that you may want to stretch even further, say, to serve 6 diners.*

Makes 4 appetizer servings

TRUFFLED MASHED POTATOES:

1 pound Yukon Gold, Yellow Finn or
    russet potatoes, peeled and halved
Kosher salt and freshly ground pepper
    to taste
½ cup heavy cream
2 tablespoons unsalted butter
1 tablespoon white truffle oil
3 ounces fresh or frozen black truffle,
    minced (2 tablespoons)

SEA URCHIN SAUCE:

4 tablespoons unsalted butter at
    room temperature
1 shallot, minced
¼ cup dry white wine
1 sprig thyme
¼ cup fish stock (page 243) or clam juice
1 ounce sea urchin roe, chopped, or
    ¼ cup crayfish essence (page 245)
Kosher salt and freshly ground pepper
    to taste

8 ounces fresh lump peeky-toe crabmeat,
    picked over for shell
Salmon or sturgeon caviar, or minced
    fresh chives for garnish

continued

To make the mashed potatoes: In a large saucepan, cover the potatoes with cold water by 1 inch. Add salt and bring to a boil. Reduce heat to a simmer and cook the potatoes until tender, about 40 minutes. Drain and return the potatoes to the saucepan. Put over low heat and cook the potatoes to evaporate their moisture, stirring and breaking them up until a film appears on the bottom of the pan and the potatoes begin to appear opaque, 3 to 4 minutes. Meanwhile, in another saucepan, heat the cream and butter until very hot. Using a food mill or ricer, puree the potatoes. Whisk the hot cream mixture into the potatoes until absorbed. Transfer the potatoes to a bowl, loosely cover with aluminum foil, and set over (but not touching) warm water for up to 1 hour before serving. Just before serving, stir in the truffle oil and chopped truffles. Season with salt and pepper.

To make the sauce: In a small saucepan, melt 1 tablespoon of the butter over low heat. Add the shallot and cook until translucent, about 2 minutes. Add the wine, increase heat to medium-high, and cook to reduce the liquid by half. Add the thyme and stock or clam juice and cook to reduce to 3 or 4 tablespoons. Reduce heat to low and whisk in the remaining 3 tablespoons butter, 1 tablespoon at a time, to make an emulsified sauce. Strain through a fine-mesh sieve. Add the sea urchins or the crayfish essence. Season with salt and pepper. Set aside near a pilot light or in a bowl set over warm water for up to 1 hour before serving.

To serve, warm the crabmeat in a bowl set over warm water. Put one-fourth of the warm mashed potatoes in the center of 4 dinner plates, glass bowls, or decorative shells. Top with the crabmeat and spoon on some of the sea urchin sauce. Garnish with caviar or chives.

IMPROVISATIONS Dungeness crab or any fresh local crab is the obvious substitution here. Lobster could be used instead of crab and the dish presented in lobster shells; lobster essence should then be used in the sauce. The mashed potatoes can be plain or flavored with roasted garlic or chives.

ADVANCE PREP The sea urchin sauce can be made 1 hour ahead and kept over warm water, near a pilot light, or in a wide-mouth thermos. Mashed potatoes will hold for 1 hour at the most, and the truffles should only be added right before serving because all their exquisite (and expensive) aromas dissipate with heat and time. The crayfish essence can be made up to 7 days ahead and frozen for use in this recipe or others.

SIMPLIFYING The most complicated thing here is the sauce; the mashed potatoes are like any other recipe (except of course for the truffles, which require nothing in the way of preparation), and the crab can be purchased already cleaned and picked out of the shell. Try anchovy butter in place of the sauce. It's quick and easy, and would be an interesting addition to this dish.

WINE NOTES Crab and Sauvignon Blanc are a lovely food-and-wine pairing, but this appetizer is a good example of how the main ingredient in a dish, depending on how it is prepared, can make a big difference in deciding which wine to serve. Although a bigger wine like a Chardonnay does not usually match crab, here it would go well with the heaviness of the final dish. A Sancerre or Pouilly-Fumé might be too crisp and austere, though, and a Napa or Sonoma Chardonnay with a bit of richness would complement the dish better.

Entrees

Chefs get typecast, just like actors. At Stars, I became known for my hearty meat dishes and charcuterie: braises, stews, sausages, spit-roasted meats, game, pâtés, and terrines. But from the time I was a kid cooking my own freshly caught trout, to my stint in the Alaskan tundra cooking hundreds of pounds of salmon in a makeshift smoker, I've learned to treasure the sublime taste of freshly caught and simply prepared seafood. At Farallon, I've been able to experiment with a mind-boggling variety of fresh fish and shellfish delivered to us from waters all over the world (about 85 percent of the items on our menu feature seafood). What has become clear to me is that few foods offer such an incredible range of culinary possibilities.

When coming up with a list of entrees for inclusion in this chapter, I wanted not only to gather the favorites from our menu, but to demonstrate that an impeccably fresh piece of fish can be the highlight of any menu, whether for a casual mid-week dinner or an important celebration. The key is to choose a technique that accentuates and doesn't obscure the unique characteristics of the fish, and to select side dishes that offer support in the way of contrasting textures or flavors. One of the great things about fish is that similar kinds are interchangeable. But to make these decisions you must first know the nature of your fish: Is it lean or fatty, delicate or dense, mild flavored or robust? Read through "Fish and Shellfish" (page 225) to learn as much as you can about the fish and shellfish we use, then choose a dish based on a technique that would be most appropriate, or choose your recipe and then see which kinds of fish would make good substitutes.

You'll find a variety of techniques represented in this chapter that can be considered master recipes for cooking fish, enabling you to use them as creative starting points. Several of the dishes feature fish that is simply seared in a hot pan on top of the stove, then finished in the oven. There are grilled dishes to encourage you to break out of the barbecued-salmon-and-swordfish rut and a few poached and steamed dishes, most user-friendly and healthful. And what fish book would be complete without something fried? Although I personally prefer fried food served as an appetizer, I've included two favorites.

Farallon's menu always includes meat or poultry, for those customers who don't want fish. But in choosing the meat dishes for this book, I had a difficult time narrowing them down, and simply decided to go with the ones that I like to serve at home. And what do you know—three are game meats. Being the avid hunter that I am, I love game meat for its rich, deep flavors, ease of cooking, and endless variety.

The entrees in this chapter are but twenty-two of the hundreds we've served at Farallon. Our menus never stay the same, and my chefs and I are always looking for new ingredients, and ways to combine them. As you flip through the pages of this chapter, I hope the dishes I've chosen will inspire you to stretch out a little bit, to try a new ingredient or technique, and to expand your own culinary repertoire.

Whenever I'm asked to name the best and worst meals I've ever had, I don't even hesitate. The best meal was a sensually rich, inky black cuttlefish risotto, a real *risotto nero*, that I had at a little trattoria in Genoa on my first trip to Italy. It was also the worst meal I ever had, because I spent the next twenty-four hours in bed, sick as a dog. It was such a delicious revelation—the first black rice dish I'd ever tasted—that to this day, I refuse to blame it for my short but extreme misery. Used in numerous risottos, paellas,

SEARED SCALLOPS *with* SQUID INK RISOTTO, SAUCE GRIBICHE, *and* CELERY ROOT SALAD

and stews throughout the Mediterranean, squid or cuttlefish ink contributes a beautiful sheen, a subtle sea saltiness, and a little thickening power to dishes in which it's deployed. In addition to the renowned Venetian black risotto, Spain, and more specifically Catalonia and Barcelona, is famous for black paellas, brimming with seafood and sausage and accompanied with aioli, a light garlic mayonnaise similar to the more familiar aioli of Provence but without the eggs. It was this pungent sauce that inspired me to serve our squid ink risotto with a gribiche, a piquant, loose French mayonnaise. As a whole, this dish is quite rich, so I serve the risotto in relatively small portions as a bed for seared sweet scallops. The crisp celery root dressed with vinaigrette offers a textural and acidic contrast to the dish.

★ CHEF'S TIPS *When working with squid ink, be aware that it stains anything it comes in contact with, and though not permanent, it's difficult to remove. | You can buy frozen squid ink in smaller quantities in Japanese markets or order it (see page 249). | Sauce gribiche is similar to a tartar sauce, but more acidic and flavorful. Classically, the mayonnaise base is made with cooked egg yolks instead of raw ones, or sieved hard-cooked eggs are stirred in at the end. Our version is more like a loose emulsified vinaigrette rather than a thick mayonnaise. It's tangy, salty, full of herbs and chopped eggs, and makes a great sauce for any cooked fish. Texture is important here, so it's best to chop the ingredients by hand rather than in a food processor. For our risotto-making techniques, see Chef's Tips, page 132.*

Makes 4 entree servings

2 ounces cleaned squid, rinsed
1 clove garlic, minced
½ teaspoon chopped fresh thyme
1 tablespoon olive oil

SAUCE GRIBICHE:
3 hard-cooked eggs, finely chopped
½ small red onion, cut into ⅛-inch dice (about ½ cup)
½ bunch chives, minced
Leaves from ½ bunch flat-leaf (Italian) parsley (about ⅓ cup), finely chopped
¼ cup fresh minced chervil
1 clove garlic, minced
1 salt-packed anchovy fillet, rinsed, and finely chopped

½ cup fish stock (page 243) or clam juice
3 tablespoons Champagne vinegar
1 cup extra-virgin olive oil
Kosher salt and freshly ground pepper to taste

CELERY ROOT SALAD:
1 tablespoon kosher salt
1 small celery root (about 1 pound), peeled and julienned
Lemon Vinaigrette (page 247)

RISOTTO:
4 cups fish stock (page 243) or water
1 tablespoon olive oil
1 small yellow onion, cut into ¼-inch dice (about ½ cup)
1 cup Arborio rice
2 tablespoons squid ink
⅓ cup dry white wine
3 tablespoons unsalted butter
1 ice cube
Kosher salt and freshly ground pepper to taste

SCALLOPS:
12 large "dry-packed" sea scallops (page 68), rinsed and patted dry
Kosher salt and freshly ground pepper to taste
2 tablespoons grapeseed, canola, or olive oil

FRIED SQUID TENTACLES (OPTIONAL):
4 cups canola oil for deep-frying
Reserved squid tentacles from squid, above
½ cup cornstarch or rice flour
Kosher salt to taste

Fresh chervil sprigs for garnish

continued

To marinate and cook the squid: Reserve the tentacles. In a small bowl, combine the squid bodies, garlic, thyme, and olive oil. Let sit at room temperature for 1 hour. In a small sauté pan or skillet over high heat, heat a little of the marinade and sauté the squid bodies until lightly browned at the edges, 3 to 4 minutes. Let cool. Cut the bodies into ¼-inch-wide rings. Set aside.

To make the gribiche: In a medium bowl, stir the eggs, onion, chives, chopped herbs, garlic, anchovy fillet, fish stock or clam juice, and vinegar together. Gradually whisk in the olive oil to make an emulsified sauce. Season with salt and pepper. Refrigerate, covered, for up to 2 days.

To make the salad: Add the salt to a medium saucepan of boiling water. Drop the celery root into the boiling water and cook until crisp-tender, 1 to 2 minutes. Using a slotted spoon, transfer to a bowl of ice water. Drain well and pat dry with a clean kitchen towel. Toss with the lemon vinaigrette and set aside for up to 30 minutes.

To make the risotto: Bring the stock or water to a low simmer on the stove. In a 3- to 4-quart heavy saucepan, heat the olive oil over medium heat and sauté the onion until translucent and just beginning to turn golden, about 5 minutes. Stir in the rice and cook until the rice grains become opaque, about 2 minutes. Add the squid ink and white wine and keep stirring until almost dry. Add ½ cup of the simmering stock or water and continue to cook, stirring constantly, until the rice has absorbed almost all the liquid. Continue cooking and stirring, adding the simmering liquid in ½-cup increments, making sure that each addition of liquid is almost completely absorbed by the rice before adding the next. Taste the rice after about 12 minutes. It should be about half cooked. Add the sautéed squid rings and butter. Continue to cook, stir, and add the stock or water as above until the rice is firm but tender, anywhere from 20 to 30 minutes, total cooking time. Immediately stir in the ice cube. Season with salt and pepper. Remove from heat and set aside.

To sear the scallops: Season the scallops with salt and pepper. In a large sauté pan or skillet, heat the oil over high heat until it shimmers. Add the scallops and sauté on each side until golden brown on the outside and almost opaque throughout, about 4 minutes. Remove the pan from heat and let the scallops sit for a few minutes to finish cooking while preparing the plates.

To fry the squid tentacles: In a medium, heavy saucepan, heat the oil and bring to shimmering, 350°F. Toss the tentacles in the cornstarch or flour, shake off any excess, and lower into the oil. Fry until golden brown, 5 minutes. Using a slotted spoon, transfer to paper towels to drain. Season with salt.

To serve, reheat the risotto over medium heat for 2 to 3 minutes. Add a little more liquid if it is too thick. Place a mound of the risotto in the middle of each of 4 warmed large shallow bowls. Place 3 scallops, evenly spaced, around the risotto. Mound the celery root salad on top of the risotto and spoon the gribiche in a circle around the outside of the scallops. Top with the fried tentacles, if using, and the chervil sprigs.

IMPROVISATIONS *The risotto can be made without the squid ink, or the squid. If it's summer and you've got the grill on, try grilling the squid (and the tentacles) and the scallops too—this would add a terrific smoky flavor.*

ADVANCE PREP *The gribiche will keep, covered, in the refrigerator for up to 2 days. The celery root salad may be made 1 day ahead and kept in the lemon vinaigrette, but is best made the day of serving. The risotto can be made ahead (see Chef's tips, page 132), but the scallops should be seasoned and seared at the last minute.*

SIMPLIFYING *Until you get the hang of it, risotto isn't particularly simple. Especially with the timing of the other components, this dish can be a little difficult. If you want to opt for an easier route, steam long-grain rice and add squid ink to the liquid. Rather than make the gribiche from scratch, you could add freshly chopped ingredients to a commercial mayonnaise that's been thinned with a little fish stock and a splash of vinegar.*

WINE NOTES *This entree is pretty much white wine territory, although a light Spanish red might also do the trick. The dish is rich and earthy and has a highly acidic sauce. A white wine that comes to mind is the Mas de Daumas-Gassac Blanc, a Viognier-and-Chardonnay blend from the Languedoc region of France. It's unoaked, with a mineral and fruit reminiscent of a white Burgundy. Other good choices would be anything from the Châteauneuf-du-Pape or Hermitage regions.*

Whenever I think of cod, I have an immediate, vivid image of a hearty New England fisherman braving treacherous seas and gale winds to haul in a catch that will feed his and his neighbors' families throughout a long, freezing winter. It was the abundance of this miraculous fish in the waters of the North Atlantic that provided sustenance for our forefathers during austere winters, and it was the cornerstone of the New England fishing industry. In fact, it would be difficult to overstate the importance of the Atlantic

JUNIPER-SEARED ATLANTIC COD *with* SAUERKRAUT, POTATO GRATIN, *and* APPLE *and* HERB SALAD

cod to the survival, nutritionally and economically, of our fledgling country from the time of the pilgrims to the end of the 1800s. But aside from its historical significance, the Atlantic cod is one of the most popular round fish in America, admired for its pristine snowy white flesh, big, dense flakes, and subtle, sweet flavor. With those bitter nor'easters in mind, it seemed natural to pair the cod with other stalwarts of the winter pantry: potatoes, apples, and cured cabbage—sauerkraut—a specialty of my talented dinner chef, Parke Ulrich.

★ *CHEF'S TIPS If you can't find Atlantic cod, use a good-sized lingcod in its place, but it's not the cod of legend, and actually isn't a cod at all—lingcod is a Pacific rockfish. To make matters even more confusing, there's also Pacific cod, often called "true cod," which is fished out of the Gulf of Alaska. If you use lingcod, it will be substantially thinner and you can omit the oven-cooking time; just cook the fillets all the way through in the sauté pan. | For traditional sauerkraut, you need to plan ahead; it takes the cabbage 10 days to cure properly. It's incredibly easy and tastes better than anything you can buy, although there is some good sauerkraut sold in better delis. Duck or chicken fat adds a terrific amount of flavor and great mouth-feel to the sauerkraut and is worth the extra cholesterol. Chicken fat can be purchased at kosher butchers—ask for schmaltz.*

Makes 4 entree servings

SAUERKRAUT:

8 juniper berries

3 pounds green cabbage, cored and thinly sliced

2½ tablespoons kosher salt

2 tablespoons sugar

COD MARINADE:

Four 6-ounce Atlantic cod fillets

1 tablespoon juniper berries, lightly crushed

½ cup Cognac

2 tablespoons olive oil

2 teaspoons minced fresh thyme

Kosher salt and freshly ground pepper to taste

POTATO GRATIN:

4 large russet (baking) potatoes, peeled and rinsed

1½ cups heavy cream

⅓ cup dry white wine

2 tablespoons minced fresh thyme, or 2 teaspoons dried thyme, crumbled

2 to 3 teaspoons kosher salt

Freshly ground pepper to taste

¼ cup rendered duck fat or chicken fat, or olive oil

¼ cup finely diced onion

1 teaspoon minced fresh thyme or ½ teaspoon dried thyme, crumbled

Kosher salt and freshly ground pepper to taste

APPLE AND HERB SALAD:

2 sweet, firm apples such as Braeburn or Fuji, peeled, cored, and quartered

¼ cup fresh flat-leaf (Italian) parsley leaves

¼ cup fresh tarragon leaves

¼ cup fresh chervil leaves

¼ cup ½-inch pieces fresh chives

1 tablespoon Champagne vinegar or fresh lemon juice

3 tablespoons extra-virgin olive oil

Kosher salt and freshly ground pepper to taste

2 tablespoons vegetable or canola oil

continued

To make the sauerkraut: In a preheated 350°F oven, roast the juniper berries for 3 to 4 minutes. Let cool and grind finely. Set aside, or cover in an airtight container for up to 3 months.

Put one-fourth of the shredded cabbage in a large bowl. In a small bowl, toss the ground juniper berries with the salt and sugar. Sprinkle the cabbage with one-fourth of the juniper mixture. Repeat to layer the remaining cabbage with the spice mixture. With a large mallet or potato masher, press down on the cabbage to slightly bruise it and break it down so that it begins to exude liquid. Transfer the cabbage to a nonreactive container, such as a plastic tub or a pottery crock. Pack it down and then cover with a dampened piece of doubled cheesecloth. Place a plate on top of the cabbage and weight the plate with a brick or a couple of heavy cans. Let the cabbage cure at room temperature in a dark, cool area for 10 days, changing the cheesecloth every 2 to 3 days. After 10 days, remove the cured cabbage, put it in a clean, airtight container, and store it in the refrigerator for up to 3 months.

To marinate the cod: Place the fish in a shallow bowl and cover with the marinade ingredients. Cover and refrigerate for at least 1 hour or up to 4 hours.

To make the gratin: Preheat the oven to 350°F. Place an oven rack in the center of the oven. Thinly slice the potatoes, with a mandoline if possible, and arrange in even layers in an 8-inch gratin dish or shallow baking dish. In a medium bowl, mix the cream, wine, thyme, salt, and pepper together and pour into the gratin dish; it should come three-quarters of the way up to the top of the potatoes. Cover with aluminum foil and cook until tender when a small knife or skewer is inserted, about 45 minutes. Remove the foil and bake until browned, 5 to 10 minutes (you may need to move the gratin to a rack on the top level). Or, remove from oven, let cool completely, and refrigerate for up to 1 day in advance. Remove from the oven and let rest for 5 minutes before cutting into squares and serving.

To cook the sauerkraut: In a small sauté pan or skillet, melt the fat or heat the oil over medium heat. Add the onion and cook until translucent, about 3 minutes. Add the sauerkraut and thyme and cook over very low heat, stirring occasionally, for 30 minutes. Season with salt and pepper. Set aside and cover to keep warm.

To make the salad: Thinly slice the apple quarters, then cut them into julienne. In a small bowl, combine the apple pieces with the herbs. Whisk the vinegar or lemon juice and olive oil together. Add to the salad and toss to coat. Season with salt and pepper. Set aside.

To cook the cod: Preheat the oven to 375°F. Drain the fish fillets, discard the liquid, and sprinkle with salt and pepper. Heat a large ovenproof sauté pan or skillet over medium-high heat. Add the oil and heat for a few seconds until the oil begins to shimmer. Slide the cod into the skillet, skin-side down. Cook until the skin is crisp and golden, about 2 minutes. Gently turn the fillets over with a slotted spatula and put the pan into the preheated oven. Cook until opaque throughout, 3 to 5 minutes, depending on the thickness of the fish.

To serve, place a square of the potato gratin, slightly off center, on each of 4 warmed plates. Mound the sauerkraut on the other side and drizzle a little of the juice around. Top with a cod fillet. Place a mound of apple and herb salad on top and serve immediately.

IMPROVISATIONS Atlantic cod is a lean, medium-firm, white-fleshed fish. Haddock, lingcod, rockfish, halibut, or sea bass are all good substitutes. You can use the braised cabbage recipe (page 154) instead of the sauerkraut.

ADVANCE PREP The cabbage needs to cure for 10 days. The herbs for the salad can be picked and kept in an airtight container for 1 day. The gratin can be cooked to the point of browning 1 day ahead, then finished in the oven up to 1 hour before serving. The salad should be tossed, the sauerkraut heated, and the fish cooked just before serving.

SIMPLIFYING You could serve plain mashed potatoes with this dish with just as much effect. The sauerkraut is terrific homemade, but you can also use 2½ cups of a good brand of sauerkraut from your local deli.

WINE NOTES This is your chance to drink a great bottle of Alsace Riesling. The wines are for the most part dry and fruity, full of refreshing acidity and a perfect foil for the flavors of juniper, sauerkraut, apple, and herbs. There are many wonderful producers from which to choose. Try Weinbach, Leon Beyer, Lucien Albrecht, Kuentz-Baz, and Albert Boxler.

I created this dish one night when I had some wonderfully fresh Monterey spot prawns that I'd brought home from the restaurant, a sprig of rosemary from the huge bush growing right outside our front door, and nothing in the refrigerator except a couple of beets. What is it that's said about the mother of invention? Although this dish sounds complicated, it actually goes together quickly and looks beautiful on the

ROSEMARY-SEARED PRAWNS *with* SAFFRON RISOTTO, ROASTED-BEET VINAIGRETTE, *and* PEA SHOOT SALAD

plate, with the magenta beets, yellow rice, pink prawns, and green pea shoots. I love rosemary, but I have to restrain myself when I use it in this dish, because a little rosemary goes a long way.

★ *CHEF'S TIPS I often use grapeseed oil for sautéing because of its high smoking point, but it can get just too darn hot, which, although great for getting a crust on fish fillets, can turn delicate prawns into rubber. Here, the prawns are sautéed in olive oil over medium-high heat. | When I was in Italy a few years ago, I attended a dinner for about five hundred guests and risotto was featured on the menu. I was wondering how the chefs could possibly make that much risotto and keep it hot, creamy, and not overcooked. The secret, I found out, was ice. Just as the risotto was cooked to perfection, they threw ice cubes into the mammoth pots. The rice immediately stopped cooking and the risotto became creamy without cooling down too much. We use this technique now at Farallon, whether we are cooking the rice ahead for a large banquet or serving it immediately after cooking. If you are preparing it in the afternoon for a dinner party, cook it until al dente, stir in the ice, and just set the pot aside. When ready for serving, reheat the rice over medium heat for about 2 minutes, and stir in the butter. Cook for 1 minute more, add a little more liquid if it's too thick, then serve piping hot.*

Makes 4 entree servings

1½ pounds jumbo prawns, shelled and deveined, tails on
1 tablespoon chopped fresh rosemary
1 tablespoon olive oil

ROASTED-BEET VINAIGRETTE:
5 or 6 ruby beets (about 12 ounces), scrubbed, greens trimmed to 1 inch
2 teaspoons olive oil
Kosher salt and freshly ground pepper to taste
1 teaspoon fresh thyme leaves
¼ cup water
1 tablespoon Champagne vinegar
¼ cup extra-virgin olive oil

RISOTTO:
5 cups water, fish stock (page 243), or a mixture of half water and half clam juice
½ teaspoon saffron threads, or scant ¼ teaspoon powdered saffron
3 tablespoons olive oil
1 medium onion, diced (about ¾ cup)
1 cup Arborio or Carnaroli rice
1 garlic clove, minced
1½ teaspoons minced fresh thyme, or ½ teaspoon dried thyme, crumbled
¼ cup dry white wine
1 ice cube
Kosher salt and freshly ground pepper to taste

Kosher salt and freshly ground pepper to taste
2 tablespoons grapeseed, canola, or olive oil
2 tablespoons unsalted butter
2 cups fresh pea shoots (see page 40)

To marinate the prawns: Toss the prawns with the rosemary and olive oil in a bowl. Set aside while you prepare the beets and risotto.

To make the vinaigrette: Preheat the oven to 400°F. Put the beets in a small, shallow baking dish, and rub with the olive oil, salt, and pepper. Add the thyme and water and cover the dish with aluminum foil. Roast until tender when pierced with a small knife, about 45 minutes. Uncover and let cool, then peel. Remove the tops and tails. Strain and reserve any of the roasting liquid. Cut the beets into ¼-inch dice and return them to the container with their liquid. Set aside, or cover and refrigerate for up to 1 day.

In a small bowl, whisk the Champagne vinegar with the extra-virgin olive oil and salt and pepper to taste. Remove 2 tablespoons of the vinaigrette and reserve it (for the pea shoot salad). Pour the reserved beet juices into the bowl with the remaining vinaigrette and whisk to combine. Stir in the diced beets.

To start the risotto: Bring the water, stock, or clam juice mixture to a low simmer on the stove and add the saffron. In a 3- to 4-quart heavy saucepan, heat the olive oil over medium heat and sauté the onion until translucent and just beginning to turn golden, about 5 minutes. Stir in the rice and cook until the rice grains become opaque, about 2 minutes. Add the garlic, thyme, and white wine and keep stirring until almost dry. Add ½ cup of the simmering saffron liquid and continue to cook, stirring constantly, until the rice has absorbed almost all the liquid. Continue cooking and stirring, adding the simmering liquid in ½-cup increments, making sure that each addition of liquid is almost completely absorbed by the rice before adding the next. Adjust the heat so that the risotto maintains a low simmer. The rice is done when firm but tender, which can take anywhere from 20 to 30 minutes, total cooking time. Immediately stir in the ice cube. Remove from heat. Season with salt and pepper. Cover and set aside in a warm place.

To cook the prawns: Sprinkle the prawns with salt and pepper. In a large skillet, heat the oil over medium-high heat until hot but not smoking. Add the prawns and sauté until evenly pink on both sides and golden brown on the edges, about 4 minutes. Remove the prawns from the pan and set aside.

To serve, reheat the risotto over medium heat for 2 minutes. Stir in the butter. Cook for 1 minute, and stir in a little more liquid if the risotto is too thick. Toss the pea shoots with the reserved vinaigrette. Place a spoonful of risotto on the center of 4 warmed large shallow bowls. Arrange 6 prawns around and on top of each serving of risotto. Spoon some of the beet vinaigrette around the rice and prawns, and top each with a handful of the pea shoots. Serve immediately.

IMPROVISATIONS *Scallops may be substituted for the prawns, and herbs such as thyme or tarragon for the rosemary. Risotto is always open to variation. A vegetable risotto with spinach, peas, or leeks would be nice with the prawns, or one with all fresh herbs. Remember that cheese and shellfish are not good partners, however. Any spicy or peppery greens, like arugula or watercress, can stand in for the pea shoots.*

ADVANCE PREP *This is a dish that is meant to be made quickly; however, the risotto can be cooked up to 1 day ahead, before adding the butter, contrary to popular cookbook wisdom (see the Chef's Tips, above). Finish the risotto as you sauté the prawns just prior to serving. The beets can be roasted and the vinaigrette made 1 day ahead.*

SIMPLIFYING *You could skip the risotto and serve the prawns with a long-grain or basmati saffron rice instead.*

WINE NOTES *This entree brings to mind Provence or the Italian Mediterranean, both visually and in its sunny seaside flavors. A medium- to full-bodied dry rosé from either of these wine-growing regions is not only a perfect choice, but the pink wine with the yellow risotto and the rosemary-flecked prawns would be beautiful. Also try a Chianti Classico, or even a California Sangiovese like the 1996 Atlas Peak from Napa.*

I think Americans have finally begun to appreciate skate; whenever it's on our menu, we always sell out. Europeans and Asians have long loved this odd-looking sea creature (a cousin of the cartilaginous shark) and over the years have developed recipes that highlight its remarkably sweet flesh. (Skate flesh is so sweet that it's been falsely rumored for years that unscrupulous fish purveyors have stamped out coins of skate and passed them off as expensive scallops.) Skate, or ray, as it's often called, is a versatile fish: It can be steamed, braised, grilled, sautéed, or poached. A classic French preparation is skate poached and served with capers and brown butter. Although skate flesh is fairly mild in flavor, ingredients that are salty or piquant seem to contrast especially well with its sweetness and decep-

SAUTÉED PACIFIC SKATE *with* WARM POTATO SALAD, SAUCE VERTE, *and* ROASTED-PEPPER RELISH

tive richness (it's actually quite lean). I think this sauce verte—my interpretation of the Mediterranean green sauce—is a particularly good foil for skate. I really like skate that has been pan-seared so that it develops a nice crisp, golden exterior, but the key to preparing it is to keep it simple—it's great for a quick midweek dinner. If you've never tasted skate, or have enjoyed it only in restaurants, try this easy recipe. I hope that you'll enjoy it so much that you'll want to experiment and develop your own recipes.

★ *CHEF'S TIPS When purchasing skate wings from your fish purveyor, ask for a whiff. If it smells strongly of ammonia, say "no thanks." It's been improperly handled and has deteriorated. If there's only a very slight ammonia smell, you can take it home and soak it in a mixture of 2 tablespoons lemon juice or vinegar to 4 cups of water for 30 minutes at room temperature or up to 3 hours in the refrigerator. This same tip also applies to shark. | Most skate sold in retail fish markets has been skinned, and that's what you want. Skinning a skate wing is a task best left to someone else—my very adept prep chefs do it for me. However, if you should somehow wind up with an unskinned skate wing, poach it first for a few minutes, making the skin easy to pull off. | It's the flat triangular wings of this member of the ray family that are edible. Each wing yields 2 triangular fillets on either side of the ribs of cartilage. If you purchase a whole wing that's been skinned but not filleted, consider cooking it whole instead. Many skate lovers, myself included, don't mind cutting the cooked meat from the cartilage on our plates, and some claim it tastes even better that way. | At Farallon, we use both Pacific and Atlantic skate, but I tend to prefer the Pacific skate for its larger size and equally good taste. I've found the smaller Atlantic skate wings to be more fragile and therefore a little bit more difficult to handle when cooked (make sure you have a large spatula to turn them over). The two fillets from one whole Atlantic skate wing can usually serve 2 people. The larger, thicker Pacific skate-wing fillets can be cut into several portions to serve 4 to 6. Since skate tastes best when it's cooked all the way through (at least I think it does—a Frenchman might disagree with me), the cooking time depends on the thickness of your fillets.*

Makes 4 entree servings

ROASTED-PEPPER RELISH:
4 yellow and/or red bell peppers
1 teaspoon olive oil
1 teaspoon fresh lemon juice
Kosher salt and freshly ground pepper
    to taste

SAUCE VERTE:
1 clove garlic, smashed
1 tablespoon fresh tarragon leaves

1 tablespoon fresh thyme leaves
2 teaspoons salt-packed capers, rinsed,
    or drained vinegar-brined capers
3 anchovy fillets, drained
3 tablespoons coarsely cut fresh chives
¼ cup fresh basil leaves
½ cup fresh flat-leaf (Italian) parsley
    leaves
¼ teaspoon freshly ground pepper
½ teaspoon green peppercorns, drained

½ teaspoon fresh lemon juice
¼ cup fresh orange juice
1 teaspoon Champagne vinegar
¼ cup olive oil
Kosher salt to taste

POTATO SALAD:
1½ pounds unpeeled Yukon Gold
    potatoes, scrubbed
⅓ cup extra-virgin olive oil

1 shallot, finely diced
1 teaspoon Champagne or sherry vinegar
Kosher salt and freshly ground pepper
    to taste

Four 8-ounce skate wings, skinned and
    filleted
Kosher salt and freshly ground pepper
    to taste
1 to 2 tablespoons grapeseed or canola oil

To make the pepper relish: Preheat the oven to 400°F. Cut the peppers in half, remove the stems and seeds, and rub the outsides with olive oil. Place, cut-side down, on a baking sheet and roast until the skin is blistered, about 20 minutes. Using tongs, place the peppers in a bowl and cover with plastic wrap. Set aside until cool, allowing the natural condensation to lift the peel from skin. Remove the skin from the peppers, wiping with a paper towel as necessary. Cut the roasted peppers into ¼-inch dice, put in a small bowl, and stir in the lemon juice, salt, and pepper. Set aside until ready to use.

To make the sauce verte: In a food processor or blender, puree all the ingredients except the olive oil and salt, scraping down the sides of the container once or twice. With the machine running, gradually add the olive oil to make the sauce the consistency of thin mayonnaise. Add a little water if necessary to thin out. Season with salt. Transfer to another container or bowl, cover, and set aside. Refrigerate for up to 4 hours.

To make the potato salad: Put the potatoes in a large saucepan and cover with cold water. Salt lightly; bring to a simmer and cook until the potatoes are easily pierced with a small knife or thin skewer, 10 to 15 minutes. You want them tender but not falling apart. Drain the potatoes and let sit until they're still warm but cool enough to handle. Cut into ¼-inch-thick slices and set aside. In a medium saucepan, heat the olive oil over medium heat and sauté the shallot until translucent, about 2 minutes. Add the sliced potatoes and stir to coat with the olive oil. Stir in the vinegar, salt, and pepper. Remove from heat, cover, and keep warm while you cook the skate.

To cook the skate: Sprinkle both sides of each fillet with salt and pepper. If you have portions of the thicker Pacific skate, you might be able to comfortably fit all 4 fillets in the pan at once. If you have small whole Atlantic skate wings, you might be able to fit 2 in the pan, in which case you'll need to do them in batches or use a couple of pans. Heat a large sauté pan or skillet over high heat, add the oil, heat for a few seconds, swirl the oil around the pan, and slide in the skate fillets, "pretty," or ridged-side, down (chefs refer to this as the "presentation side"). Cook the skate until a golden brown crust has formed on the bottom, 2 to 4 minutes. With a broad spatula, carefully turn the fillets over and cook until almost opaque throughout, 1 to

4 minutes longer, depending on the thickness of the fillets. Turn off the heat but leave the pan on the burner while you prepare the plates.

To serve, place a scoop of warm potatoes on each of 4 warmed plates. Top with a skate fillet and then a spoonful of pepper relish. Pour a ribbon of sauce verte around each dish and serve with extra sauce at the table.

IMPROVISATIONS *The first thing that comes to mind here is to use scallops in place of the skate. Just about any other white-fleshed fish would be good too, from delicate and mild sole or flounder to robust and firm tuna or shark. The recipe for sauce verte welcomes improvisation, so eliminate or change ingredients to suit your mood or pantry. Just make sure you include fresh herbs, an acid, and oil.*

ADVANCE PREP *While the skate in this recipe should be cooked right before serving, it's a common secret in professional kitchens that skate is one of the few fishes that keeps well under refrigeration, providing that it was properly handled to begin with. In fact, the texture seems to improve and become more firm, even up to 3 days. The sauce verte will keep for 4 hours, covered and refrigerated, and the pepper relish for 2 days. The potato salad is best made no more than 4 to 5 hours ahead and then briefly rewarmed. (It will still taste good even 2 days later, but it loses some of its fresh potato flavor.)*

SIMPLIFYING *The skate is easily prepared and cooked, but if you don't want to make the sauce verte, consider using a good-quality pesto instead. The potato salad is the simplest one you could imagine. For the pepper relish, you could purchase peeled, roasted peppers from a good deli or market.*

WINE NOTES *The wine pairings for skate are numerous, depending upon how it is cooked and what the accompaniments are. For white wines that match all the fresh herbs and roasted peppers in this preparation, try a full-bodied "New World" Sauvignon Blanc or Semillon (from Australia, New Zealand, or South Africa) or a Côtes-du-Rhône Village from France. A Californian Syrah (the next big thing) and a lighter-bodied Rhône red like Saint Joseph, or a rosé from Provence, are fine choices as well.*

The method used here for cooking fish fillets—searing them on top of the stove and then finishing them in the oven—is common in restaurants. It's an easy technique used for all kinds of meats. One of the most frequent questions I receive, whether in cooking classes or at Farallon, is "How did you get such a crispy crust on this fish?" Fish cooked this way develops a wonderful, crispy exterior that contrasts with the moist, tender meat. Pan-roasting is a simple technique that can be also be used to get a crispy skin on chicken breasts. It helps to have a good exhaust fan and a nonstick skillet. But the

PAN-ROASTED WALLEYED PIKE *with* ENGLISH PEA RAVIOLI, BRAISED ENDIVE, CRAB, *and* MINT PESTO

best part of this dish is not the fish—it's the combination of the pea ravioli with the mint pesto, a classic pairing. The pea puree is so incredibly good that I could eat it straight from the pan with a spoon. And I have.

★ CHEF'S TIPS *I can immediately qualify someone seeking a job as a line cook by asking him or her to sear a fish fillet. The test is in keeping the fish from sticking to the pan, because the pans we use are all stainless steel—teflon nonstick pans are not durable enough for the high heat and multiple dishwashings that they undergo on the line. An experienced cook will heat an empty stainless pan over high flame for a minute or so, add a little oil, and slide the fish fillet in with one hand, while simultaneously shaking the pan with the other hand. The friction and movement of the fish in the pan prevents it from sticking. All that said, when I pan-roast fish at home, I use a nonstick skillet.*

Makes 4 entree servings

ENGLISH PEA RAVIOLI:
2 tablespoons unsalted butter
1 pound English peas, shelled (about 1 cup), or 1 cup frozen peas
1 teaspoon chopped fresh tarragon
Kosher salt and freshly ground pepper to taste
40 wonton wrappers
1 egg beaten with 1 tablespoon water
Flour for dusting

MINT PESTO:
¾ cup loosely packed fresh mint leaves (from 1 small bunch)
¼ cup loosely packed fresh flat-leaf (Italian) parsley leaves
4 tablespoons canola oil
1 tablespoon pine nuts, toasted
½ teaspoon fresh lemon juice
1 teaspoon grated orange zest
Kosher salt and freshly ground pepper to taste

BRAISED ENDIVE:
4 heads Belgian endive, halved lengthwise
¼ cup dry white wine
¼ cup fish stock (page 243) or clam juice
¼ cup heavy cream
1 teaspoon chopped fresh tarragon
1 teaspoon chopped fresh thyme

BUTTER SAUCE:
¼ cup dry white wine
¼ cup fish stock (page 243) or clam juice
½ cup (1 stick) cold unsalted butter, cut into tablespoon-sized pieces
Kosher salt and freshly ground pepper to taste

Four 6-ounce walleyed pike fillets (skin on), pin bones removed (see Chef's Tips, page 46)
Kosher salt and freshly ground pepper to taste
4 tablespoons grapeseed, canola, or olive oil

1 cup fresh lump crabmeat, picked over for shells

Preparation

To make the pea ravioli filling: In a medium sauté pan or skillet, melt the butter over medium heat, add the peas, and cook until warmed through and slightly softened, about 3 minutes. (If you are using frozen peas, it's not necessary to defrost them first.) Add the tarragon, salt, and pepper. Transfer to a blender or food processor and puree. Let cool. Use now, or cover and refrigerate for up to 2 days.

To assemble the ravioli: Lay out 20 wonton wrappers on a work surface. Place a heaping teaspoonful of pea puree in the center of each wonton and brush the edges of the wrappers with the egg wash. Top each with another wrapper and firmly press the edges to seal, creating a small round mound in the center as you push out as much air as possible. Either leave square or cut with a round biscuit cutter. Put the ravioli on a parchment paper–lined baking pan that has been lightly dusted with flour. Store, uncovered, in the refrigerator for up to 1 day. Or, freeze on a baking sheet, then transfer to a covered container and freeze for up to 3 weeks.

To make the pesto: In a large pot of boiling water, blanch the mint and parsley leaves for about 10 seconds.

continued

Drain and transfer the herbs to a bowl of cold water to set the color and stop the cooking. Using your hands, squeeze out as much moisture as possible. In a food processor or blender, puree the herbs with 2 tablespoons of the oil, scraping down the sides of the container once. With the machine running, gradually add the remaining 2 tablespoons of oil. Add the pine nuts, lemon juice, and orange zest and process until the mixture forms a smooth sauce, a few seconds longer. Season with salt and pepper. Transfer to a small plastic container, press a piece of plastic wrap onto the surface of the pesto, and seal with the container top. Use now or refrigerate for up to 2 days. Return to room temperature before serving.

To braise the endive: Preheat the oven to 375°F. Arrange the endive, cut-side down, in a gratin or baking dish just large enough to hold them in one layer. Pour the wine, stock or clam juice, and cream over the endive and sprinkle with the tarragon and thyme. Cover with aluminum foil and braise in the oven until a sharp knife slides easily into the core of the endive and the cream has thickened, about 45 minutes. Remove the dish from the oven and serve immediately, or let cool if preparing in advance. Reheat before serving.

To make the butter sauce: In a small saucepan, combine the wine and fish stock or clam juice and bring to a boil over medium-high heat. Cook to reduce the liquid by half. Reduce heat to very low and whisk in the butter, 2 tablespoons at a time, allowing the sauce to emulsify each time before adding more butter. Season with salt and pepper. Keep the sauce warm near a pilot light or in a bowl set over (but not touching) warm water for up to 4 hours. Whisk occasionally if the sauce begins to separate.

To cook the ravioli and pike: Preheat the oven to 375°F and bring a large pot of water to a boil. Heat a large, ovenproof sauté pan or skillet over medium-high heat and sprinkle the fish fillets with salt and pepper. Add the oil to the skillet and heat for a few seconds. Slide the pike into the skillet, skin-side down. Cook until the skin is crisp and golden, about 2 minutes. Gently turn the fillets over with a spatula and put the pan into the oven. As soon as the fillets go in the oven, generously salt the boiling water and drop in the ravioli. Immediately turn the heat down so that the water just simmers. After 3 minutes, test for doneness by cutting off and biting into the corner of a ravioli. When al dente, use a slotted spoon to transfer the ravioli to a bowl and add a large spoonful of the butter sauce. Gently turn the ravioli to coat with the sauce. Check the pike for doneness and remove the skillet from the oven.

To serve, put the crabmeat in a small bowl and toss with some of the warm butter sauce. Arrange 5 ravioli on each of 4 warmed dinner plates. Using a slotted spoon, transfer 2 halves of endive to the top of each serving of ravioli. Place the pike fillets, crispy skin-side up, on top of the endive. Drizzle some mint pesto on the plate around dish, and garnish with a mound of crabmeat on top of the pike.

IMPROVISATIONS *We make this dish almost year-round at Farallon, using seasonal ingredients. In the spring we fill the ravioli with peas, and in the winter we might use celery root or potato. Any medium-firm, mild-flavored fish works here. While mint and peas are a classic combination, you could use another herb for the pesto, particularly if you use another filling for the ravioli. Cooked shrimp and lobster could fill in for the crabmeat.*

ADVANCE PREP *All of the components of this dish, except the fish, may be done in advance.*

SIMPLIFYING *You could use good-quality purchased ravioli, but I'd just serve the fish on a bed of the pea puree, it's that tasty. Instead of making butter sauce and mint pesto, you could save time by just tossing the ravioli with melted butter seasoned with a little minced fresh mint, salt, and pepper.*

WINE NOTES *The white wines of the Rhône Valley are nice and dry, usually not oaky. They're also unique, with grapes like Marsanne and Roussanne, Clairette, and Viognier. They have flavors that are—unlike Chardonnay and Sauvignon Blanc—more like stone fruits, honey, herbs, and minerals, maybe with a touch of anise or fennel. The vintages are variable, but when the grapes were warm and ripe and not plagued by rain, these wines are gorgeous—and perfect with this dish.*

Turbot, a member of the sole family, is on my list of favorite fish, but I don't just love it for its firm, sweet, and mellow white flesh; I love it for its bones, which make the best, most flavorful, gelatinous fish stock. At the restaurant we order only whole fish—an option I realize is not often afforded the retail fish shopper. The advantage to buying whole fish and filleting it yourself is that not only is it cheaper, you're also able to make use of the bones. Often, fishmongers will label any kind of flatfish *turbot*

PAN-ROASTED EUROPEAN TURBOT *with* FENNEL *and* ARTICHOKE HEART SALAD *with* PRESERVED LEMON–LAVENDER VINAIGRETTE

if they think that they can charge more for it. Most of what they try to pass off as turbot is caught in waters around Greenland and also the Pacific but has a soft, sort of mushy meat that doesn't even come close in flavor to its European flatfish cousin. My preferred way to prepare this dish is to quickly brown individual pieces of turbot on the bone, then finish them in a hot oven. After that, it's an easy task for diners to separate flesh from bone at the table. This Mediterranean-inspired salad of shaved artichokes and fennel with preserved lemons and lavender contrasts with the sweetness of the fish but doesn't overpower its delicacy.

★ CHEF'S TIP *Usually, what you'll find identified as turbot is not the real thing, and you should always ask where your fish is from; it could be the so-called Greenland turbot, the most undesirable kind, or it may actually be a flounder. Be suspicious if the fishmonger says that it's European turbot and the price is under six or seven dollars per pound.*

Makes 4 entree servings

FENNEL AND ARTICHOKE SALAD:
4 sprigs thyme
2 sprigs lavender, or ½ teaspoon dried lavender blossoms
8 juniper berries
1 tablespoon kosher salt
1 teaspoon freshly ground pepper
¼ cup olive oil
½ cup Champagne vinegar or white wine vinegar
4 extra-large artichokes (about 1½ pounds total)
2 to 3 fennel bulbs, trimmed and cored
Fresh juice of 1 lemon

PRESERVED LEMON–LAVENDER VINAIGRETTE:
1 tablespoon rinsed and minced Moroccan preserved lemons, rind included (page 242)
¼ cup extra-virgin olive oil
2 teaspoons minced lavender flowers, or 1 teaspoon dried lavender blossoms

1 tablespoon minced fresh flat-leaf (Italian) parsley
2 teaspoons fresh lemon juice
Kosher salt and freshly ground pepper to taste

Four 6- to 8-ounce turbot fillets, skinned
Kosher salt and freshly ground pepper to taste
¼ cup grapeseed or canola oil

2 cups arugula leaves

continued

To start the salad, first cook the artichokes: Fill a small stockpot with cold water and add the thyme, lavender, juniper berries, salt, pepper, oil, and vinegar. Add the artichokes, cover, and bring to a boil. Reduce heat, partially cover, and simmer, until tender, about 25 minutes. Drain. Discard all the outer leaves and trim away the stem. Using a large spoon, carefully scoop out the fuzzy inner leaves and discard. Trim away any stringy pieces. Slice thinly and set aside. Meanwhile, using a mandoline or a very sharp knife, cut the fennel into very thin slices. Add the lemon juice to a bowl of water and immerse the fennel slices in the water. These can be kept for up to 8 hours.

To make the vinaigrette: Combine all the ingredients and whisk well. Set aside or cover and refrigerate for up to 1 day.

To roast the turbot: Preheat the oven to 425°F. Season the turbot with salt and pepper on both sides. In a medium, ovenproof sauté pan or skillet, heat the oil over high heat and sear the turbot until lightly browned, 2 minutes on each side. Transfer to the oven and roast until opaque throughout, about 8 minutes. Remove from the oven and let rest while the dish is assembled.

To finish the salad, drain the fennel. Combine the fennel, artichoke hearts, and arugula in a medium bowl with 2 to 3 tablespoons of the vinaigrette and toss to coat evenly.

To serve, place an equal amount of the salad in the middle of each of 4 plates and place a piece of turbot on top. Drizzle a little remaining vinaigrette around.

IMPROVISATIONS *Substitute halibut or cod. For a winter version of this dish, you could slice the fennel and sauté it in a little butter and oil, then toss it with brown sugar before roasting it in a preheated 300°F oven until deep brown, about 40 minutes. At the last minute, toss in the artichoke hearts and some warm vinaigrette.*

ADVANCE PREP *The artichokes and fennel can be prepared 1 day ahead. Instead of immersing the fennel in the lemon water, toss it and the artichokes in a little of the vinaigrette. Add the arugula and more of the vinaigrette before serving.*

SIMPLIFYING *This is a very basic recipe where most of the components can be done a day ahead. If preserved lemon is not available, substitute an equal amount of lemon zest or Lemon Vinaigrette (page 247).*

WINE NOTES *This is a pretty rich plate of food, but with lots of bright accents. A white Burgundy or Chardonnay would be fine, but try a white Bordeaux with Semillon in the mix, something with exotic vanilla notes and bracing acidity. They are amazing wines.*

Tilefish should get an agent because it oughta be a star. Unfortunately, it rarely makes an appearance in markets other than those on the East Coast, where it's fished commercially in deep waters from Nova Scotia to the Gulf of Mexico year-round. It has all the characteristics that consumers love: It is lean, firm, white, and inexpensive, with a flavor so delicate (often compared to lobster in taste) that I've

GRILLED BACON-STUDDED TILEFISH *with* POTATO RAVIOLI, BRAISED CARDOONS, *and* MADEIRA SAUCE

heard it makes a terrific sashimi. Its beautiful olive-green, gold-spotted skin crisps up well and is also particularly tasty. What I like to do with a thick fillet like tilefish is to lard it: I insert small pieces of blanched bacon into the flesh, which adds moisture to the meat with a slight smokiness. The potato ravioli, braised cardoons (a native Mediterranean vegetable that tastes a little like artichokes), and Madeira sauce all play supporting roles, cast strictly to support the smoky bacon-studded tilefish—the real star.

★ *CHEF'S TIPS Larding is a fairly old-fashioned technique from the days when big lean cuts of meat were injected with fat by using a special larding needle. This should not be confused with barding, which means to wrap meat with strips of bacon before cooking. At the restaurant, we still use larding needles, but if you don't have one you can just stud the fish by poking holes in the meat with a sharp paring knife, then pushing the bacon in with the end of a chopstick. | Buy Atlantic tilefish if you see it in the markets, not Pacific tilefish, or ocean whitefish, as it is called, as it can have a bitter taste. | Rather than grill the fish, you can pan-roast it (see Walleyed Pike, page 137). | Cardoons are thistles, closely related to the artichoke, which they resemble in taste. They're prized in the Mediterranean but uncommon here.*

Makes 4 entree servings

POTATO RAVIOLI FILLING:
1 pound Yukon Gold potatoes, peeled
    and cut into even pieces
¼ cup mascarpone cheese
1 tablespoon extra-virgin olive oil
1 tablespoon minced fresh thyme
Kosher salt and freshly ground pepper
    to taste

16 to 20 round wonton wrappers
1 egg beaten with 1 tablespoon water
Flour for sprinkling

CARDOONS:
Juice of 1½ lemons
1 pound cardoons
½ cup dry white wine
½ cup extra-virgin olive oil
1 bay leaf
4 sprigs thyme
2 cloves garlic, crushed
Kosher salt and freshly ground pepper
    to taste

MADEIRA SAUCE:
2 shallots, minced
2 teaspoons minced fresh thyme
½ cup Madeira
1 cup fish stock (page 243) or clam juice
Kosher salt and freshly ground pepper
    to taste

4 ounces good-quality smoked slab
    bacon, cut into ¼-inch-by-1-inch pieces
Four 6-ounce tilefish fillets
2 tablespoons grapeseed, canola,
    or olive oil
Kosher salt and freshly ground pepper
    to taste

To make the ravioli filling: In a medium saucepan, combine the potatoes in salted water to cover. Bring to a boil and cook until just tender, about 20 minutes. Drain and let dry for about 10 minutes. Push the potatoes through a ricer or a food mill fitted with a medium-hole disk. Add the remaining filling ingredients and stir to blend. Set aside to cool for up to 1 day.

To assemble the ravioli: lay out half of the wonton wrappers on a work surface. Place 1 heaping teaspoon of potato puree in the center of each wonton and brush the edges of the wrappers with the egg wash. Top each with another wrapper and firmly press the edges to seal, creating a small round mound in the center as you push out as much air as possible from the ravioli. Store the ravioli on a baking sheet lined with parchment paper and dusted with flour; refrigerate for up to 1 day or freeze for up to 3 weeks until ready to cook.

To braise the cardoons: Add the juice of 1 lemon to a bowl of water. Trim off the leaves of the cardoons and remove any spiny skin from the stalks. Remove the outer strings by cutting into one end of the stalk and then pulling the strings down and away. Cut the stalks into 4-inch lengths, dropping them into the lemon water as you go. The cardoons can be kept in the lemon water for up to 24 hours. To cook, drain and cut the cardoons into ½-inch thick slices. In a medium saucepan combine the wine, olive oil, juice of ½ lemon, bay leaf, thyme, garlic, salt, and pepper. Add the cardoons, bring to a boil, reduce heat to a simmer, and cook until tender, about 30 minutes. Remove from heat and let the cardoons cool in their liquid. Strain and serve, or store overnight in their poaching liquid.

To make the Madeira sauce: In a small saucepan, combine all the ingredients except the salt and pepper and simmer over low heat until reduced by about three-fourths. Season with salt and pepper. Set aside and keep warm, or let cool, cover, and refrigerate for up to 1 day. Reheat to serve.

To cook the ravioli and tilefish: Bring a large pot of water to a boil. In a medium sauté pan or skillet of simmering water, blanch the bacon pieces for 3 to 4 minutes. Using a slotted spoon, transfer the bacon to paper towels to drain. Use a sharp paring knife to make 7 to 10 holes through each fillet. Using a chopstick, gently poke the bacon into the holes. Rub the tilefish with the oil and season with salt and pepper. Heat a grill pan over high heat. Cook until grill-marked on the outside and opaque throughout, 3 to 4 minutes on each side, depending on the thickness of the fish. Transfer to a plate and keep warm. Generously salt the boiling water and drop in the ravioli. Immediately turn the heat down so that the water just simmers. After 3 minutes, test for doneness by cutting off and biting into the corner of a ravioli.

To serve, place the warm ravioli in a ring in the center of each of 4 warmed plates. Fill the center with some of the warm cardoons and place the tilefish on top. Spoon a little of the Madeira sauce over and around the plate.

IMPROVISATIONS Any thick fish fillets from cod, monkfish, halibut, or grouper would do well in this dish. The ravioli are quite rich, and you can try playing around with the ravioli filling, but keep in mind that this dish is well balanced and quite light. I love the flavors of the smoky bacon, potatoes, rich mascarpone, and Madeira. Artichoke hearts are good substitutes for cardoons.

ADVANCE PREP The Madeira sauce, cardoons, and ravioli filling can all be made 1 day ahead. The ravioli can be assembled 1 day before and kept, well covered, in the refrigerator. Or they can be frozen for up to 3 weeks.

SIMPLIFYING You could omit the Madeira sauce, but you would miss out on some of the depth of flavor. Use the liquid from the cardoons to lightly coat the ravioli for a simpler dish. You could just wrap the bacon around the fish and secure it with a toothpick.

WINE NOTES Red wine and fish? Why not? Especially when elements like bacon and a red wine sauce are featured. Pinot Noir is an incredibly versatile wine, and Americans are making huge strides in capturing all the fruit, finesse, and complexity this grape has to offer. Talk to someone at your local wine store and try Handley Cellars in the Anderson Valley, or Saintsbury and Domaine Carneros, Rochioli and Merry Edwards from Sonoma. From Oregon, try Domaine Drouhin and Archery Summit, and from Santa Barbara, try Au Bon Climat and Babcock.

If you've skimmed through this book at all, you will know that I'm a truffle fanatic. And truffles go with lobster. It's one of the all-time great pairings in which the two ingredients seem to accentuate and intensify each other's qualities. In the case of truffles and lobster, the earthy, aromatic truffles

GRILLED WHOLE TRUFFLED LOBSTER *with* CAULIFLOWER GRATIN *and* GRILLED ASPARAGUS

underscore the intensely sweet ocean flavor of the lobster. I don't remember the exact moment when I discovered this combination (apparently it wasn't the epiphany that it should have been), but I do know that at some point I heard about a dish prepared many years ago by Georges Garin at his restaurant in France. He had injected a lobster with truffle butter before roasting it. At Farallon, I was inspired to create a similar dish, and it's been wildly popular. For the sake of simplification here, I eliminated the injection of the truffle butter and elected to brush the lobster with a butter and truffle oil mixture instead. You still get the essence of lobster and truffles together.

★ CHEF'S TIPS *Once opened, a can of truffle peelings will last, refrigerated in an airtight container, for up to 2 weeks. Any remaining liquid can be cooked to reduce it by half and used in, say, black truffle vinaigrette or to add a sexy flavor boost to sauces. | Truffle shavers are beautiful tools designed particularly for the hardness, size, and desired shaving thickness of truffles. It can also be used for decorative chocolate shavings.*

Makes 4 entree servings

CAULIFLOWER GRATIN:
1 large head cauliflower (about 2
    pounds), cut into small florets
¾ cup heavy cream
¾ cup mascarpone cheese
¼ cup dry white wine
1 teaspoon chopped fresh thyme
1 teaspoon chopped fresh marjoram
1 teaspoon chopped fresh sage
Kosher salt and freshly ground pepper
    to taste

1 cup panko (Japanese bread crumbs)
    or dried bread crumbs (page 240)
1 tablespoon chopped fresh flat-leaf
    (Italian) parsley
2 tablespoons olive oil

GRILLED ASPARAGUS:
1 pound medium to large asparagus
    stalks, tough white ends cut off
2 tablespoons olive oil
Kosher salt and freshly ground pepper
    to taste

TRUFFLE BUTTER:
1 cup (2 sticks) unsalted butter, at room
    temperature
2 teaspoons white truffle oil, or
    ⅓ ounce fresh black truffle, minced
    (2 teaspoons)
1 tablespoon chopped fresh tarragon
1 tablespoon chopped fresh chervil
Kosher salt and freshly ground pepper
    to taste

Four live Maine lobsters
    (about 1½ pounds each)
Kosher salt and freshly ground pepper
    to taste

continued

To make the cauliflower: Preheat the oven to 350°F. Butter a large gratin dish or 4 individual gratin dishes. In a medium saucepan of lightly salted boiling water, cook the cauliflower florets for 4 minutes and drain. In a medium stainless-steel bowl, combine the cream, mascarpone, wine, and herbs. Put the hot cauliflower into the cream mixture, stir to coat, and season with salt and pepper. Pour into the prepared gratin dish or dishes. Bake until tender when pierced with a knife and heated through, 15 to 20 minutes. In a small bowl, mix the panko or bread crumbs, parsley, and olive oil. Remove the gratin from the oven and sprinkle the mixture on top. (At this point, you can cool, cover, and refrigerate the gratin for up to 1 day.) Increase the oven temperature to 450°F and return the gratin to the oven until the mixture starts to bubble and brown on top, 5 to 10 minutes. If the gratin is not browning, either move it to a rack closer to the top of the oven or put it under a broiler for a minute or so. Set aside until serving.

To grill the asparagus: Light a fire in a charcoal grill. If the asparagus spears are thick, bring a large pot of salted water to a boil and blanch the spears for 2 minutes; drain and pat dry. Toss the asparagus spears with the olive oil, salt, and pepper until well coated. Place on the grill at a right angle to the grill grids or place in a grill basket. Grill, turning frequently, until marked and crisp-tender, 5 to 8 minutes. Set aside in a warm place.

To make the truffle butter: In a small bowl, mash all the ingredients together until well combined. Set aside at room temperature for up to 30 minutes, or cover and refrigerate for up to 1 day. Bring back to room temperature before using.

To grill the lobster: Bring a large pot of salted water to a boil and plunge in the lobsters, head first. Cook for 4 minutes. Remove from the pot. Split the lobsters in half lengthwise. Clean out the pink coral and tomalley in the head area and any intestines running down the back. Brush the lobster meat with the truffle butter and season with salt and pepper. Grill, flesh-side up, until opaque and cooked through, 3 to 5 minutes. Serve immediately.

To serve, place a scoop of the cauliflower gratin in the center of each of 4 warmed plates with the asparagus (tips pointing in the same direction) placed alongside. Top with 2 lobster halves, each head half facing the same direction, leaning slightly.

IMPROVISATIONS *Colossal or jumbo prawns could stand in for lobster. Technically speaking, all the elements of this dish are very "mix 'n match"; you could serve the lobster with a potato gratin, or you could serve the cauliflower gratin with a grilled piece of filet mignon, and the asparagus can go with virtually anything. The combination of all three together, however, is unique and worth trying at least once. Don't make this dish without the white truffle oil, because you will lose the very essence of the recipe.*

ADVANCE PREP *The cauliflower for the gratin can be blanched 1 day ahead. Or, you can cook the whole gratin 1 day ahead and brown it just before serving. The asparagus too, if they are thick, can be blanched 1 day ahead. The butter can be frozen, then thawed for brushing on the lobster. The lobster should be grilled right before serving, but you can partially cook it earlier in the day.*

SIMPLIFYING *If you're not up for grilling, broil the lobster, or roast it in a preheated 500°F oven for 5 to 7 minutes. The asparagus can also be oven-roasted or sautéed in a little olive oil over medium-high heat until tender and lightly browned. Instead of preparing a whole gratin, serve the cauliflower steamed and lightly drizzled with butter and seasonings.*

WINE NOTES *Nothing can match the luxurious flavors of lobster and truffles except a bottle of fabulous white Burgundy. Certainly a Chardonnay from California or Australia would match the heaviness of the dish, but take the opportunity to get to know the wines of Etienne Sauzet, a first-rate domaine in the Côte d'Or. They're powerful and graceful, not unlike the avid rugby player who makes them. They age beautifully, so if a premier or Grand Cru '90 or '92 is available, now is the time.*

All of us at Farallon look forward to soft-shell crab season, which runs roughly from May through August, and every year I catch one of my chefs or cooks popping a soft-shell crab into his mouth. While this is not accepted professional behavior, I do understand the allure of these tasty little creatures. When I was at Stars, we used to serve as many as one hundred orders a night of breaded and fried soft-shell crab, which meant frying twice that many (2 per order). It was a nightmare for my line cooks,

FRIED SOFT-SHELL CRABS *with* GARLIC BELUGA LENTILS *and* SLOW-ROASTED TOMATO *and* BASIL SAUCE

because the crabs had to be breaded right before the frying and serving. If you've ever breaded something using your fingers, you know what a mess it is and how often you need to rinse your hands. One night, after closing, I decided to throw a crab into the fryer for myself (I'm not immune to temptation), but was too tired to bread it. I tossed it in, uncoated, and 2 minutes later I had a crispy morsel that tasted like sweet crab instead of breading. It was a revelation, and from that moment on, I haven't breaded soft-shell crab. Occasionally we'll pat on some bonito flakes, which adds a slight crunch, salty taste, and lacy appearance. The following dish is extremely popular at the restaurant and is easy to duplicate at home.

★ CHEF'S TIPS *Many home cooks suffer from "fear of frying," but this recipe is relatively easy and worth the trouble to set up a fryer. One word of warning: The crabs bubble up like crazy when they hit the hot oil, so use either a covered electric fryer or a deep Dutch oven filled only half full with oil; anything with a heavy bottom and deep sides should do. You can also fill a large, deep skillet with about ½ inch of oil and pan-fry the crab. Whichever method you choose, make sure the oil is hot, so that the crab gets crispy without absorbing a lot of fat, and use fresh oil (I never use the same oil twice). It's important to use a deep-frying thermometer to make sure your oil is the correct temperature. To save time, have your fishmonger clean the crab for you. | Beluga lentils are black in color and smaller than regular lentils; they're named after their resemblance to caviar. If you can't find them, look for French green lentils, especially those from Le Puy. They hold their texture and shape better than the other kinds, especially the reds and yellows that can quickly turn to mush.*

Makes 4 entree servings

SLOW-ROASTED TOMATO AND BASIL SAUCE:
3 tablespoons olive oil
1 clove garlic, lightly smashed
1 cup coarsely chopped fresh basil leaves
¼ cup fish stock (page 243), shellfish stock (page 244), or clam juice
¼ cup dry white wine
¾ cup coarsely chopped, peeled slow-roasted tomatoes (page 247)
¼ cup extra-virgin olive oil
Kosher salt and freshly ground pepper to taste

GARLIC BELUGA LENTILS:
2 tablespoons olive oil
½ cup finely diced onion
1 heaping cup beluga lentils or French green lentils (*lentilles du Puy*)
1½ teaspoons minced fresh thyme, or ½ teaspoon dried thyme, crumbled
1 teaspoon kosher salt, plus salt to taste
3 cups water
1 clove garlic, minced
1 tablespoon fresh lemon juice
Freshly ground pepper to taste

Peanut or canola oil for deep-frying
8 soft-shell crabs, cleaned (see page 233)
Bonito flakes (optional)
Kosher salt and freshly ground pepper to taste

continued

To make the sauce: In a small sauté pan or skillet, heat the olive oil over medium heat and sauté the garlic until just golden. Remove and discard the garlic (all you want is a subtle flavor of garlic). Add the chopped basil and sauté for 30 seconds. Add the stock or clam juice and the wine. Increase heat to high and bring to a boil. Remove the pan from heat. Add the tomatoes and whisk in the extra-virgin olive oil, salt, and pepper. Set aside for up to 1 hour. Reheat briefly before serving, if necessary, whisking to reemulsify.

To make the lentils: In a small saucepan, heat the olive oil over medium heat and sauté the onion until translucent, about 4 minutes. Add the lentils, thyme, and salt. Increase heat to medium-high and sauté until the lentils begin to lighten slightly in color, about 2 minutes. Add the water, bring to a simmer, and cook the lentils, uncovered, for 20 minutes. Cover and remove from heat. Let stand undisturbed for 10 minutes, then taste a few lentils for doneness. They should be tender to the bite but still retain their shape. If they're still too crunchy for your taste, simmer them 5 minutes longer, uncovered, and let stand, covered, off heat for 5 minutes. If they're too dry, add a little more water. Stir in the minced garlic and season the lentils with the lemon juice, salt, and pepper. Set aside for up to 1 hour before serving.

To fry the soft-shell crabs: In a Dutch oven or deep fryer, heat 2 to 3 inches of peanut or canola oil to 365°F. Pat the soft-shell crabs dry with paper towels and lightly pat on the bonito flakes, if using. Don't worry if they don't adhere well; it's only going to be a loose coating. Carefully slide the crabs, 2 at a time, into the hot oil. Be careful, because the crabs will bubble and spit. Fry the crabs until golden and crispy, 2½ to 3 minutes. Using a wire-mesh skimmer, transfer the crabs to a wire rack set on a baking sheet and place in a low oven to keep warm while frying the rest of the crabs.

To serve, season the crabs with salt and pepper. Place a mound of lentils in the center of each of 4 warmed dinner plates. Top each serving of lentils with 2 soft-shell crabs and spoon warm tomato-basil sauce around the edges.

IMPROVISATIONS *Any kind of lentil may be substituted for the belugas. You might even try this dish with some braised cannellini or small white beans. Pasta would also be nice, tossed with the tomato sauce, and rosemary or thyme could stand in for the basil.*

ADVANCE PREP *The lentils and tomato sauce may be prepared 1 day ahead, refrigerated, and reheated up to 1 hour before serving. The crabs should be served as soon as all of them have been fried.*

SIMPLIFYING *The beauty of this dish is how simply the crab is cooked. The lentils take less than 30 minutes, which is not much longer than it takes to heat the oil to fry the crabs. The most time-consuming part of this dish is making the slow-roasted tomatoes, so if you don't have them on hand, just use good-quality canned Italian tomatoes.*

WINE NOTES *The earthy lentils, bright tomatoes, and rich fried crab allow for a wide selection of wines, such as a barrel-fermented California Sauvignon Blanc; a ripe and oaky white Graves from Bordeaux; an Italian white wine such as Soave or Greco di Tufo; or an Albariño from Spain. All are medium-full wines that would marry well with this dish. Medium-bodied red wines are a great option, too. Rioja or Ribera del Duero, from two premium growing regions in Spain, would work, but avoid too powerful a style. A soft, fruity Côtes-du-Rhône is a good, inexpensive choice.*

For a while there, I was really tired of squid. Over the last twenty years, I've prepared at least a zillion dishes of squid at both the Santa Fe Bar & Grill and Stars, and I swore when we opened Farallon that I didn't want to see any more tentacles. But gradually, this sneaky cephalopod began to make brief appearances on our menu. At first it was when Brad put some tempura-fried squid with my favorite black bean sauce on the lunch menu. Then, George made a grilled-squid and squid-ink risotto to go with the seared scallops for a dinner entree. Suddenly, without realizing it, I was starting to think

GRILLED STUFFED SQUID *with* WARM SPINACH, FLAGEOLETS, *and* CARAMELIZED SALSIFY

about using squid again. The first dish I created after my squid sabbatical was this one. Squid bodies are like nature's little purses, perfect vehicles for stuffing, and grilling is my preferred way of cooking them. If you too are feeling a little squid-weary, try this for an unusual and casual entree; it might be just the right antidote.

★ CHEF'S TIPS *Stuffing squid tubes can be rather tedious, so a few words of advice: The larger squid bodies make for shorter work, although the smaller ones tend to be more tender and tasty. The stuffing mixture needs to be rather wet and pasty; a dry, crumbly mixture is difficult to put into the tubes. The quickest way to stuff them is with a pastry bag, but a small espresso spoon will work too. Fill them only about three-fourths full, since the squid will shrink. If you turn the tubes inside out first, they will naturally close up, eliminating the need for toothpick closures. | Small squid make great hors d'oeuvres, if you have the patience to stuff them (or if you have a pastry bag). | To make turning squid on the grill easier, thread the stuffed tubes onto skewers (with the bodies perpendicular to the skewer). | Flageolets are delicate-tasting, pale green French legumes, something like less starchy kidney beans. They're mostly found dried, though occasionally you can find them fresh or frozen. | We love to use just barely wilted greens at Farallon, because texturally they are not quite raw but not mushy either, and they have a quick "firing" time. It takes only a few seconds, and I mean one-thousand-and-one, one-thousand-and-two, one-thousand-and-three, to get the right degree of "wiltedness." We heat a stainless-steel bowl with the dressing in the bottom right over the gas flame, take it off, toss for 3 seconds, then serve. This also works with other greens like spinach, arugula, chopped cabbage, or chard.*

Makes 4 entree servings

FLAGEOLETS:
3 tablespoons unsalted butter
2 tablespoons olive oil
1 onion, cut into ¼-inch dice
Leaves from 1 bunch fresh thyme, chopped
1½ cups fresh, frozen, or dried flageolets or dried small white beans
4 cups water
2 dried bay leaves
2 teaspoons kosher salt, plus salt to taste
1 carrot, cut into ¼-inch dice
¾ cup heavy cream

¼ cup dry white wine
¼ cup minced fresh flat-leaf (Italian) parsley
Freshly ground pepper to taste

STUFFED SQUID:
1 shallot, minced
½ bunch chives, minced
½ bunch flat-leaf (Italian) parsley leaves, stemmed and minced (about ⅓ cup)
¼ cup minced fresh chervil
1 clove garlic, minced
1 salt-packed anchovy fillet, rinsed and finely chopped

¼ cup extra-virgin olive oil
Kosher salt and freshly ground pepper to taste
1 cup dried bread crumbs, moistened with a little water
2 tablespoons unsalted butter
2 pounds squid, cleaned

CARAMELIZED SALSIFY:
Juice of 1 lemon
1 pound salsify or burdock root
2 tablespoons olive oil
2 tablespoons sugar
2 tablespoons water
Kosher salt and freshly ground pepper to taste

2 tablespoons grapeseed, canola, or olive oil
Kosher salt and freshly ground pepper to taste

WARM SPINACH:
2 tablespoons fresh lemon juice
⅓ cup extra-virgin olive oil
Kosher salt and freshly ground pepper to taste
1½ pounds savoy (crinkly-leaf) spinach, stemmed and rinsed

To prepare the flageolets: In a medium saucepan, melt 2 tablespoons of the butter with the oil over medium-low heat. Add the onion and thyme and cook until the onion is softened, 3 to 4 minutes. Add the flageolets, water, bay leaves, and 2 teaspoons salt. Increase heat to a simmer and cook the fresh or frozen beans, if using, until tender, about 20 minutes. Simmer, if using dried beans, for 1 hour or longer, adding an extra cup or two of water if they become dry. In a separate sauté pan or skillet, melt the remaining 1 tablespoon of butter over medium heat and cook the carrot for 1 minute. Add the cream and wine and bring to a simmer. Cook for 2 minutes, then remove from heat and set aside. When the beans are fully cooked, drain, reserving 1 cup of the bean broth. To prepare ahead, cool the beans, broth, and cream mixture separately and refrigerate for up to 1 day. Return the beans to the saucepan and add the parsley and cream mixture, stirring to combine. Add some of the bean broth if necessary to create a loose sauce consistency. Season with salt and pepper to taste. Set aside.

To make the stuffed squid: In a food processor, combine the shallot, herbs, garlic, anchovy, olive oil, salt, and pepper. Pulse off and on for 15 seconds. Scrape down the sides of the container, then pulse for another 15 seconds to chop finely. Put the mixture in a small bowl and stir in the moistened bread crumbs. Melt the butter in a small sauté pan or skillet over medium heat. Increase the heat to high and cook the squid tentacles for 1 minute. Remove, finely chop, and add to the bowl with the stuffing. Stir well to combine. The mixture should be moist and pasty; add more water if necessary. Turn the squid bodies inside out. Using either a small espresso spoon or a pastry bag, push about 1 tablespoon of the stuffing into each body, making sure it's no more than three-fourths full. Use now or cover and refrigerate for up to 2 hours.

To make the caramelized salsify: Add the lemon juice to a bowl of water. Peel the salsify and cut it into ½-inch-long diagonal pieces, immersing it in the lemon water as you go. Use now or keep in the lemon water for up to 24 hours. Drain. Heat a large sauté pan or skillet over high heat and add the olive oil. Add the salsify, sprinkle with the sugar, and cook, stirring, until beginning to brown, about 3 to 4 minutes. Stir in the water. Reduce heat to low and cook until just tender, 3 to 4 minutes. Season with salt and pepper and set aside.

To grill the squid: Heat a grill pan over high heat.

Coat the squid with oil and season each side with salt and pepper. Cook for about 3 minutes, then turn over and grill until opaque and grill-marked, about 3 minutes. Set aside in a low oven while you cook the spinach.

To cook the spinach: In a medium stainless-steel bowl, whisk the lemon juice and olive oil together. Set over medium-high heat. Season with salt and pepper and add the spinach, tossing to coat and just barely wilt the leaves, about 1 minute.

To serve, place a mound of spinach on each of 4 warmed plates and spoon some of the flageolets around the spinach. Top with the stuffed calamari.

IMPROVISATIONS *Try playing around with the stuffing: mushrooms, spinach, pine nuts, and tomatoes are all ingredients that taste good with squid. Sometimes salsify or burdock can be difficult to find. If that is the case, you could omit this vegetable altogether or simply caramelize some sliced fennel or sliced yellow onions.*

ADVANCE PREP *The ravigote stuffing can be made 24 hours ahead, and the calamari can be stuffed 2 hours ahead and both stored in the refrigerator. The beans may be cooked up to 1 day in advance and reheated with the warm cream just prior to serving. The spinach should be cooked just before serving. The salsify or burdock can be held in the lemon water overnight, then cooked just before serving.*

SIMPLIFYING *If you don't want to stuff the squid, cut open the bodies, lightly score them on both sides, and weave them onto skewers. Grill on both sides until just opaque. Make the stuffing without the bread crumbs and add a bit more olive oil to make it more like a sauce that you can drizzle over the grilled calamari.*

WINE NOTES *This dish includes rich flageolets and naturally sweet caramelized salsify, plus the green accent from the wilted spinach. A bottle of "New World" Chardonnay or a nutty, spicy, smoky Meursault is a shoo-in for a good white-wine match. Red wine might also be appropriate since the calamari is grilled and the stuffing is spicy. Good vintages for Italian Dolcetto are 1996, '97, and '98; this spicy, fruity, and zesty red might be a good foil for this combination. A California Sangiovese or the even lighter-bodied Zinfandel is a good choice as well.*

For years, beginning in the early eighties at the Santa Fe Bar & Grill in Berkeley, I've been putting whole fish on my menus, but back then few customers would go near them. Today, at Farallon, I notice that more and more people are ordering whole fish; it seems that Americans have finally discovered what Europeans and Asians have known forever: whole fish on the bone is juicier and has more flavor. Here, in one of our most-requested dishes, a whole, small fish is coated lightly with bonito flakes

BONITO-CRUSTED WHOLE YELLOWTAIL SNAPPER *with*
SPICY CHINESE BLACK BEAN SAUCE *and* SAFFRON NOODLES

and deep-fried, giving the fish a crackling exterior and moist, flaky flesh. It's served with a spicy Chinese-inspired sauce that I created in 1984 after returning from a trip to Hong Kong: plump fermented black beans, chili paste, tomatoes, and butter. The sauce is simply put together but has a complexity of flavor that works well with all kinds of fried foods. My son, Charles, even loves it with barbecued ribs.

★ *CHEF'S TIPS Frying a whole fish is a rather risky business, but the return on effort makes it a worthwhile technique to master. Read through the frying tips (page 147), and remember that you should have good ventilation, a few open windows, or a good exhaust system. I've read that burning incense during the cooking process will help eliminate lingering odors. I guess it's a matter of taste, because I think I'd prefer the smell of fish. | One of the main ingredients used to make the Japanese base stock dashi, bonito flakes come from a Japanese mackerel that has been preserved, dried, and shaved. They're commonly sold in plastic packets. Once opened, they can be stored at room temperature in an airtight container for several months. | Chili paste (sambal oelek) is a very spicy ground and fermented paste found all over Southeast Asia. Some varieties include garlic, soybeans, or Chinese black beans. It is available at most supermarkets.*

Makes 4 entree servings

BLACK BEAN SAUCE:
- ½ cup Chinese fermented black beans, soaked for 1 hour and drained
- 2 large cloves garlic, minced
- 1 tablespoon minced fresh ginger
- 2 tablespoons soy sauce
- ½ teaspoon Asian sesame oil
- 1 tablespoon fresh orange juice
- ½ teaspoon Chinese chili paste or red pepper flakes

- 2 tablespoons rice vinegar
- 1 cup tomato concassé (page 247) or diced canned tomatoes
- ½ cup fish stock (page 244) or clam juice
- 4 tablespoons unsalted butter, cut into tablespoon-sized pieces
- ½ cup thinly sliced (diagonally) green onions, including some green parts
- ½ cup chopped fresh cilantro

SAFFRON NOODLES:
- Generous pinch of saffron threads
- 4 ounces bean thread (cellophane) noodles
- Kosher salt to taste

- 4 whole yellowtail snappers (about 1¼ pounds each), scaled and dressed
- Peanut or canola oil for deep-frying
- 2 cups bonito flakes
- Cilantro sprigs for garnish

To make the black bean sauce: In a small, medium saucepan, combine all the ingredients except the butter, green onions, and cilantro. Bring to a gentle simmer. Gradually whisk in the butter, 1 tablespoon at a time. Remove from heat and stir in the green onions and cilantro. Set aside in a warm place.

To make the noodles: In a medium bowl, combine the saffron and noodles. Add boiling water to cover. Season with salt and let the noodles sit until very tender, about 20 minutes. Drain and set aside, or cover and refrigerate for up to 1 day. Reserve the liquid for another use.

To fry the snapper: Score the flesh of the fish with deep slashes, spaced about ½ inch to 1 inch apart, from fin to belly without cutting through to the bone. Fill a large wok or Dutch oven one-third full with oil. Over high heat, heat the oil to 375°F. Pat the bonito flakes onto the fish. Using tongs, carefully place one fish at a time in the oil, being very careful not to let it spatter, and cook until brown and crispy, about 7 minutes. Using a wire-mesh skimmer (don't use tongs, as they will tear the cooked flesh), transfer to several layers of paper towels to drain, taking care to set the fish upright and gently curve the tail while it continues to crisp. Keep warm in a low oven while frying the remaining fish.

To serve, use warmed shallow bowls or plates with a slight lip and ladle a generous amount of black bean sauce on the bottom of each. Place a mound of noodles towards the front of the bowl or plate and carefully place a curled fish behind that. Garnish with fresh cilantro sprigs. Serve the remaining sauce on the side or drizzled over the plate.

IMPROVISATIONS *Any small, whole fish, about 1 to 1½ pounds, can be used, such as skinned catfish, bass, pike, or whitefish. Or, coat a lot of calamari rings and tentacles with a little rice flour and fry them instead. They're fabulous with the sauce.*

ADVANCE PREP *The black bean sauce can be made 2 days ahead to the point of adding the last 3 ingredients. Add the butter, cilantro, and green onions up to 30 minutes before serving. The noodles can be made early on the day of serving, then reheated in a sauté pan with a little water. The fish should be cooked within 1 hour of serving to keep its crispy texture.*

SIMPLIFYING *Coat the fish with oil and roast in a preheated 375°F oven for 10 to 12 minutes, depending on the size and type of fish. Serve the fish and sauce with plain steamed jasmine rice instead of noodles. The black bean sauce, however, is essential.*

WINE NOTES *The word* spicy *should not be overlooked here. This sauce has some heat. Don't overlook a cool pilsner from Full Sail in Oregon. However, the oak in Chardonnay would clash, and a Semillon, which is fuller than a Sauvignon Blanc, goes well with spicy foods. The residual sugar of a German Spätlese or a demi-sec Vouvray might quench the fire. If you really want a red, go for a Beaujolais. Avoid anything with wood, high alcohol, or tannin that might accentuate the heat.*

Many people familiar with my cooking were surprised when I opened a restaurant that specializes in seafood. Although I'm an avid fisherman and spent my early culinary years cooking freshly caught fish over campfires in Alaska, I've always been known as a "meat guy." At Stars, with its brasserie menu and atmosphere, I was able to indulge my passion for lusty and hearty dishes like braised lamb shanks, oxtail ragout, grilled sweetbreads, house-cured prosciutto, and homemade sausage. At Farallon, it's a different story, of course, but in the interest of balance and for those customers who just can't abide fish, we always include poultry and red meat on our menu. Wild boar, when we have

ROASTED RACK *of* WILD BOAR *with* CHESTNUT SPAETZLE, BRAISED CABBAGE, *and* SAGE JUS

it, is a favorite. Here, it's paired with braised red cabbage and chestnuts, but instead of glazing whole chestnuts, Parke Ulrich, our talented dinner chef, created an awesome chestnut spaetzle, sweet and slightly nutty, perfect with the boar.

★ *CHEF'S TIPS* *Wild boar is sweet and lean, and similar in taste and texture to its domesticated cousin, the pig, but not at all gamey. For the most part, wild boar can be treated and cooked just as you would "the other white meat." While trichinosis is largely a thing of the past in American pork products, you do need to exercise a bit more caution in the handling and cooking of any wild game, although the wild boar sold by reputable companies must meet federal inspection guidelines that are quite stringent. Bruce Aidells, co-author of* The Complete Meat Cookbook *(Houghton Mifflin), notes that trichinosis is killed at 137°F and recommends that for maximum flavor and moisture, small, lean cuts of pork like loin or tenderloin should be cooked to a temperature of no more than 155°F. Some cookbooks say to cook pork to 160°F, but I think it's way too dry at that temperature. A rack of boar is similar in size, but not flavor, to a rack of lamb and is easily overcooked. We're talking about just a few degrees here, which make the difference between meat that's moist and tender or chewy and dry, so it's imperative that you have a reliable instant-read thermometer for this recipe. Remember that the temperature of the meat will rise by up to 10 degrees after resting for 20 minutes.* | *A colander produces small spaetzle, the size of a thin pencil, and a box grater produces larger, gnocchi-shaped spaetzle. Spaetzle makers can also be purchased in some cookware shops. Making spaetzle is a little tricky at first, but it's supposed to look homemade and oddly shaped.* | *Chestnut flour is made from finely ground chestnuts and is popular in Europe. It is usually mixed with other types of flours to make breads, pastas, and pastries.*

Makes 4 entree servings

MARINADE:
1 cup dry red wine
2 cloves garlic, crushed
½ bunch thyme sprigs
6 juniper berries, crushed
½ cup red wine vinegar
2 bay leaves
Kosher salt and ground pepper
    to taste

2 racks of wild boar (about 1 to
    1½ pounds each), trimmed

SAGE JUS:
½ cup Cognac
1½ cups veal stock (page 246)
3 shallots, minced
½ bunch *each* thyme and sage

BRAISED CABBAGE:
2 tablespoons duck fat, chicken fat,
    or unsalted butter
½ cup finely diced white onion
Leaves from ½ bunch thyme, chopped
1 clove garlic, minced
2 to 3 juniper berries, crushed to a paste
1 tablespoon sugar
1 cup Calvados
1 small head red cabbage, halved, cored,
    and thinly sliced
2 to 4 tablespoons red wine vinegar
Kosher salt and freshly ground pepper
    to taste

SPAETZLE:
One 8-ounce can vacuum-packed peeled
    chestnuts, drained, or one 8-ounce can
    chestnut puree plus 2 tablespoons
    water (optional)
1 cup whole milk
2 large eggs
2 tablespoons olive oil, plus more for
    greasing
½ cup chestnut flour
½ teaspoon baking powder
2 cups all-purpose flour
1 tablespoon unsalted butter
Kosher salt and freshly ground pepper
    to taste

Kosher salt and freshly ground pepper
    to taste
¼ cup grapeseed, canola, or olive oil

To marinate the boar: Whisk all the marinade ingredients together and put the boar in a large self-sealing plastic bag. Add the marinade, seal, and refrigerate overnight.

To make the sage jus: In a small saucepan, combine all the ingredients and bring to a simmer over medium heat. Reduce heat and cook to reduce the liquid by half. Strain, discarding the solids. Set aside in a warm place until ready to serve. Or, let cool, cover, and refrigerate for up to 1 day. Gently reheat for serving.

To make the braised cabbage: In a large sauté pan or skillet, melt the fat or butter over low heat and cook the onion until soft but not browned, about 10 minutes. Add the thyme, garlic, juniper berries, and sugar. Increase heat to medium and cook for 10 minutes. Increase heat to high and carefully pour in the Calvados, stirring for 2 minutes to reduce the liquid and evaporate the alcohol. Add the cabbage, reduce heat to low, and cook, uncovered, stirring occasionally, for 1 hour. Season with the vinegar, salt, and pepper and remove from heat. Set aside and keep warm for up to 1 hour before serving.

To make the spaetzle: If using whole chestnuts, process in a food processor with the water until pureed. Add the milk, eggs, and 1 tablespoon of the olive oil. Process briefly to combine, then add the dry ingredients. Pulse on and off to knead the dough until it begins to ball up, about 3 minutes. Let rest for a few minutes. It should be the consistency of sticky bread dough. If using chestnut puree, combine all the wet ingredients except 1 tablespoon of the olive oil in a food processor and puree, and then add the dry ingredients. Knead by pulsing for 2 to 3 minutes. Bring a large saucepan of lightly salted water to a boil over high heat. Lightly grease a metal colander or a box grater with olive oil. Put about ¼ cup dough in the colander or grater, and, using a rubber spatula, push the dough through the large holes of the colander or the grater into the boiling

water. Stir the water so the spaetzle rise to the surface and cook for 1 minute. Using a slotted spoon or wire-mesh skimmer, transfer to a bowl of ice water. Repeat until all the dough is used, wiping the colander or box grater each time with olive oil to prevent sticking. Drain the spaetzle well and let cool. The spaetzle may be made to this point up to 24 hours ahead and refrigerated in a covered container.

In a large sauté pan or skillet, heat the remaining 1 tablespoon olive oil over medium-high heat and add the spaetzle. Cook and toss until lightly browned and beginning to crisp on the outside, about 5 minutes. Add the butter and stir to combine. Season with salt and pepper. Remove from heat, cover, and keep warm, or set aside and reheat briefly before serving.

To roast the boar: Preheat the oven to 350°F. Remove the boar from the marinade and wipe off any bits of thyme or juniper. Season generously with salt and pepper. In a large sauté pan or skillet, heat the oil over high heat and brown the boar on all sides for about 2 minutes. Pour off and discard all but 1 tablespoon of oil, turn the boar so that it's bone-side down, and put the pan in the oven. Cook until the meat registers 140° to 145°F on an instant-read thermometer inserted in the middle of the rack and not touching any bones, 12 to 15 minutes. Remove from the oven and cover the boar with a double thickness of kitchen towel. Let sit for 20 minutes. The temperature will rise anywhere from 5 to 10 degrees as it sits. The final temperature should be 150° to 155°F for medium-well. If you prefer your meat to be a little less done, remove it at 137° to 140°F.

To serve, and mound the red cabbage in the center of each of 4 warmed plates. Spoon the spaetzle around the cabbage and drizzle with the sage jus. Cut the racks into chops and place 3 or 4, bones up and crossed in a teepee shape, in the center of each serving of cabbage.

continued

IMPROVISATIONS *You'll need to plan ahead for this dinner; wild boar must be either ordered from your butcher or a mail-order source. The obvious stand-in for boar is pork. Use a center-cut loin, on the bone or boneless, or a tenderloin. Adjust your cooking times accordingly, but follow the same guidelines for final temperatures. You could substitute regular green cabbage for the red, as napa cabbage is a little too delicate. Use white wine, sherry, or apple cider vinegar in place of the red wine vinegar.*

ADVANCE PREP *The sage jus can be made 1 day before, cooled, covered, and refrigerated. Gently reheat just before serving. The spaetzle will keep in a covered container for up to 24 hours and should be sautéed just before serving. The cabbage tastes best if it's cooked at the last moment. The boar can be left in the marinade for up to 2 days. It needs to rest for 20 minutes before serving.*

SIMPLIFYING *If using pork tenderloin, remember that it cooks quickly. You could also sear and roast some thick-cut pork chops. On a week night, make a warm red cabbage salad while roasting the meat. Toss shredded cabbage with a little vinegar, salt, and pepper. In a skillet, cook some pancetta or bacon in a couple tablespoons of olive oil until crisp. Pour over the cabbage and toss until slightly wilted. Use a purchased veal stock in the sage jus, and if the spaetzle seem too daunting, just cook some fresh fettuccine and toss it with a little butter and the sage jus.*

WINE NOTES *Zinfandel. The red stuff. Fruity and spicy and unpretentious wine that can be drunk young or aged for a couple of years, a great contrast with the dish. Barolo and Barbaresco will echo and complement it. An older Nebbiolo from Piedmont would be a more expensive, classy kind of evening drink, with its soft tannins and complexity.*

I love little game birds. They're quick to cook, take well to flavorful marinades, and are fun to eat. I first learned to hunt with my uncle, and some of my fondest childhood food memories are of pulling quail from the campfire, juicy, smoky, and still hot enough to burn my fingers. As a young man, I learned

ROASTED QUAIL STUFFED *with* ARMAGNAC-LACED PRUNES, FOIE GRAS, CORN CAKES, *and* RED CURRANTS

in Tuscany to wrap the quail first in grape leaves and then in pancetta before putting them on a fire made with the grapevine cuttings. At Stars, we marinated the quail in berry purees or served them in warm salads with fruit salsas. In this preparation for Farallon, quail are stuffed with prunes and foie gras, grilled, and served with sweet corn cakes, chard, and red currants. Although it sounds like an elaborate dish, it's quite easily executed and the juxtaposition of flavors is extraordinary. Although my tastes have become more sophisticated over the years, it's still the simple grilled quail at the heart of this dish that I love the most.

★ CHEF'S TIP *Farm-raised domestic quail are commonly available now and can be ordered from good butchers, fresh or frozen, whole or boneless (only the ribcage is removed). If you're having your butcher bone your meat, always aks for the bones and trimmings; you will need to supplement with other poultry bones to have enough for the jus.*

Makes 4 entree servings

16 pitted prunes
½ cup Armagnac or Cognac
6 ounces fresh foie gras
2 teaspoons chopped fresh thyme
Kosher salt and freshly ground pepper
   to taste
8 boneless quail

QUAIL JUS:
1 tablespoon olive oil
2 pounds bones and trimmings from
   quail, duck, chicken, or squab
½ cup reserved prune-soaking liquor,
   above
5 shallots, minced
2 cups chicken stock (page 243) or
   canned low-sodium chicken broth
4 or 5 sprigs thyme
Kosher salt and freshly ground pepper
   to taste

CORN CAKES:
½ cup boiling water
½ cup cornmeal
1 large egg, separated
1 cup fresh or frozen corn kernels
½ cup heavy cream
2 tablespoons milk
3 tablespoons all-purpose flour

¼ teaspoon kosher salt
¼ teaspoon baking powder
Pinch of freshly ground pepper
½ tablespoon white truffle oil
1 teaspoon chopped fresh thyme
2 tablespoons grapeseed, canola, or
   olive oil

CORN PUREE:
2 tablespoons unsalted butter
1½ cups fresh or frozen corn kernels
⅓ cup water
2 tablespoons white truffle oil
Kosher salt to taste

BRAISED SWISS CHARD:
3 tablespoons unsalted butter
½ red onion, thinly sliced
2 bunches red or white Swiss chard (about
   2 pounds), ribs removed and leaves
   thinly sliced into ¼-inch shreds
3 tablespoons dry white wine
Kosher salt and freshly ground pepper
   to taste

Olive oil for coating
Kosher salt and freshly ground pepper
   to taste
Red currants for garnish (optional)

Preparation

To stuff the quail: Soak the prunes in the Armagnac or Cognac for 2 hours or as long as overnight. Drain, reserving the liquid. Dice the foie gras and season with the thyme, salt, and pepper. Push a cube of foie gras into the cavity of each prune and stuff two prunes into the cavity of each quail. Tie the legs together or make a small slit in the lower leg of one side of the quail and slide the other leg through that. Set aside.

To make the quail jus: In a medium saucepan, heat the oil over medium-high heat and add the quail bones and any trimmings. Cook, stirring occasionally, until well browned, 8 to 10 minutes. Pour off and discard the oil. Return the pan to medium heat. Add the prune soaking liquid and stir to scrape up the browned bits from the bottom of the pan. Add the shallots, stock or broth, and thyme. Bring to a boil, reduce the heat, and simmer for 1 hour. Strain through a fine-mesh sieve, discard the solids, and return the liquid to the saucepan. Cook over high heat to reduce by half. Season with salt and pepper. Set aside until serving.

To make the corn cakes: In a medium bowl, pour the boiling water over the cornmeal. Stir briefly and let sit in a warm place for 10 minutes. In a medium bowl, beat the egg white until stiff peaks form. In a small sauté pan or skillet,

continued

cook the corn kernels with the cream and milk over medium heat until just hot. Remove from heat, let cool slightly, then puree in a blender or food processor. In a medium bowl, combine the corn puree with the egg yolk and the cornmeal mixture; stir to blend. Add the flour, salt, baking powder, pepper, truffle oil, and thyme and mix thoroughly. Fold in the beaten egg white. Heat a nonstick sauté pan or skillet over medium heat and brush with a little oil. Drop heaping tablespoons of the mixture into the pan and cook until bubbles cover the surface, about 2 minutes. Using a metal spatula, flip the corn cakes over and cook another minute or two. Check for doneness by breaking one open and making sure it's cooked through. Remove and set aside while cooking the remaining batter.

To make the corn puree: In a medium sauté pan or skillet, melt the butter over low heat and sauté the corn for 4 minutes without browning. Add the water, bring to a simmer, and cook until the corn is tender, 2 to 3 minutes. Remove from heat. Drain, reserving the corn liquid. In a blender or food processor, puree the corn on high while gradually adding the truffle oil. Add the salt. Depending on the kernels, you may need to add a little of the reserved liquid to loosen the mixture. Push through a medium-mesh sieve.

To cook the chard: In a large sauté pan or skillet, melt the butter over medium heat and cook the onion until softened, 2 to 3 minutes. Add the chard, stir, and let wilt for about 4 minutes. Add the wine, salt, and pepper. Stir and cook to reduce until almost dry. Drain the chard. Keep in a warm place for up to 15 minutes.

To cook the quail: Prepare a fire in a charcoal grill or heat a grill pan over high heat. Coat the quail with olive oil and sprinkle with salt and pepper. Grill, turning every couple of minutes, until deep brown on both sides, 7 to 10 minutes; the quail breasts should feel firm to the touch and the juices should run just barely pink when the thigh is pierced. You can also pan-roast the quail, which gives them a more even browning: Preheat the oven to 450°F. In a medium ovenproof sauté pan or skillet over high heat, heat the olive oil until shimmering. Place the quail, breast-side down, in the pan and cook for 2 minutes. Put the pan in the oven and cook for 5 minutes, then turn the quail and cook another 4 minutes.

To serve, spread a circle of the corn puree in the middle of each of 4 warmed plates. Place 2 corn cakes side by side and put a quail on top of each corn cake. Mound some of the braised chard in the center and spoon the quail jus around the outside of the corn cakes. Scatter the plates with the currants, if using.

IMPROVISATIONS *Stuff the quail with fresh or soaked dried figs. Blueberries, huckleberries, or Champagne grapes are all good substitutes for the hard-to-find red currants.*

ADVANCE PREP *The corn cakes, quail jus, and corn puree can be cooked 2 days ahead and reheated just before serving. The quail can be stuffed and cooked 1 day ahead and reheated in a preheated 350°F oven for 20 minutes just before serving.*

SIMPLIFYING *You could omit either the corn puree or the jus; you'll need at least one of these to give the right textural balance to the dish. A reduced good chicken stock or broth would be fine in place of the quail jus.*

WINE NOTES *A Pinot Noir or red Burgundy is a "sure thing" with this dish. Both wines have a natural sweetness and spiciness that is a lovely match with the taste of grilled quail, corn, foie gras, and fruit.*

For years, I couldn't give rabbit away. I think people had a hard time getting past their childhood images of Peter Cottontail, Thumper, and Bugs Bunny. And at Easter, well forget it. But beginning a few years ago at Stars, I noticed that slowly, almost imperceptibly at first, our sales of rabbit started to increase. Now, at Farallon, I can put rabbit on the menu and feel confident that we'll sell out. Americans have finally realized that it's really rabbit and not pork that is "the other white meat." Commercially farmed domesticated rabbit—and we're not talking here about wild hare—is almost indistinguishable in

ROASTED SADDLE *of* RABBIT *with* FAVA BEANS, MORELS, *and* CRISP SPANISH HAM

taste and texture from chicken. Rabbit meat is like that of its feathered friend: white and fine-grained, with a slightly sweet, delicate flavor. And if that's not enough to recommend it, it's extremely low in fat and cholesterol. In this dish, boned rabbit saddles, or loins, are partnered with their perfect springtime companions: fava beans and morel mushrooms. One of the best parts of this dish is the crispy ham; slowly dried, it becomes brittle and intensely flavorful.

★ *CHEF'S TIPS Two- to 3½-pound rabbits are called fryers, and anything larger than that is called a roaster. Either size will work here, but roasters can be a bit tough. Rabbits are usually sold whole. Ask your butcher to cut them into pieces and then bone out the saddles (loins) for you. I like to save the rabbit legs for braising or to use in a confit. | Serrano and Iberico are kinds of Spanish ham that are salted, dried, and aged; they are similar to prosciutto but with a sweeter flavor. | You'll need the rabbit livers for this recipe, so make sure they're included in your purchase. If they're not, buy chicken livers instead. | Mustard is a traditional flavoring for rabbit, and this dish uses mustard oil as an optional garnish. You'll need only 1 tablespoon from a recipe that makes about ½ cup, but the oil keeps refrigerated for about 1 week and can be used in other dishes—try it to add a little zip to your standard salad dressing. | This recipe uses the bones and trimmings plus chicken stock to make a rabbit stock and then the rabbit stock is used to make a pan sauce. It's an easy and relatively quick technique that adds another level of flavor to the final dish. Consider this a master recipe that can be used with lamb, squab, quail, and veal. If you're having your butcher bone your meat, always ask for the bones and trimmings and, if not using them right away, freeze them to make a stock at a later date.*

Makes 4 entree servings

4 ounces thinly (but not paper-thin) sliced
    Serrano or Iberico ham or Italian
    prosciutto

½ cup Madeira
1 tablespoon chopped fresh sage
Kosher salt and freshly ground pepper to
    taste
Saddles from 4 rabbits, boned (reserve
    bones and trimmings)
8 rabbit or chicken livers

RABBIT STOCK:
2 tablespoons grapeseed, canola, or
    olive oil
Bones and trimmings from 4 rabbits,
    above
½ cup Madeira
3 shallots, minced
3 cups chicken stock (page 243) or
    canned low-sodium chicken broth
4 whole black peppercorns
½ bunch thyme sprigs

4 pounds fava beans, shelled
    (about 2 cups)

3 tablespoons grapeseed, olive,
    or canola oil
8 ounces morels, porcini, or other
    wild mushrooms, cleaned (see
    page 53) and halved (quartered
    or sliced if large)
1 clove garlic, minced
1 teaspoon chopped fresh rosemary

Kosher salt and freshly ground pepper
    to taste
1 tablespoon unsalted butter
1 teaspoon chopped fresh flat-leaf
    (Italian) parsley

1 tablespoon infused mustard oil
    (page 242) for garnish

To dry the ham: Preheat the oven to 200°F. Put the ham or prosciutto slices on a baking sheet and bake for about 2 hours, or until completely dry and crisp.

To marinate and prepare the rabbit: In a medium bowl, combine the Madeira, sage, salt, and pepper. Add the rabbit loins and marinate at room temperature for 1 hour. Remove the rabbit from the marinade and pat dry with paper towels. On a work surface, spread the rabbit out with the flaps open and season the insides with salt and pepper. Place 2 livers along each backbone. Trim the flaps square (saving the trimmings for the rabbit stock) and fold one side, then the other, over the center of the rabbit. Using twine, tie the loins into a tight roll in 1-inch intervals. Season the outside with salt and pepper. The rabbit may be made to this point up to 1 day ahead.

To make the stock: In a large saucepan, heat the oil over medium-high heat and add the bones and any trimmings from the rabbits. Cook, stirring occasionally, until well browned, 8 to 10 minutes. Pour off and discard the oil. Return the pan to medium heat. Add the Madeira and stir to scrape up the browned bits from the bottom of the pan. Add the shallots, stock or broth, peppercorns, and thyme. Bring to a boil, reduce heat to a simmer, and cook for 1 hour. Strain through a fine-mesh sieve and discard the solids. Return the liquid to the saucepan and cook over high heat to reduce to about 2 cups. Set aside until serving, or let cool, cover, and refrigerate for up to 2 days, or freeze for up to 3 months.

To blanch and peel the fava beans: Drop the beans in a large pot of salted boiling water. Cook for 1 to 2 minutes, then plunge them into ice water to stop the cooking. Drain and cool. Break the skin of each bean with your thumbnail at the stem end and slide the bean out. Use immediately or store the beans in a self-sealing plastic bag in the refrigerator for up to 1 day.

To cook the rabbit and make the pan sauce: Preheat the oven to 350°F. In a large ovenproof sauté pan or skillet, heat 2 tablespoons of the oil over high heat and cook the rabbit, beginning with the seam-side down, on all sides until golden. Transfer the pan to the oven and roast another 7 minutes. Remove the rabbit from the pan and let rest for 15 minutes. Pour off and discard any fat in the pan. Add the remaining 1 tablespoon oil and sauté the mushrooms over high heat until softened and golden, about 4 minutes.

Add the fava beans and stir. Add the rabbit stock, garlic, rosemary, salt, and pepper and cook for 3 minutes. Remove from heat and stir in the butter and parsley.

To serve, divide the pan sauce with the mushrooms and favas among 4 shallow bowls. Place the rabbit loins on top and drizzle with mustard oil. Lean dried ham slices against the rabbit.

IMPROVISATION *Chicken is the obvious stand-in for rabbit, but this dish could be made with other poultry as well—squab, quail, or poussin. Prosciutto can be used in place of the Spanish ham as long as it's not sliced too thin. Any kind of wild mushroom, and even cremini, will work here. A nice addition to this dish is glazed pearl onions: Peel 20 small onions by blanching them for 2 minutes, then slipping off the outer skins. Sauté in a little butter or oil until golden, add stock or water, cover, and cook until tender, about 20 minutes. Cook over high heat to reduce the liquid to a glaze and season with salt and pepper.*

ADVANCE PREP *The rabbit stock can be made up to 2 days ahead or frozen for 3 months. You can tie the rabbit loins and store them in the refrigerator for up to 24 hours before cooking. After drying, the ham can be kept, well wrapped in plastic, for 2 days. Make the mushroom and fava broth no more than 2 hours before serving.*

SIMPLIFYING *Instead of making a rabbit stock to use in the pan sauce, simply use a good quality purchased or homemade chicken or veal stock. Instead of tying the loins, just cut 2 rabbits into 6 or 8 pieces each, sauté them, and finish the dish in one pan. Fava beans are time-consuming to peel, so use lima beans or shelled edamame (soybeans) instead. Instead of drying the ham, just julienne it and sprinkle over the final dish as a garnish.*

WINE NOTES *Savory and refined, this entree also has a rustic appeal. The white meat of rabbit goes well with many wines, from fuller whites to more medium-bodied reds, like the wonderful, somewhat rare white wines from Châteauneuf-du-Pape. Côtes-du-Rhône, like the 1998 Jean-Louis Chave Selection, is still a great bargain in red wines. Italy has also enjoyed several successful recent vintages; for a delicious dry red wine, check out a 1997 Chianti Classico from Tuscany or an earthy Sangiovese.*

I've noticed that something happens to people when they get dressed up and go out to dinner for a special occasion: A mysterious transformation occurs that makes even the most laid-back personalities turn self-conscious and uptight. One night, shortly after we opened, I was watching the activities in the dining room and noticed, perhaps for the first time, how long it took for people to relax. What is it? The chairs are comfortable, the lighting soft, and the wait staff is friendly. I'm no psychologist, but I thought maybe we could loosen people up a bit if we put a dish on the menu that engaged them and made them participate more in their dining experience. My chefs and I decided to serve a hot pot, a

FARALLON HOT POT

dish that requires diners to cook their own morsels of food by submerging them in a little pot of hot broth. Communal dishes are common in many cultures; the Swiss have fondue and *raclette*, the Chinese have Mongolian firepots, Koreans have barbecues, and the Japanese have *shabu-shabu* and *nabemono*, both one-pot dishes. At Farallon, we serve our hot pot along Japanese lines, in a small cast-iron pot heated with a candle, accompanied with a platter of sliced raw seafood and vegetables and one or two dipping sauces. The act of cooking together at the table is convivial and fun, and from the first evening we put the hot pot on the menu, there was almost a noticeable collective sigh in the dining room. People even began to socialize with diners at neighboring tables. Try a hot pot at your next dinner party; it's a great way to break the ice, particularly if your guests are unacquainted. The added bonus for the cook is that the guests do all the cooking.

★ *CHEF'S TIPS* Dashi *is the Japanese equivalent to our fish stock but is made from dried fish flakes* (bonito) *and seaweed* (konbu). *It's a clear, light broth, the base for miso soup and other Japanese soups. | Shiso leaves are a member of the mint family and have a very distinctive nutty flavor that matches well with other Asian ingredients. Also known as* perilla, *the pretty pointed leaves can be substituted with fresh spearmint or basil, or sometimes cilantro, depending on the particular dish. Found only in Asian supermarkets, they'll keep for 3 or 4 days in the refrigerator before the leaves turn brown. | We use individual cast-iron pots, called* tetsunabe, *that we found in a Japanese market. They have handles, a wooden lid, and a stand with a votive-candle holder underneath. They come in many sizes but at the restaurant we use small ones for 1 or 2 diners. Fondue pots or chafing dishes can substitute. Or, invest in one of those traveling propane-fueled burners with a metal pot or casserole set over it. | Japanese* ichimi, *("one spice"), made of dried red pepper flakes, is a common flavorful condiment for soups, noodles, or salads.*

Makes 4 entree servings

8 ounces sushi-grade ahi or yellowtail tuna

8 ounces salmon fillets, pin bones removed

8 oysters, shucked, bottom shells reserved

8 "dry-packed" sea scallops, rinsed and patted dry

1 cup bite-sized pieces mixed Asian vegetables such as bok choy, lotus root, and daikon

4 ounces shiitake, enoki, or cremini mushrooms, stemmed

4 ounces rice stick noodles (rice vermicelli) softened in hot water for 15 minutes and boiled for 45 seconds

8 large shrimp, shelled, deveined, and butterflied

2 lobster tails, cooked and cut into 6 thin diagonal medallions (optional)

DOUBLE-STRENGTH DASHI:

6 cups cold water

1 ounce konbu (dried kelp) plus 1½ ounces dried bonito flakes (see page 152), or 1½ ounces instant dashi

PONZU DIPPING SAUCE:

¼ cup soy sauce

1 tablespoon fresh lemon juice

1 tablespoon fresh lime juice

1 tablespoon sugar

1 teaspoon minced fresh ginger

1 green onion, finely chopped, including green parts

OPTIONAL GARNISHES:

Fresh shiso leaves

Sesame seeds, lightly toasted for garnish

Ichimi (Japanese chili flakes) for garnish

Wakame seaweed for garnish

continued

To prepare the seafood and vegetables: Carefully cut the tuna and salmon into ¼-inch-thick pieces. Put the oysters into the reserved shells. Cut the scallops into ¼-inch-thick rounds. Blanch any hard vegetables like lotus root until crisp-tender. Cut large mushrooms into halves or quarters. Arrange the noodles, seafood, and vegetables in an attractive pattern on 1 large platter or 4 dinner plates. Refrigerate, covered with plastic wrap, for up to 2 hours before serving.

To make the double-strength dashi: In a large saucepan, combine the cold water, the konbu, and two-thirds of the bonito flakes. Bring to a boil. Reduce heat to a simmer and cook to reduce broth by half, 15 to 20 minutes. Add the remaining bonito flakes and remove from heat. Let the flakes settle to the bottom and skim off any foam from the surface. Strain through a fine-mesh sieve lined with cheesecloth and discard the solids. If using instant dashi, bring the water to a boil and add, stirring to dissolve. Set aside, or cover and refrigerate for up to 3 days.

To make the ponzu dipping sauce: In a small saucepan, whisk all the ingredients together and bring to a boil over high heat. Continue to boil gently until reduced by half. Let cool to room temperature, then strain into 4 small bowls or ramekins. Set aside, or cover and refrigerate for up to 3 days.

To serve, return the dashi to a boil, remove from heat, and pour into the hot pot. Light the heat source under the hot pot and serve with the platter of seafood and vegetables. Serve each diner a bowl of dipping sauce alongside, with optional garnishes.

IMPROVISATIONS *You can serve from 3 to 10 ingredients to be cooked in the hot pot, depending on your mood and what looks good at the market. Try to stay with ingredients that make sense together, such as fish and vegetables, tofu and vegetables, or just fish and shellfish with, say, cilantro for garnish. The amounts given in the recipe are suggestions only; you can increase or decrease amounts to suit individual preferences.*

ADVANCE PREP *The beauty of this dish is that everything can be sliced and organized up to 2 hours before serving, placed on platters or plates and stored in the refrigerator covered with plastic wrap. The dashi and dipping sauce may be made up to 3 days ahead and stored in a covered container in the refrigerator. The noodles can be cooked 1 day ahead and tossed with a little canola oil to keep them from sticking together.*

SIMPLIFYING *The most difficult part of this dish is assembling the equipment. Once that hurdle has been crossed, the dish can become a weeknight standard.*

WINE NOTES *With so much going on in this dish, try drier styles of German Riesling, or demi-sec or rosé Champagne or sparkling wine. The slightly salty stock and natural sweetness of these wines work well together, and the wines are delicate enough to complement the just-cooked seafood. A good bottle of Sauvignon Blanc is also a solid match. For something more exotic, try a bottle of excellent sake, or a clean, crisp beer.*

Duck confit has become a familiar item on many contemporary American menus today because chefs have fallen in love with this amazing old-fashioned method of preserving meat and poultry, which was developed in the days before refrigeration. The word *confit* comes from the French verb *confire*, meaning "to preserve," and while the technique is no longer a necessity, we now appreciate it for what it does

CONFIT *of* TUNA *with* ONION CONFIT, ENDIVE SALAD, *and* SAUCE VERTE

for the flavor and texture of meat. In Gascony, where the making of confit is considered an art, meat of some kind—duck, geese, rabbit, pork, or wild birds—is salted, seasoned with herbs and spices, covered in rendered fat, and cooked very slowly until it's falling-off-the-bone tender, and then stored under its protective seal of fat. Anything prepared this way develops an intense flavor and succulent texture that is unique in the food world, but what many people don't realize is that this technique can be applied with equal success to fish as well. In this dish, lush olive oil–poached tuna fillets are paired with sweet, red-wine-braised onions, a piquant sauce verte, and bitter endive, creating a wonderful play of colors, textures, and tastes, all on the same plate.

★ CHEF'S TIPS *You'll often see the word* confit *used in connection with vegetables and fruits: tomato confit, onion confit, lemon confit. These slowly cooked mixtures are more like jams or preserves, called* confiture *in French. | The olive oil used for cooking the tuna can be strained and reused for sautéing fish or to make a delicious mayonnaise for a tuna salad.*

Makes 4 entree servings

ONION CONFIT:
5 tablespoons unsalted butter
1 bay leaf
5 juniper berries, lightly crushed
3 large yellow onions, cut into 8 wedges
¾ cup dry red wine
Kosher salt and freshly ground pepper
  to taste

TUNA CONFIT:
2 tablespoons cardamom pods
Four 5-ounce tuna fillets, 1½ to 2 inches
  thick
Kosher salt and freshly ground pepper
  to taste
3 to 4 cups olive oil

ENDIVE SALAD:
4 heads Belgian endive, cored and cut
  into thin diagonal slivers
½ cup watercress leaves
1 tablespoon Lemon Vinaigrette
  (page 25)

Sauce Verte (page 134)

Preparation

To make the onion confit: In a small saucepan, combine the butter, bay leaf, and juniper berries. Melt the butter over medium-low heat. Add the onions and cook, stirring, until soft, about 15 minutes. Add the wine, salt, and pepper. Cover and cook for about 30 minutes. Uncover and cook to reduce until syrupy, about 15 minutes. Keep warm, or cover and refrigerate for up to 2 days.

To make the tuna confit: In a small dry pan over medium heat, toast the cardamom pods for 3 to 4 minutes. Let cool. Remove the seeds from the pods and coarsely grind the seeds in a mortar. Sprinkle the tuna with the salt, pepper, and ground cardamom. Put the seasoned tuna in a medium saucepan and add olive oil to cover by at least ½ inch. Over high heat, bring the oil to 180°F. Remove from heat, cover, and let sit for 5 to 10 minutes, depending on the desired doneness. Using a slotted spoon, transfer the tuna to a plate. Strain and reserve the oil for another use.

To make the salad: Toss the endive and watercress with the lemon vinaigrette.

To serve, place a pool of sauce verte on each plate. Put one-fourth of the onions to one side of the sauce and a tuna fillet on the other. Place the salad on top of the tuna and onions so that it falls slightly over the side.

continued

IMPROVISATIONS *This technique works particularly well with thick fillets of medium-dense to dense and moderately fat fish, like salmon, swordfish, or sturgeon. Consider using tuna confit as the star of an entree salad or in place of canned tuna in a favorite recipe. Any kind of leafy green salad is a nice, crisp contrast to the satiny fish. The onion confit is great in any kind of salad as well as a nice addition to sandwiches—in fact, everything here, the tuna, sauce, endive, and onions, would work just as well piled into a French roll.*

ADVANCE PREP *The tuna confit can be made up to 1 day ahead and refrigerated, but it should be brought to room temperature before serving. The onion confit and lemon vinaigrette will keep for 2 days in the refrigerator. Toss the salad with the vinaigrette just before serving.*

SIMPLYING *This is possibly the easiest fish preparation in the book. If you're short on time, instead of making a sauce verte, simply serve the fish sprinkled with a generous amount of fresh herbs chopped with capers.*

WINE NOTES *This rich and savory entree is easily paired with white or red wine. A white wine should be full-bodied, such as a Burgundy or a Californian Chardonnay; look to the Rhône Valley for a big Châteauneuf-du-Pape, or to Australia for a barrel-fermented Semillon. The dish can also take red wines. The onion confit and meaty tuna, and the assertive endive and watercress, all call for a medium-bodied spicy red. Try a Ribera del Duero from Spain, a Sangiovese from California or Italy, a California Syrah, or blends from the Rhône Valley and Provence.*

This dish is the very essence of Japanese cooking, where each element stands out yet melds together. Several years ago, I had an unforgettable dinner at the Japanese-styled Matsuhisa in Los Angeles, where chef Nobu served us a dish of halibut poached in a ginger-miso broth with fresh black truffles. I was

NORI-STEAMED TRUFFLED LOBSTER TAILS *with* SOMEN NOODLES *and* GINGER-MISO BROTH

stunned. At first, it was the aroma of the truffles in the hot broth that bowled me over, but ultimately it was the unique yet simple combination of flavors—miso, ginger, and truffles—that made such a lasting impression. Here, I've taken the dish one step further and added lobster, which is fabulous paired with truffles and ginger, the miso being the background element that ties it all together.

★ *CHEF'S TIPS For all of its luxury ingredients, this dish tastes incredibly light and healthy, and in fact, it is—there's no oil or butter anywhere! I keep thinking I've missed something here . . . | Somen noodles are Japanese wheat noodles that are traditionally served cold in the summer. They are available dried in varying degrees of thickness. | Most people recognize nori as the dried sheets of seaweed that are used in sushi. Toasting it briefly over a flame intensifies its flavor, but packets of pretoasted nori are available in Asian markets (see method for toasting nori in the Black Bass and Sea Urchin Tartare in a Crisp Nori Sandwich, page 40). A diverse array of colors and quality are available in Asian markets, and you should try a few different brands to find the ones you prefer. Nori keeps for 6 months in self-sealed plastic bags.*

Makes 4 entree servings

MISO BROTH:
1 tablespoon instant dashi
3 cups water
1 tablespoon yellow (shiro) miso paste
1 teaspoon minced fresh ginger

3 ounces dried somen noodles
4 cooked lobster tails (see page 233)
½ ounce fresh truffle, cut into
⅛-inch matchsticks
2 nori sheets, toasted (see page 40)
4 green onions, green parts included, cut
into thin diagonal slices for garnish

Preparation

To make the miso broth: In a small saucepan, stir the dashi into the water. Bring to a boil and reduce heat to a simmer. Add the miso paste and ginger and stir until dissolved, about 3 minutes. Set aside, or cover and refrigerate for up to 2 days.

To cook the noodles: In a medium saucepan of lightly salted boiling water, cook the noodles, stirring occasionally, until tender, about 8 minutes. Drain and immediately rinse under cold running water. Set aside.

To assemble the lobster tails: Using a small, sharp knife or scissors, cut the shells on each side and remove the tail meat in one piece. Make an incision down the length of the back, remove the digestive track, and wipe the lobster meat free of any grit. To make the lobster tail lie flat, score the underside of the tail crosswise in 2 places without cutting all the way through. Slide the pieces of truffle in a line down the back of the lobster, just underneath the skin. Put a sheet of nori on a work surface and cut in half. (There is no need to season the lobster with salt, as the nori provides ample flavor without it.) Place the lobster tail across the bottom of the nori sheet so that the ends stick out a bit over the edges (you may have to trim the nori slightly to have it fit, depending on the size of the lobster tail). Roll up the lobster in the nori very loosely; the dried seaweed will cling to the lobster and split if it is wrapped too tightly. Moisten the ends and press to seal closed. Repeat with the remaining lobster tails and nori. Steam the wrapped tails in a covered steamer over simmering water until the lobster is heated through and the nori has become wet and "fits" the tail, 2 to 3 minutes. Remove and set aside for up to 20 minutes.

To serve, bring the miso broth to a boil, remove from heat, and strain. Divide the noodles among 4 warmed, shallow bowls, curling them in the center. Cut each lobster tail into 3 or 4 diagonal medallions and spread them on top of the noodles. Spoon the miso broth over and around. Sprinkle with the green onions and serve.

IMPROVISATIONS *Use giant shrimp instead of lobster tails, or firm white fish fillets. Soba (Japanese buckwheat noodles) could be used in place of somen.*

SIMPLIFYING *This elegant dish relies on so few components that I wouldn't try to simplify anything here.*

ADVANCE PREP *The miso broth can be made up to 2 days ahead of serving and refrigerated. Reheat and strain it just before pouring over the noodles. The noodles can be cooked until al dente, about 3 minutes, up to 2 hours ahead of time, then rewarmed in the broth. The lobster tails can be cooked and cleaned a few hours ahead, but they need to be studded and wrapped within 20 minutes of serving. The nori should be kept dry in a self-sealing plastic bag or it may break down and become unusable.*

WINE NOTES *The elements in this dish are unique and complex: miso, nori, rich lobster, earthy truffles, and spicy ginger. This is a good time for Viognier, with all its exotic fruit flavors and floral notes. This fickle grape, originally from the Rhône Valley in France, is becoming increasingly popular with wine makers and the public in the United States. The wine is rich enough for lobster, but tropical enough for miso and ginger and fruity enough for the salty nori. Check out Qupe, Alban, and Cold Heaven from the California Central Coast; Pride Mountain and Araujo Estate from Napa; Calera from Monterey; and Bon Terra from Mendocino.*

Although naming my favorite dish is a little like choosing a favorite child, I think this dish might qualify as number one. It's really a study in contrasts and it represents everything I love in one dish. It's sexy and voluptuous but classy and understated. It's rustic but elegant, classic yet modern. It's also a proletarian dish (stuffed cabbage) that uses sophisticated ingredients (foie gras). And it looks like you spent all day in the kitchen but is actually quite simple to prepare. Well, I take that back. You might have to spend an afternoon in the kitchen, but it will be time well spent and your guests will love you for it.

STEAMED SALMON and WILD STRIPED BASS PILLOWS with SHELLFISH MOUSSE, VEGETABLE BRUNOISE, and FOIE GRAS SAUCE

★ *CHEF'S TIPS The only tricky technique here is in forming the cabbage packages. Make sure you use the larger outside to middle-outside leaves from the head of a napa cabbage and blanch a few more than you think you're going to need (4 to 6 per package). After the leaves have been blanched, the tough and thick rib from the leaf needs to be trimmed or removed so that the packages are easy to roll up. What we like to do at Farallon to make the leaf thinner is to lay a blanched leaf on a work surface and, with the blade of a very sharp knife held parallel to the board, cut off the large "bump" of the rib. Another way would be to just remove the rib by cutting along each side of the leaf in a "V" shape (but not cutting the leaf in half). If you choose the latter method, just make sure that when you lay out the cabbage to form the packages, you overlap the leaves where any ribs have been removed. Otherwise you'll have too many holes. | You'll need a steamer for this dish, preferably one that's large enough to steam all the pillows at the same time. If you don't have a steamer you can improvise one by placing a wire rack on top of a ring mold or an inverted metal measuring cup in a large sauté pan, Dutch oven, casserole, or roasting pan. If the pan doesn't have a lid, cover it with aluminum foil. | See Basic Techniques and Recipes (page 233) for cutting the vegetables into brunoise, a very precise ⅛-inch dice.*

Makes 4 entree servings

SHELLFISH MOUSSE:
4 ounces shrimp, shelled and deveined
4 ounces "dry-packed" sea scallops
1 large egg white
½ cup heavy cream
2 teaspoons fresh lemon juice
Pinch of cayenne pepper
1 tablespoon coarsely chopped fresh
   tarragon
1 teaspoon kosher salt
Pinch of freshly ground pepper

16 to 20 large outer napa cabbage leaves
   from 2 large cabbages
Four 3-ounce salmon fillets, skin and
   pin bones removed (see Chef's Tips,
   page 46)
Four 3-ounce wild striped bass fillets,
   skin and pin bones removed
   (see Chef's Tips, page 46)
Kosher salt to taste

FOIE GRAS SAUCE:
1 cup fish stock (page 243), shellfish
   stock (page 244), or clam juice
¼ cup dry white wine
½ cup chilled foie gras butter (page 241),
   cut into tablespoon-sized pieces
Kosher salt and freshly ground pepper
   to taste

VEGETABLE BRUNOISE:
1 tablespoon unsalted butter
1 tablespoon grapeseed, canola, or
   olive oil
1 cup finely diced celery
1 cup finely diced peeled carrot
1 cup finely diced onion
1 tablespoon chopped fresh thyme or
   1 teaspoon dried thyme, crumbled
Kosher salt and freshly ground pepper
   to taste

Thyme sprigs for garnish (optional)

Preparation

To make the shellfish mousse: Put the bowl and metal blade of a food processor in the refrigerator to chill for about 30 minutes. In the food processor, puree the shrimp and scallops until a smooth paste forms, about 30 seconds. Using the feed tube and with the machine running, quickly pour in the egg white and cream and continue to process until the mixture is just combined. (Overprocessing can turn the cream to butter.) Add the lemon juice, cayenne, tarragon, salt, and pepper and process for a few seconds more. Set aside, or cover and refrigerate for up to 8 hours.

To cook the cabbage leaves for the pillows: In a large pot of boiling water, blanch the cabbage leaves until just wilted, about 1 minute. Quickly drain and immerse in a large bowl of ice water to stop further cooking. Drain each leaf and lay out on clean kitchen towels. Cover the leaves with another towel and pat to remove the excess water. Remove the tough and thick center rib from each of the leaves (see Chef's Tips, above).

continued

To make the pillows: Tear off a sheet of plastic wrap about 14 inches long and lay it out smoothly on a work surface. (If you have a large work area, you can make all 4 pillows at the same time, assembly-line style.) On top of the sheet of plastic wrap, spread out 4 or 5 of the blanched cabbage leaves so that they overlap slightly and form a rough rectangle about 9 by 11 inches. It doesn't matter whether you lay the leaves side by side or end to end. If some of the cabbage leaves are small, use as many as you need to create the rectangle. Place 2 to 3 tablespoons of shellfish mousse in the center of the cabbage rectangle and spread it out slightly to form a small rectangle of fairly even thickness. Place 1 salmon fillet on top of the mousse. Spread another 2 to 3 tablespoons of shellfish mousse on top of the salmon and place 1 bass fillet on top of the salmon and mousse. Spread the bass with another 2 to 3 tablespoons of the mousse and sprinkle with a little salt and pepper. Fold the cabbage leaves up to enclose the fish as if you were wrapping a gift package, then do the same with the plastic wrap, pulling the plastic snugly around the pillow. Roll the plastic up and twist both ends together, making sure that the pillow is tightly wrapped and completely sealed so that the mousse doesn't leak out during steaming. Repeat the process to make 3 more pillows. Refrigerate the pillows for up to 1 day.

To make the foie gras sauce: In a small saucepan, bring the stock or clam juice and wine to a boil. Cook over medium heat to reduce the liquid by one-half. Reduce the heat to very low and whisk in the foie gras butter 1 tablespoon at a time, waiting until it emulsifies before adding more butter. Season with salt and pepper. Keep the sauce warm for up to 1 hour over a bowl of hot water or near a pilot light. Whisk if the sauce begins to separate.

To sauté the brunoise: In a small to medium sauté pan or skillet, melt the butter with the oil over medium heat. Add the diced vegetables, reduce heat to low, and cook until the vegetables have softened but not browned, about 7 minutes. Add the thyme, salt, and pepper.

To steam the pillows: In a covered steamer over briskly simmering water, steam the pillows for 10 minutes. Turn off heat and leave the pillows in the steamer until firm when lightly pressed with your finger, about 10 minutes. Remove from the steamer and let cool slightly.

To serve, place equal portions of the vegetable brunoise on each of 4 warmed dinner plates. Cut the still-wrapped pillows in half diagonally and remove the plastic. Place 2 halves on each bed of vegetables, sitting one half cut-side up against the other half, with the cut sides facing out a little. Ladle the warm foie gras sauce around the plate. Garnish with thyme sprigs, if desired.

IMPROVISATIONS Other firm, flavorful fish may be used here, like mahi-mahi, Chilean sea bass, or tuna. You could also use all salmon or a combination of salmon and large sea scallops. The pillows are also good served cold with a frisée or arugula salad.

ADVANCE PREP The pillows and the mousse can be prepared, wrapped in the plastic, and refrigerated for up to 1 day and steamed at the last minute. The vegetables for the brunoise can be cut 1 day ahead and sautéed before serving. The foie gras sauce should be made no more than 1 hour before using.

SIMPLIFYING Use plain butter instead of the foie gras butter in the sauce. You could save quite a bit of time by mincing the vegetables in a food processor; be careful, though, that you don't puree the onions.

WINE NOTES This is a very "wine-friendly" dish with lots of options. For white wine, you want something full-bodied and luscious; these lusty, rich ingredients can stand up to a classic white Burgundy from the Côte d'Or or a "New World" Chardonnay from a top producer like Peter Michael or Pahlmeyer. An alternative choice for white wine would be a Grand Cru Pinot Gris from Alsace: rich and exotic, plump and tropical. Red Burgundy and American Pinot Noir, light- to medium-bodied red wines bursting with pretty fruit and complex, earthy aromas and flavors, also match beautifully. Sanford in Santa Barbara County and Handley in Mendocino are two good wineries to search out. Whatever wine you choose, uncork a special bottle. This dish deserves it.

Veal cheeks? Cauliflower puree? I know this recipe might be in danger of being passed over, because Lisa, my coauthor, gave me one of those "Are you kidding?" looks when I first suggested it for this book, but she trusted me and you should too, because the dish is worth a leap of faith. Veal cheeks, beef

BRAISED VEAL CHEEKS *with* LOBSTER TAILS, CAULIFLOWER PUREE, *and* LOBSTER SAUCE

cheeks, and even fish cheeks have become popular restaurant items lately, and for good reason. They are incredibly succulent and surprisingly easy to prepare. The only difficult part of this is locating a source for the veal cheeks. Wholesale purveyors have no trouble obtaining veal cheeks for restaurants, because they purchase them in such large quantities. Luckily, we found a very good, high-quality, mail-order source (page 249) that will sell and ship any size order, so I really hope you'll give this dish a try for your next special-occasion dinner party. We jokingly call this dish Farallon's "surf and turf." The veal cheeks have a meaty quality that marries well with the sweet lobster and earthy cauliflower. It's an incredibly rich dish, though, so keep the portions small and the first course light and simple. Be sure to bring out one of your best bottles of wine, and get ready to bask in the raves.

★ CHEF'S TIP *The braising liquid makes a wonderful, deep, rich, dark sauce and is a fine finish for the dish. Freeze any leftover braising liquid for another dish or the next time you make veal cheeks, or even pot roast.*

Makes 4 entree servings

MARINADE:
1 tablespoon olive oil
¼ cup balsamic vinegar
1 teaspoon kosher salt
½ teaspoon freshly ground pepper
1 tablespoon minced fresh thyme
1 tablespoon minced fresh marjoram, or
    1 teaspoon dried marjoram, crumbled

Four 4-ounce veal cheeks
Kosher salt and freshly ground pepper
    to taste
3 tablespoons olive oil
½ cup chopped celery
½ cup chopped carrot
½ cup chopped onion

1½ cups veal stock (page 246)
1 cup dry red wine
½ cup port wine
½ cup sweet Marsala wine
3 sprigs rosemary
15 black peppercorns
1 bay leaf

CAULIFLOWER PUREE:
1 small head cauliflower (about 1 pound),
    cut into florets
2 tablespoons unsalted butter
2 tablespoons heavy cream
Kosher salt and freshly ground pepper
    to taste

LOBSTER SAUCE:
1 tablespoon unsalted butter
1 tablespoon grapeseed, canola, or
    olive oil
2 tablespoons minced shallots
¼ cup dry white wine
1 cup fish stock (page 243), shellfish
    stock (page 244), or clam juice
½ cup water
¼ cup lobster essence (page 245)
¾ cup (1½ sticks) cold unsalted butter,
    cut into tablespoon-sized pieces
Kosher salt and freshly ground pepper
    to taste

4 cooked lobster tails (see page 233)
Thyme sprigs for garnish

continued

To marinate the veal: In a small bowl, whisk all the marinade ingredients together. Put the veal cheeks in a heavy-duty self-sealing plastic bag, pour in the marinade, and seal tightly. Marinate them in the refrigerator for at least 4 hours, or overnight if possible.

To braise the veal: Preheat the oven to 275°F. Season each side of the veal cheeks liberally with salt and pepper. In a heavy, medium Dutch oven, heat the oil over high heat until shimmering. Cook the cheeks until well browned on both sides, about 8 minutes. Remove and set aside. Add the celery, carrot, and onion to the pan, reduce heat to medium, and sauté the vegetables until slightly colored, about 8 minutes. Add the stock, wine, port, and Marsala and stir to scrape up the browned bits on the bottom of the pot. Increase heat to high and add the rosemary, peppercorns, and bay leaf. Return the veal to the pan. Cover and braise in the oven until the meat is tender when pierced with a fork, 2 to 2½ hours. Remove from the oven and, using a slotted spoon, transfer the veal to a plate. Set aside, or let cool, cover, and refrigerate for up to 3 days. Let the braising liquid cool. Strain the braising liquid and, using a large spoon, gently skim any fat off the top. Set aside, or cover and refrigerate for up to 3 days.

To make the cauliflower puree: Add the cauliflower to a medium saucepan of lightly salted, boiling water. Reduce heat to medium-low, and simmer until the cauliflower is soft when pierced with a knife, 15 to 20 minutes. Drain and let cool, reserving the cooking liquid. In a blender or food processor, puree the cauliflower with the butter, cream, salt, and pepper, adding some of the cooking liquid as necessary to create a thick, smooth puree. Set aside, or cover and refrigerate for up to 1 day.

To make the lobster sauce: In a medium saucepan, melt the butter with the oil over medium heat and sauté the shallots until softened, about 4 minutes. Add the wine, stock or clam juice, water, and lobster essence. Increase heat to high and cook to reduce the sauce by one-third. Reduce heat and whisk in the butter, 1 tablespoon at a time, until the sauce is emulsified. Remove from heat and season with salt and pepper. Keep in a bowl over hot water or near a pilot light until ready to serve, or let cool, cover, and refrigerate for up to 1 day. Reheat gently, whisking to reemulsify the sauce.

To serve, reheat the veal cheeks in the reserved braising liquid. Reheat the cauliflower puree over low heat until warmed through. Cook over low heat for 5 minutes. Reheat the lobster sauce, and if the lobster tails have been refrigerated, warm them gently in the sauce. If you aren't using the lobster sauce, warm the lobster tails in a covered pan of lightly salted simmering water. On each of 4 warmed dinner plates, place a large spoonful of cauliflower puree and top with a veal cheek. Ladle a spoonful of braising liquid over and around. Place a lobster tail on top of the veal. Spoon some lobster sauce around the dish and garnish with thyme sprigs.

IMPROVISATIONS *Jumbo shrimp, crayfish, or crab are perfect stand-ins for the lobster. Small filet mignon steaks may be sautéed over high heat for 7 to 8 minutes and used instead of the veal, or ask your butcher for a good beef braising cut. Mashed potatoes or turnip puree are good choices to replace the cauliflower. Soft polenta would also be a perfect partner.*

ADVANCE PREP *The veal cheeks can be cooked 3 days ahead and will even benefit from advance preparation. The sauce, puree, and lobster tails may all be prepared 1 day ahead and reheated up to 1 hour before serving.*

SIMPLIFYING *These veal cheeks are so good they can be served just with crusty bread to soak up the braising liquid and a little prepared horseradish as a condiment.*

WINE NOTES *This is an elegant special-occasion dish and a special-occasion wine is recommended. Uncork a killer bottle of Burgundy, like a 1990 Chambolle-Musigny or a Williams Selyem Pinot Noir. A white Burgundy can work as well; just make sure it is full-flavored enough to stand up to the dish. Then kick back and savor every bite.*

There is not much better food in this world than the hot dog. From brats to kielbasa, chorizo to salami, and boudin noir to andouille, I have no limits or prejudices. And not only do I love to eat sausage, I love to make it. It seems that as long as humans have been eating meat they've been making frugal use of the scraps and odds and ends that are leftover after the larger cuts had been consumed; Homer,

SEAFOOD SAUSAGE *with* HAZELNUT MASHED POTATOES *and* CARDAMOM-SAFFRON SAUCE

Aristophanes, and Athenaeus all make references to chopped-meat preparations that had been stuffed into casings. Today, we make sausage not just to use up lesser cuts of meat but also as an expression of culinary creativity. It is a such a versatile medium that it can be made of just about anything you can imagine—seafood, meat, poultry, and vegetables, seasoned with an infinite variety of spices—but what most home cooks don't realize is that they can be easily made at home without casings. Here, I use our standard seafood mousse as a binder, add chunks of lobster meat, form them into logs, and wrap them in plastic wrap; the sausages are then poached and browned before serving. It's a terrific recipe for entertaining, because the sausages can be made in advance and your guests will be impressed when they find out you've made the sausages yourself.

★ CHEF'S TIP *The base for this sausage is seafood mousse, and the trick to getting a good and safe emulsification is to make sure all your ingredients are cold; as added insurance, refrigerate the food processor bowl and blade for at least 15 minutes before beginning. | Dry-packed scallops are preferable for the mousse. If they're unavailable, use all prawns.*

Makes 4 entree servings

SEAFOOD SAUSAGE:

12 ounces shrimp, shelled and deveined

12 ounces scallops, preferably dry-packed

4 egg whites

½ cup heavy cream

2 teaspoons fresh lemon juice

1 teaspoon kosher salt

Meat from 2 whole cooked lobsters, cut into ¼-inch pieces (see page 233)

Pinch of cayenne pepper

Pinch of freshly ground pepper

2 teaspoons chopped fresh tarragon, parsley, or chervil

CARDAMOM-SAFFRON SAUCE:

¾ cup fish stock (page 243) or clam juice

⅓ cup dry white wine

2 shallots, minced

5 black peppercorns

1 teaspoon chopped fresh tarragon

Pinch of saffron threads

Seeds from 5 cardamom pods, crushed

½ cup (1 stick) plus 2 tablespoons cold unsalted butter, cut into tablespoon-sized pieces

Kosher salt and freshly ground pepper to taste

HAZELNUT MASHED POTATOES:

1½ pounds Yukon Gold, Yellow Finn, or russet potatoes, peeled and quartered

¾ cup heavy cream

6 tablespoons unsalted butter

3 tablespoons hazelnut oil, or to taste

Kosher salt and freshly ground pepper to taste

2 tablespoons unsalted butter

HERB SALAD:

2 cups fresh parsley, chervil, or tarragon leaves; 1-inch pieces fresh chives; frisée leaves; or a combination

2 tablespoons Lemon Vinaigrette (page 247)

continued

To make the sausages: Chill the bowl and blade of a food processor in the refrigerator for 30 minutes. In the food processor, pulse the shrimp and scallops until coarsely chopped. With the machine running, add the egg whites, cream, lemon juice, and salt, and puree until emulsified, no more than 1 minute. Using a rubber spatula, transfer the mousse into a stainless-steel bowl placed over a bowl of ice. Fold in the chopped lobster meat, cayenne, pepper, and herb. Spread a square of plastic wrap on a work surface. Scoop a 4-ounce portion of the lobster mixture into the center of the lower third of the square. Fold the plastic in half and, using a gentle rolling motion, form the mixture into a rough "sausage" shape, with no visible air bubbles. Tightly twist the ends in opposite directions to push the filling into a perfect cylinder shape about 5 inches by 1½ inches. Wrap another piece of plastic over the roll to hold the ends in tightly. Prick a couple of holes in the plastic with a sharp knife. Repeat to make 3 more sausages. Refrigerate for up to 1 day.

To make the sauce: In a small saucepan, combine all the sauce ingredients except the butter, salt, and pepper. Cook over low heat to reduce by half. Whisk in the cold butter, 2 pieces at a time, to make a thick pale yellow sauce. Season with salt and pepper. Strain through a fine-mesh sieve and set aside over tepid water for up to 1 hour.

To make the mashed potatoes: In a large saucepan, combine the potatoes in salted water to cover. Bring to a simmer, partially cover, and cook until tender when pierced with a knife, 30 to 40 minutes. Meanwhile, in a small saucepan, gently heat the cream and butter. Drain the potatoes and transfer to a large bowl. Use a potato masher or ricer to puree the potatoes. Gradually whisk in the cream mixture until the potatoes are light and fluffy (you may not need all of the liquid) but still a little dry. Add the hazelnut oil, 1 tablespoon at a time, to taste. Season with salt and pepper to taste. Set aside over hot water for up to 1 hour.

To cook the sausages: In a medium saucepan of simmering water, cook the sausages until pink and firm to the touch, 10 to 15 minutes (or until an instant-read thermometer inserted into a sausage reads 120°F). Transfer to an ice-water bath. Use now, or refrigerate for up to 1 day.

To serve, slice the ends of the plastic wrap off and gently squeeze the sausages onto a plate. In a medium sauté pan or skillet over low heat, heat the butter until foaming. Add the sausages and brown evenly on all sides, about 5 minutes. Transfer to paper towels and cut each sausage crosswise in half on a slight angle. Lightly toss the herbs and/or frisée with the vinaigrette. Place a mound of mashed potatoes in the center of each of 4 warmed plates and place 2 sausage halves off to one side. Spoon some of the cardamom sauce over and around the sausages. Top with a little of the herb salad.

IMPROVISATIONS Any kind of shellfish can be substituted for the lobster meat: prawns, crab, scallops, or even mussels. The mousse can be made with all white-fleshed fish or even salmon. Vary the herbs and spices according to your taste. The recipe for the sauce (a basic beurre blanc made with fish stock) can be modified to your taste by omitting the cardamom and saffron entirely and flavoring it with minced fresh parsley or chives.

ADVANCE PREP The sausage can be made 1 day ahead and browned prior to serving. The mashed potatoes can be kept over hot water for up to 1 hour and the sauce can be kept over tepid water for up to 1 hour. The lemon vinaigrette can be made 1 day before. Don't toss the salad until the last minute.

SIMPLIFYING Buying cooked lobster makes this dish much easier. You could also serve the sausages with a simple green salad.

WINE NOTES This entree, with the trio of rich, succulent seafood, earthy potatoes, and exotic saffron sauce, is a natural for white Burgundy. Some of the lesser appellations, like Saint-Aubin and Monthélie, Saint-Romain, and Savigny-les-Beaune, would be delicious here. "New World" Chardonnays from California, Australia, or New Zealand are also a natural choice. Keep in mind the level of oak; you don't want that taste overwhelming these complex flavors.

The evolution of this dish began with Russian *kulebiaka*, or *coulibiac*, a traditional large pie similar to a beef Wellington but filled with salmon, mushrooms, rice, hard-cooked eggs, and dill. When Jeremiah was at Chez Panisse, with fond memories of his Russian uncle he created his own contemporary Russian-French version using wild rice and wild mushrooms, which proved extremely popular. At Stars, I was responsible (and became known) for making coulibiacs, but by that time they had become increasingly more elaborate and difficult for the cooks because we always made the traditional large loaf-shaped

MONKFISH CHAUSSONS *with* MUSHROOM DUXELLES, ROOT VEGETABLES, *and* MUSHROOM BROTH

pastries that were cut into individual slices. The one constant was the brioche dough, but the filling changed according to my whim; sometimes pheasant or sweetbreads, other times brains or squab. When we opened Farallon, I wanted to put a fish coulibiac on the menu and decided that it would be easier on the line cooks and make a better presentation if we did individual ones. In the most recent and refined version, I combined monkfish with foie gras, a perfect textural match in which the foie gras provides a rich but subtle meaty flavor. These individual pastry packages are designed to be made ahead and cooked just before serving, making them perfect for entertaining, but I have to admit that my favorite way to eat them is by hand, like a sandwich, in my car going home after the restaurant has closed.

★ *CHEF'S TIPS Classically, a chausson is a French turnover, usually made with puff pastry or short dough. This dish is a combination of both a coulibiac and a chausson, using brioche dough as an individual turnover. You could make this dish with another pastry rather than brioche, but the brioche provides a buttery flavor and is very elastic and easy to work with. Though it may seem like a difficult added step to make your own dough, Emily's recipe is foolproof and can be made 1 day ahead. | Brunoise is a classic vegetable cut that's supposed to be an exact ⅛ inch square. It's a lot of work to prep a large amount of brunoise vegetables, unless you're quite deft with a knife, but the end result will give you a great return for your effort. Because they're cut so small, the vegetables cook quickly and meld into a wonderful sweet mixture that's somewhere between a sauce and condiment in texture. It's a technique that we use frequently. See page 233 for information on cutting brunoise.*

Makes 4 entree servings

Four 2-ounce slices fresh foie gras
6 juniper berries
1 cup Cognac
2 sprigs thyme
Kosher salt and freshly ground pepper
    to taste

MUSHROOM DUXELLES:
2 tablespoons unsalted butter
2 tablespoons grapeseed, canola, or
    olive oil
1 pound cremini mushrooms, cleaned
    and halved
1 teaspoon minced fresh thyme
Kosher salt and freshly ground pepper
    to taste

VEGETABLE BRUNOISE:
1 tablespoon unsalted butter
1 tablespoon olive oil
1 cup finely diced celery root
1 cup finely diced carrots
1 cup finely diced onions
1 cup finely diced parsnips
1 tablespoon minced fresh thyme, or
    1 teaspoon dried thyme, crumbled
Kosher salt and freshly ground pepper
    to taste

MUSHROOM BROTH:
2 tablespoons olive oil
3 cups cremini mushrooms, cleaned
    and coarsely chopped
2 tablespoons minced shallots
3 or 4 sprigs thyme
½ cup Cognac
3 cups water
Kosher salt and freshly ground pepper
    to taste

CHAUSSONS:
Four 5-ounce monkfish fillets, as even
    and equal in shape as possible
3 tablespoons olive oil
1 teaspoon minced fresh thyme
Kosher salt and freshly ground pepper
    to taste
1½ pounds brioche dough (page 237)
1 large egg beaten with 1 tablespoon
    water

2 tablespoons minced fresh flat-leaf
    (Italian) parsley for garnish

continued

To marinate the foie gras: Put the foie gras in a glass or ceramic bowl and sprinkle with the juniper berries, Cognac, thyme, salt, and pepper. Cover and refrigerate for at least 2 hours or up to 8 hours.

To make the duxelles: In a medium sauté pan or skillet, melt the butter with the oil over medium heat and cook the mushrooms until they've released their liquid and begin to brown slightly, 8 to 10 minutes. Add the thyme, salt, and pepper. Reduce heat to medium-low and cook until almost dry. Transfer to a bowl and let cool. In a food processor, pulse the mushroom mixture until finely chopped, being careful not to puree. Let drain in a fine-mesh sieve until almost dry. Set aside, or cover and refrigerate for up to 2 days.

To sauté the brunoise: In a medium sauté pan or skillet, melt the butter with the oil over medium heat. Add the diced vegetables, reduce heat to low, and cook until the vegetables have softened but not browned, about 7 minutes. Add the thyme, salt, and pepper. Set aside in a warm place, or cover and refrigerate for up to 2 days.

To make the mushroom broth: In a small sauté pan or skillet, heat the oil over medium-high heat and sauté the mushrooms, shallots, and thyme until the mushrooms are lightly browned and have released their juices, about 8 minutes. Remove from heat and add the Cognac. Return to medium heat and cook until almost evaporated. Add the water and cook to reduce to about 1½ cups. Season with salt and pepper. Set aside, or cover and refrigerate for up to 2 days.

To start the chaussons: Rub the monkfish fillets on all sides with 1 tablespoon of the olive oil and sprinkle with thyme, salt, and pepper. In a medium sauté pan or skillet, heat the remaining 2 tablespoons olive oil over high heat until almost smoking. Sear the fish for 1 to 2 minutes on each side, or until browned on the outside and opaque throughout. Using a slotted spoon, transfer the fish to a plate, pat dry with paper towels, and set aside to cool.

To assemble the chaussons: Preheat the oven to 325°F. On a lightly floured board, roll the brioche dough out into a 16-inch square about ¼ inch thick. Cut into four 8-inch squares. Brush one square with some of the egg mixture and spread with a fillet-sized layer of mushroom duxelles. Top with a monkfish fillet, then 1 piece of foie gras. Finish by spreading 1 tablespoon duxelles over the foie gras. Fold up all the sides and pinch tightly together to form a raised X on top. Flip over and tuck the edges under. Prick holes in the top with a fork and brush with some more of the egg mixture. Assemble the other 3 chaussons and place them all on a parchment-lined baking sheet. You can refrigerate for up to 2 days at this point (don't freeze, or the foie gras will lose its texture). Bake until golden brown, about 15 minutes. Remove from the oven.

To serve, spoon the mushroom broth onto 4 warmed plates. Place a mound of vegetable brunoise in the center of each and nestle a chausson into the brunoise. Garnish with a sprinkling of parsley.

IMPROVISATIONS *Any medium-to-firm fatty fish would be good here. Even squab, pheasant, or sweetbreads would work. You can eliminate the foie gras (although it gives an incredible rich, meaty flavor to the final dish). Any kind of mushroom can be used instead of cremini, and any combination of mixed root vegetables can be used for the brunoise.*

ADVANCE PREP *This is the perfect do-ahead entree for a special-occasion dinner. You can prepare all the different components 2 days ahead, although the fish should be sautéed right before assembling the chaussons.*

SIMPLIFYING *This is a rather complex dish that really can't be simplified. However, as long as you're going to the trouble, why not double or even triple the recipe and then cook the chaussons for another dinner? Without the brunoise vegetables, and if you can purchase some brioche dough from a local bakery, it's one of the easier dishes in the book. It can also be made with a purchased puff dough.*

WINE NOTES *Time to break out the Pinot Noir: Williams-Selyem, Dehlinger, Rochioli, Etude, Au Bon Climat, Littorai, or Flowers, to name several. California wineries are making huge strides in capturing that grape's soft, velvety texture; complex, earthy aromas; and the naturally sweet and sexy fruit. It's also a great match with this rich and meaty entree, especially if the bottle has a couple of years of age.*

This is macaroni and cheese for grown-ups. A recipe dear to my heart, it takes advantage of the height of the truffle season. The very rich sauce is a perfect vehicle for the flavor and aroma of fresh truffles. It would be a wonderful appetizer for 6 people, in the tradition of the Italian *primo piatto*, or first course, of a grand dinner. The fonduta makes an incredible sauce for pasta, but I also like to pour it

FONDUTA *with* FRESH TRUFFLES

over a platter of grilled or toasted French bread and serve the whole dish family style during the winter holidays. And don't skimp on the truffles!

★ CHEF'S TIPS *Keep the truffles in the refrigerator wrapped in tissues or paper towels in a sealed container for up to 10 days. Remember that they will lose flavor and aroma over time. Some cooks like to keep them buried in raw risotto rice, claiming that they get a bonus because the truffle perfumes the rice. Personally, I don't think the process does much for the truffle or the rice, and I think the truffle loses too much moisture. If you don't use up your whole truffle, cover it with olive oil in an airtight container for up to 1 month. Truffle oil should be stored in a cool, dry place, but once opened it can be kept in the refrigerator for up to 2 months. | To clean a fresh truffle, brush it with a soft, damp cloth or toothbrush to remove any surface dirt. If it's particularly dirty, you can use a little water. Black truffles can be cooked or used raw, and while some chefs like to peel them, I never do. White truffles are extremely aromatic but their perfume dissipates when exposed to heat, so they're best shaved directly over a dish at the table. (Hand-held truffle slicers, resembling small mandolines, are available from specialty stores.) | The fonduta needs to be cooked very slowly over low heat so that the eggs don't curdle—a double boiler is an added protection against overcooking, but it's not necessary. The sauce can be made up to a day ahead, refrigerated, and then reheated in a double boiler over simmering water.*

Makes about 4 entree servings

FONDUTA:

1 cup heavy cream

2 large egg yolks

8 ounces Italian fontina cheese, cut into
½-inch cubes (about 2 cups)

2 tablespoons unsalted butter

½ ounce fresh black or white truffle,
minced, plus ½ whole fresh black or
white truffle for garnish

Freshly grated nutmeg to taste

Kosher salt and freshly ground pepper
to taste

1 pound fresh tagliatelle or fettuccine

To make the fonduta: In a heavy, medium saucepan, combine the cream and egg yolks and whisk over low heat for 2 minutes. Add the cheese and butter and cook, stirring constantly, until the cheese melts and the mixture has thickened, 10 to 15 minutes. Add the minced truffle, nutmeg, salt, and pepper. The sauce can also be made in a double boiler set over simmering water. Set aside and keep warm for no more than 15 minutes.

To cook the pasta: In a large pot of salted boiling water, cook the pasta until al dente, 1 to 2 minutes. Drain and immediately place in a warmed large bowl.

To serve, pour the fonduta over the pasta and toss well to coat. Divide among 4 warmed shallow bowls, then shave the remaining truffle over all. Season with a little more nutmeg and freshly ground pepper and serve immediately.

IMPROVISATIONS *I think this is a dish to make only if you have a fresh truffle; otherwise it would be similar to a classic fettucine Alfredo: still good, but not the same.*

ADVANCE PREP *Both the fonduta and the pasta should be cooked and served as close to eating as possible.*

SIMPLIFYING *You can use a frozen truffle in place of fresh, but if you do, drizzle a little white truffle oil over each serving at the last minute to boost the truffle aroma.*

WINE NOTES *Vintage Champagne! Try something a little complex and citrusy that can cut through the cream and still stand up to the truffles, like the fabulous Bouzy 1990 Comtesse Marie de France.*

Just Desserts *by Emily Luchetti*

When people ask what kind of food we serve at Farallon, I explain that we call it coastal cuisine because 75 percent of the menu is seafood. As pastry chef and promoter of all things sweet, I always like to add ". . . and 100 percent dessert!" I'm also often asked how we plan the pastry menu and if it is designed around the main menu. The answer is yes and no. It's important that the styles of the two menus mesh and that they match the feeling of the restaurant, but we seldom sit down and plan it that way. Luckily, Mark and I have the same approach to food, so the creative process of writing the menus at Farallon is not necessarily a conscious effort, but more instinctual. We have worked together for over fifteen years and have always shared the same sense of style, which has evolved along parallel paths over time. That is what makes our relationship unique: not much needs to be explained, because it is understood on the gut level. I believe, as does Mark, that flavor is the first and most important factor in food. Technique and visual appearance are important, but unless the flavor is there, everything else will fall flat.

Our approach to both the savory and the sweet menus at Farallon is to offer enough diversity that diners can create their own menu. For instance, if they've had a rich foie gras and monkfish entree they can opt for a lighter dessert, such as Lemon Ravioli. On the other hand, if they've had the grilled scallops, they may feel ready to indulge with Double-Chocolate Pudding Cake. We also offer tiers of desserts: several of our favorite desserts served in smaller portions.

Much of the credit for the creation and production of the desserts goes to a team of people. My responsibilities are developing the overall dessert menu, helping the pastry chef to manage the department, and promoting the restaurant through teaching and writing. Don Hall, our pastry chef, works very hard training the cooks, developing and producing the desserts on the menu, and explaining the desserts to the front of the house.

The dessert recipes included in this book have been carefully chosen and tested for the home cook. I'd like to note that while most of the savory dishes in this book are designed to serve four, these desserts are written to serve eight. We found it easier to write our recipes in larger amounts, and besides, we think that a little leftover dessert is a good thing. We hope you enjoy making the desserts for your family and friends as much as we enjoy making them for the diners at Farallon. For me, making sweet dishes gives me personal satisfaction in creating something "extra-special" with my own hands, as well as the pleasure of adding a sense of occasion to any dining experience.

These ethereal gratins are actually more like soufflés, and much more predictable for the cook, because once prepared, they're frozen in their ramekins (actually we use hemisphere molds at the restaurant), then unmolded, and baked just before serving. They make a perfect ending to a rich, formal meal because they're sweet, a bit tart, and light on the tongue. The recipe may seem a little sensitive, but

BLOOD-ORANGE GRATINS *with* BLOOD-ORANGE SEGMENTS *and* CANDIED ORANGE SLICES

it's actually very forgiving. The fact is that the gratins taste very good, and they can be made completely ahead, up to 2 days in advance of your party. Just pop them in the oven to bake, with no fuss or muss.

★ CHEF'S TIPS *For taking the temperature of the syrup for the meringue, use an instant-read thermometer rather than a candy or deep-fry thermometer; they're easier to read and tend to be more accurate. | You'll need 4 blood oranges for the entire recipe, for the zest, juice, and segments. Some of the segments will be baked into the gratins, and some will be used for garnish. | This is a bit of an exercise in timing, where everything needs to be warm to work properly. Make sure that you don't add the gelatin mixture to the pastry cream until you're ready to fold the pastry cream into the meringue; once the gelatin is added to the pastry cream, it will begin to set up. | At Farallon, we unmold the gratins (using Flexipan molds in a hemisphere shape, as shown in the photograph, see Resources, page 249) into shallow 4-ounce gratin dishes and then bake them, allowing the sides of the gratins to brown as well as the tops. They can also be baked right in their ramekins if you prefer. If you don't use the gratin dishes, serve the blood orange segments on the side.*

Makes 8 servings

BLOOD-ORANGE PASTRY CREAM:
¼ cup heavy cream
2 tablespoons fresh blood-orange juice
2 tablespoons fresh lemon juice
3 large egg yolks
2 tablespoons granulated sugar
1 tablespoon all-purpose flour
Grated zest of 1 blood orange

1 envelope plain gelatin
3 tablespoons water

ITALIAN MERINGUE:
6 tablespoons granulated sugar
2 teaspoons light corn syrup
3 tablespoons water
3 large egg whites, at room temperature

3 blood oranges, peeled and cut into
    segments (see page 236)
1 to 2 tablespoons confectioners' sugar
1½ cups crème anglaise (page 239)
8 candied orange slices (page 237)
    for garnish (optional)

Preparation

To make the pastry cream: In a small saucepan, combine the cream, blood-orange juice, and lemon juice. In a medium bowl, whisk the egg yolks and sugar together, then whisk in the flour. Bring the cream mixture to a boil, then remove from heat. Whisk a few tablespoons of the hot mixture into the egg and sugar mixture. Return the egg mixture to the saucepan and place the pan over low heat. Cook, stirring constantly, first with a rubber spatula, then whisking, until the cream is smooth and thickened, about 2 minutes. Remove the pan from heat, stir in the zest, and place a piece of plastic wrap on the surface to prevent a skin from forming. Set aside in a warm place.

To prepare the gelatin: In a small bowl, stir the gelatin into the water and let sit for 2 minutes. Place the bowl of gelatin in a small saucepan of barely simmering water until it's liquid and translucent. Remove and set aside. If the gelatin later becomes cloudy, it may have cooled too much, and you might need to reheat the gelatin before you mix it with the pastry cream, so reserve the saucepan of warm water.

continued

To make the meringue: In a small, heavy saucepan, combine the granulated sugar, corn syrup, and water and cook over medium heat until the mixture registers 230°F on an instant-read thermometer, about 7 minutes. In a heavy-duty mixer on medium speed, start beating the egg whites. By now the syrup should be at 240°F. With the machine running, gradually pour the hot syrup into the egg whites. Try to avoid pouring the syrup on the whisk or the sides of the bowl, but don't worry if some of it sticks to the sides of the bowl; it's inevitable. After the syrup has been added, increase the speed to high and beat until the outside of the bowl has cooled to the touch, about 4 minutes.

Stir the warm liquid gelatin, rewarming in the reserved pan of warm water if necessary (it should be translucent), into the orange pastry cream. Fold about half of the orange cream into the meringue until blended, then gently fold in the remaining half. Place 2 or 3 orange segments in the bottom of each of eight 4-ounce ramekins or Flexipan hemisphere molds (reserving the rest for garnish), then fill the ramekins three-quarters full with the meringue cream. Cover with plastic wrap and freeze until firm, 3 to 4 hours, or up to 2 days.

To cook the gratins: Preheat the oven to 350°F if keeping the gratins in the ramekins, 450°F if unmolding. To unmold the meringues, quickly dip the ramekins in a bowl of warm water, run a knife around the edge, and invert the meringues into shallow gratin dishes. (If you used Flexipan molds, just pop the meringues out.) Heavily dust the meringue with confectioners' sugar and bake until golden brown and cooked through, about 15 minutes. Or, bake the meringues in their ramekins, without unmolding, 20 to 25 minutes. Remove from the oven.

To serve, if you unmolded the meringues into gratin dishes, pour some crème anglaise around them and scatter a few orange segments inside the dish. If you baked the meringues in their ramekins, put them on larger plates for serving and just put a few orange segments around the ramekins. Serve the remaining crème anglaise in a small pitcher on the side to allow guests to pour it into the center of the gratin. Place an optional candied orange slice on top of each meringue and serve immediately, while they're still warm.

IMPROVISATIONS *The citrus flavors in this dessert are open to change, but keep in mind that the sweetness of the fruit needs to be balanced with a little acid. That's why I added lemon juice to the blood-orange juice in this recipe. Regular oranges combined with lemon juice will work instead of blood oranges (although the color is not quite as pretty). Tangerine juice or lemon juice will work too, as will passion fruit or a combination of passion fruit and lemon (one of my favorites).*

ADVANCE PREP *The gratins must be made in advance (except for the baking) and frozen for at least 3 to 4 hours. They can be kept frozen for up to 2 days. They don't reheat, however, so make sure you bake them just before serving, as you would a soufflé. Store the candied orange slices in an airtight container for up to 2 weeks.*

SIMPLIFYING *Skip the unmolding step and bake the meringues in their ramekins, as explained in the recipe. You could also omit the crème anglaise and just strew a serving plate with a few orange segments.*

WINE NOTES *A light and refreshing ending to a meal, this dessert is also striking in its different shades of orange. Try a fresh and fruity Muscat Beaumes de Venise from the southern Rhône, or if you find one of the delicately sweet, pale pink dessert wines made by Brachetto in northwest Italy, snap it up. An Italian Moscato would be a wonderful match as well.*

POACHED PEAR–CHESTNUT FINANCIERS *with* MILK CHOCOLATE SAUCE

Don Hall, our pastry chef, created this recipe. I like to call it his "Armani" dessert: it's sophisticated and understated, in gorgeous shades of gold and brown. A miniature pear, simply poached, is suspended in a dense little cake made with chestnut flour and presented in a pool of chocolate. It's the perfect finale to an elegant fall or winter meal. For a dessert that requires no last-minute fuss, you can also prepare the pears and cake batter in advance and then bake the financiers the day you want to serve them. If you have never seen or cooked with tiny, precious Seckel or Forelle pears, make an effort to seek them out. They're sweet and buttery, and make this dessert even more special.

★ CHEF'S TIP *The pears should be poached 1 day ahead and left to infuse overnight before using; the batter for the cakes can also be refrigerated overnight.*

Makes 8 servings

POACHED PEARS:
1½ cups sugar
1½ cups water
1½ cups Riesling, Sauternes, or other sweet white wine
1 vanilla bean, halved lengthwise, or 2 teaspoons vanilla extract
8 small ripe Seckel or Forelle pears

CHESTNUT CAKES:
¾ cup (1½ sticks) unsalted butter
1 heaping cup sliced almonds
½ cup chestnut flour
5 tablespoons unbleached all-purpose flour
Pinch of kosher salt
1 cup confectioners' sugar
2 tablespoons canned chestnut puree or peeled and pureed vacuum-packed chestnuts
¾ cup egg whites (about 6)
⅔ cup granulated sugar

MILK CHOCOLATE SAUCE:
6 ounces milk chocolate, coarsely chopped
7 tablespoons hot water

Preparation

To poach the pears: In a medium saucepan, stir together the sugar, water, wine, and vanilla bean. Bring the mixture to a boil and cook for 1 minute to dissolve the sugar. Core the pears from their bottoms, leaving the stems intact, by cutting out a little cone with a sharp paring knife or grapefruit knife. Peel them and slice a thin layer off the bottom of each pear so it can stand upright. Place the pears in the hot liquid and cover the saucepan tightly with plastic wrap. Bring the mixture to a boil again. Remove the pot from heat and let cool to room temperature. Refrigerate the pears in their poaching liquid overnight, or up to 3 days.

To begin the chestnut cake batter: In a small saucepan, melt the butter over low heat. Increase heat to medium-high and let the butter bubble up for about 1 minute. When the bubbles begin to decrease, watch carefully and, in about 2 minutes (depending on the heat), the butter will begin to turn a pale brown. Be careful that the butter does not become too dark. If it becomes dark brown or blackened, throw it out and start over—burned butter is bitter and cannot be salvaged. Set aside to cool to room temperature while you make the batter.

In a food processor, process the almonds, chestnut flour, all-purpose flour, salt, and confectioners' sugar until the almonds are finely ground. In a large bowl, whisk the chestnut puree while gradually adding the egg whites a little at a time until thoroughly incorporated. Add the granulated sugar and whisk until smooth. Add the flour mixture, again whisking until smooth. Whisk in the brown butter. Cover and refrigerate for at least 2 hours or as long as overnight.

continued

To prepare and bake the cakes: Preheat the oven to 350°F. Remove the pears from the saucepan and place them on paper towels to drain. Place the saucepan of poaching liquid on the stove and cook to reduce over high heat until slightly golden and syrupy. Remove from heat and set aside. While the liquid is reducing, butter eight 3½-inch tartlet pans. Fill each tartlet pan with about ¼ cup batter. Put the pans on a baking sheet and bake for 5 minutes. Remove from the oven and nestle an upright poached pear in the middle of each cake. Return the pans to the oven and bake until the cakes are beginning to brown at the edges and appear less shiny on top, 15 to 20 minutes. Let cool before unmolding.

To make the sauce: In a double boiler over barely simmering water, melt the chocolate. Whisk in the hot water. Set aside and keep warm, or let cool and reheat over very low heat to serve. Be careful not to boil, or the sauce will separate.

To serve, spoon some of the warm milk chocolate sauce onto each of 8 dessert plates. Place a cake on top of the sauce. Warm the poaching liquid, if necessary, and drizzle a little over each pear and cake.

IMPROVISATIONS *Halved apples or pears could be poached if you can't find the small pears. If you're unable to find chestnut flour, use almond cake batter (page 194).*

SIMPLIFYING *Purchase a good-quality chocolate sauce or omit the sauce altogether. But do use the pear syrup; it's easy enough to reduce.*

ADVANCE PREP *The pears should be prepared at least 1 day ahead and can be prepared up to 3 days in advance. The cake batter can be refrigerated overnight. The pear syrup keeps well for a week covered in the refrigerator. The chocolate sauce can be made a few hours ahead and reheated briefly over very low heat.*

WINE NOTES *A vanilla-scented, velvety tawny port is a nice choice here. For something more extravagant, choose a colheita (single-vintage) tawny from a producer like Neipoort or Warre's. An older Madeira is another option.*

ALMOND CAKES *with* CARAMEL-PINEAPPLE COMPOTE *and* COCONUT SHERBET

These wonderful little almond tea cakes are traditional in France, and you'll often find French children nibbling on them after school. You won't believe how easy they are to prepare. Grind some almonds in a food processor with confectioners' sugar, whisk in eggs, a little flour, butter, and rum, spread into individual tartlet pans, and bake for 15 minutes. Voilà! That's it. We can't resist dressing them up a little bit, however, by spooning a caramelized pineapple compote over the cakes, then topping them off with a scoop of either coconut sherbet or vanilla bean ice cream. I particularly love this pineapple compote—it has just the right balance of sweet and acid and is delicious served on its own with vanilla ice cream.

★ CHEF'S TIP *You will need 1 large pineapple, about 1½ pounds, peeled, cored, and cut into ½-inch chunks, to make the compote and to top the cakes.*

Makes 8 servings

COCONUT SHERBET:
¾ cup sugar
2 cups milk
One 13½-ounce can coconut milk
½ cup corn syrup
¼ teaspoon salt

CARAMEL-PINEAPPLE COMPOTE:
1 tablespoon unsalted butter
3¼ cups ½-inch chunks fresh pineapple
2 tablespoons sugar
Pinch of kosher salt
One 6-ounce can pineapple juice
½ vanilla bean, split lengthwise,
    or 1 teaspoon vanilla extract

ALMOND CAKES:
¾ cup slivered almonds
½ cup confectioners' sugar
4 large eggs
3 tablespoons plus 1 teaspoon cake flour
2 tablespoons plus 1½ teaspoons
    cornstarch
Pinch of kosher salt
1½ teaspoons dark rum
6 tablespoons unsalted butter, melted
¾ cup ½-inch chunks fresh pineapple

Preparation

To make the sherbet: In a medium, heavy saucepan, combine the sugar and milk. Heat over medium-low heat until the sugar is dissolved. In a bowl, whisk the remaining sherbet ingredients together. Whisk in the milk mixture. Let cool, then refrigerate for at least 2 hours or up to 1 day. Freeze in an ice cream maker according to the manufacturer's instructions.

To make the compote: In a large sauté pan or skillet, melt the butter over medium-high heat. Add the pineapple, sugar, and salt. Cook until the sugar has completely melted. Continue to cook until the pineapple begins to caramelize and the sugar begins to turn golden. Add the pineapple juice and stir briskly. Remove from heat. If using the vanilla bean, scrape out the seeds and add to the mixture with the pod. Or, add the vanilla extract. Set aside, or let cool, cover, and refrigerate for up to 2 days. Remove vanilla bean pod before serving.

To make the almond cake batter: In a food processor, combine the almonds and confectioners' sugar. Process for about 20 seconds, pulsing a few times, until the almonds are finely ground. Scrape down the sides of the container and transfer the mixture to the bowl of a heavy-duty mixer fitted with a paddle. Add one of the eggs and beat on medium speed for 1 minute. Add the remaining 3 eggs, one at a time, and continue to beat until the mixture is smooth and forms a slowly dissolving ribbon on the surface when the beater is lifted. Sift the cake flour, cornstarch, and salt together onto a piece of waxed paper. Add to the almond mixture and beat on low speed until combined, about 30 seconds. Stir the rum into the melted butter, then add this mixture to the mixer. Beat on low speed until thoroughly combined.

To bake the almond cakes: Preheat the oven to 350°F. Spray eight 4-inch tartlet molds with vegetable-oil cooking spray and set aside. Ladle equal amounts of batter into each mold and put a few of the pineapple pieces into each, pressing the fruit slightly to submerge it in the batter. Place the tartlets on a baking sheet and bake until the edges of the tartlets begin to turn golden and pull away from the sides of the molds, 15 to 20 minutes.

To serve, reheat the compote and the almond cakes, if necessary. Put 1 cake on each of 8 dessert plates and spoon some of the compote around. Top with a scoop of coconut sherbet.

IMPROVISATIONS *Fresh berries would be nice in the cake batter and made into a berry sauce to serve alongside the cakes instead of the caramelized sauce. Try hazelnuts in place of almonds.*

ADVANCE PREP *The sherbet will keep frozen for up to 3 days. The almond cakes and the pineapple compote can be made up to 2 days in advance. The cake batter can also be made 1 or 2 days in advance. Cover and refrigerate the compote, and wrap the cakes in plastic and keep them at room temperature. Reheat the compote over low heat until warm, and reheat the almond cakes in a preheated 350°F oven for 5 to 7 minutes.*

SIMPLIFYING *This is a fairly simple, homey dessert, but you can simplify it further by just serving almond cakes with diced, fresh pineapple or fresh berries. Instead of making the sherbet, buy a high-quality coconut or vanilla ice cream or sorbet.*

WINE NOTES *Desserts can be tricky matches with wine; the sweetness of the dessert can strip the wine of its fruit, leaving acid and/or tannin behind. Keep in mind the relative sweetness of the dessert, and try to "one up" it with the dessert wine. Bonny Doon Vin de Glacière, an ice wine made from California Muscat grapes, can match beautifully. Also try a 1989 Sauternes or a late-harvest Vouvray, for something a bit more extravagant.*

Babas au rhum—I love that name—are wonderful little yeast cakes, soaked in a rum-flavored sugar syrup, that owe their ancestry to Eastern Europe and Russia, though they were adopted and made famous by the French. According to one legend, a Polish king in the 1600s doused his favorite sweet bread,

BABAS AU RHUM *with* CARAMELIZED BANANAS *and* CRÈME ANGLAISE

kugelhopf, with his favorite alcohol, rum, then named the dessert after his favorite storybook character, Ali Baba. Other legend has it that they were called babas as a diminutive of the Polish term for grandmother, *babka*. They are also said to resemble chefs' toques. Whatever their origin, these "cakes" are an exceptional dessert that will captivate your guests, young and old.

★ CHEF'S TIPS *Babas are traditionally baked in small, thimble-shaped molds that can be purchased in many cookware shops. Some are nonstick, which is helpful for unmolding, but not necessary. Four- or 5-ounce ramekins, or cleaned tomato-paste cans, with tops and bottoms removed, can substitute for baba molds. | Be careful to not let the babas rise above the rims of the molds on their second rising, or they will mushroom and spill over during baking and the finished cakes will be too porous. | The babas don't need to be hot as long as the syrup is. The crème anglaise should be at room temperature. | I prefer dark rum for its deeper flavor.*

Makes 8 servings

BABAS:
1 package instant dry yeast
3 tablespoons warm (105° to 110°F) water
2¼ teaspoons sugar
3 tablespoons warm (105° to 115°F) milk
3 large eggs, at room temperature
1½ cups plus 3 tablespoons all-purpose flour

6 tablespoons unsalted butter, cut into ½-inch cubes, at room temperature
¼ teaspoon salt

RUM SYRUP:
1 cup sugar
¾ cup water
3 tablespoons dark rum
2 teaspoons fresh lemon juice
Pinch of salt

CARAMELIZED BANANAS:
1 cup sugar
½ cup water
4 tablespoons cold unsalted butter
4 peeled bananas, sliced into ¼-inch-thick rounds

1½ cups Crème Anglaise (page 239)

To make the baba dough: In the bowl of a heavy-duty mixer fitted with a paddle, whisk the yeast and water together. Whisk in the sugar and let sit for 10 minutes. Add the warm milk and eggs and beat on low speed for 1 minute. Beat in the flour on low speed, then increase the speed to medium-high and beat for 3 to 4 minutes until the dough is smooth and satiny. The dough will be quite sticky. Put the softened butter on top of the dough and sprinkle the salt over the dough as well. Cover the bowl with plastic wrap and let rise in a warm place until doubled, 1 to 1½ hours. Stir in the butter and salt until completely incorporated.

Butter eight 4-ounce baba molds (if they are not non-stick) and divide the dough among them. Cover the babas with a large inverted bowl or plastic container and let sit until they rise ¼ inch from the rim of the molds, about 30 minutes. (Do not cover with plastic wrap or it will stick to the dough as it rises.)

To bake the babas: Preheat the oven to 350°F. Bake the babas until golden brown, about 25 minutes. Remove the babas from the oven and immediately remove them from the molds, transferring them to a baking dish that will hold them all comfortably. If you notice that the sides of the babas are not golden brown when you remove them from the molds, slide them back into their molds and bake for another 2 minutes or so before proceeding. Set aside, or let cool and wrap tightly in plastic wrap to keep at room temperature for up to 2 days, or freeze for up to 3 months.

To make the rum syrup and soak the babas: In a small saucepan, combine the sugar and water. Bring to a boil over high heat and cook until the sugar is dissolved, about 1 minute. Don't cook the syrup for too long or it will get too thick and not absorb properly into the babas. Stir in the rum, lemon juice, and salt. Let sit until lukewarm, or let cool, cover, and refrigerate for up to 3 days.

With a wooden skewer or toothpick, poke holes in the babas and pour the warm syrup over them. Let the babas soak for a few minutes, then turn them over to soak on the other side. Remove them from the syrup and place them on a platter.

To make the caramelized bananas: In a large sauté pan or skillet, combine the sugar and water. Without stirring, cook over medium-high heat until light golden brown;

don't allow it to become too dark or the burned sugar will taste bitter. Turn off heat but keep the pan on the burner. Add the butter and bananas and stir just until the butter is melted and the bananas are heated through.

To serve, put a little pool of the crème anglaise on each of 8 dessert plates. Using a slotted spoon, place some bananas in the middle. Place 1 baba on top of each serving of bananas and drizzle with a little of the caramel sauce from the bananas. Serve immediately.

IMPROVISATIONS As a substitute for rum, try Amaretto or Grand Marnier mixed with orange or apple juice. Champagne- or Sauternes-soaked babas would be delicious. Fresh berries or ripe peaches could replace the bananas. For a totally different flavor, add 1 teaspoon of instant espresso powder to the flour when you make the baba dough, then soak the cakes in Amaretto or Grand Marnier. Sprinkle with toasted sliced almonds.

ADVANCE PREP The rum syrup can be made up to 3 days in advance. Refrigerate in a covered container and reheat on top of the stove. The unsoaked baked babas will keep up to 2 days at room temperature, wrapped in plastic, or they can be frozen for up to 3 months. The crème anglaise can be covered and refrigerated for up to 1 day.

SIMPLIFYING You can heat the bananas in a good-quality purchased caramel sauce or eliminate it altogether and heat them in some of the rum syrup. Instead of crème anglaise, try the simple trick of melting your favorite vanilla-bean ice cream and serving it as a sauce. Lightly sweetened whipped cream is also hard to beat (no pun intended!).

WINE NOTES Sauternes and similar wines, like Far Niente Dolce, a late-harvest Sauvignon Blanc and Semillon blend from California, are a fine match with the flavors in this rich finale. The cakes are rich but not too sweet, and the caramelized bananas will nicely echo the vanilla-oaky flavors in the wine. For a different experience, try a rich style of Madeira.

If you love apples, as I do, and you've tried every variation of apple tart and pie you can think of, as I have, this dessert will give you new inspiration. It has all the same flavors and textures as a traditional apple tart, but with a twist. Instead of apples baked into a sugar crust, the apples are lightly sautéed

CINNAMON-APPLE STACKS

and sandwiched between layers of crisp sugar cookies and dollops of crème fraîche. It's light and delicate both in flavor and texture, and is much less complicated to prepare than a tart or pie. It also has one other quality I love: All the components can be prepared in advance, which guarantees the cook peace of mind during dinner.

★ CHEF'S TIPS *Choose a great apple variety that is grown in your region. Here on the West Coast I like Golden Delicious, Pink Pearls, Braeburns, Galas, and Black Jonathans. By sautéing the apples rather than baking them in a pastry crust, you're able to make adjustments for a particular variety's texture and flavor. Cook them longer, add more liquid, or add more sugar, as your taste dictates. | The pastry dough I used here is a favorite of mine—it's incredibly easy to work (as long as you don't let it get too soft). You can flavor the dough with ground nuts or spices later. Anything you make with the dough can be rolled out and frozen, or baked and kept at room temperature in an airtight container. Because the yolks in the dough are cooked, you can also keep the unbaked dough in the refrigerator, wrapped in plastic, for up to 5 days.*

Makes 8 servings

COOKIES:

4 hard-cooked egg yolks

1 cup (2 sticks) unsalted butter, at room temperature

½ cup plus 2 tablespoons granulated sugar

2 cups unbleached all-purpose flour

1 teaspoon ground cinnamon

⅛ teaspoon salt

APPLE FILLING:

8 large apples, preferably locally grown, peeled, cored, and cut into quarters

1 cup granulated sugar

1 cup hard apple cider or apple juice

2 cups crème fraîche

2 tablespoons confectioners' sugar for dusting

Preparation

To make the cookie dough: In a food processor, combine the egg yolks, butter, and granulated sugar and process until well combined, about 10 seconds. Add the flour, cinnamon, and salt and process until smooth. Remove the dough and divide it into 2 equal portions. Shape the dough into 1-inch-thick disks and wrap tightly in plastic. Refrigerate the dough for at least 1 hour or up to 5 days.

To roll out and bake the cookies: Preheat the oven to 350°F. Remove one dough disk from the refrigerator. If the dough has been refrigerated for more than 1 hour, let sit at room temperature until it's malleable enough to roll out, about 15 minutes. On a lightly floured surface, roll out the cookie dough, flouring your rolling pin or the dough as necessary to prevent sticking, to an even ⅛-inch thickness. Using a lightly floured 3-inch biscuit or cookie cutter, cut into 12 rounds. You may need to reroll the dough scraps. If at any point the dough becomes too soft to work with, refrigerate it in plastic again for 5 or 10 minutes. Place the rounds on baking sheets lined with parchment paper. Repeat with the second disk for a total of 24 cookies. Bake the cookies until the edges turn golden, about 10 minutes. Remove from the oven and let cool.

To make the apple filling: Slice the apple quarters crosswise into ⅛-inch-thick slices. Put the apple slices in a large skillet with the sugar and apple cider. Cook the apples over medium heat, stirring occasionally, until they're soft but still hold their shape, about 10 minutes. You may have to do this in batches, depending on the size of your skillet. The time it takes will depend on the kind of apple you're using; some varieties will cook more quickly than others. If the apples aren't very juicy, you may have to add more cider or even 1 or 2 tablespoons butter. Taste them, and if they're not sweet enough for you, add a little more sugar, stirring until it's dissolved. Set aside and reheat before serving.

To serve, put 1 cinnamon cookie on each plate. Mound 2 tablespoons of warm apples in the center of each cookie and spoon on 1 tablespoon of the crème fraîche. Carefully place another cookie on top of each serving (watch out—the cookies are fragile), then more apples, another tablespoon of crème fraîche, and one more cookie. Dust the stacks with confectioners' sugar and place one more dollop of crème fraîche in the center of the top cookie. Serve immediately.

IMPROVISATIONS *This is a perfect dessert for improvisation. Instead of apples, I've used sautéed pears in the fall and fresh berries in the summer. Try flavoring the dough with ground nuts (grind them with the sugar before adding the butter), other spices, seeds, or ginger. Even though I prefer crème fraîche for its slightly tangy flavor which plays well against the apples, it can be replaced with sour cream or softly whipped cream.*

ADVANCE PREP *Everything here can be prepped ahead. The cookie dough can be made up to 5 days ahead, wrapped in plastic, and kept in the refrigerator. The cookies can be rolled out and frozen for 1 week, or baked and stored at room temperature, in an airtight container, for 4 to 5 days. The apples may be sautéed earlier on the day you plan to serve them, then reheated.*

WINE NOTES *There are a lot of wine options to try with apple stacks: White wines that are not oaky, like a late-harvest Viognier from the Cambria Winery in Santa Barbara, are good. So is a classic younger Sauternes (save the ultra-expensive bottle of D'Yquem!). Even a Tokaji Aszu or a tawny East India sherry, port, or Madeira could be fun.*

PERSIMMON PUDDING CAKES *with* ORANGE SAUCE *and* RUM RAISIN ICE CREAM

Tasting an unripe persimmon is an extremely unpleasant experience. Imagine sucking on a super-intense lemon and then magnify that pucker about ten times. But an unripe persimmon is actually a sheep in wolf's clothing. Give an unripe persimmon a little time on your kitchen counter, and it magically transforms itself from bitingly astringent to sweet and unbelievably mellow. This is a contemporary twist on an old-fashioned dessert, a cross between a pudding and a cake: dense but moist, and aromatic with spices. Serve these little cakes warm from the oven with homemade rum raisin ice cream, and you'll have a perfect ending to an informal fall or winter dinner.

★ *CHEF'S TIPS There are two main varieties of persimmons available today: the pointy-ended Hachiya, which is the kind that needs to be super soft before eating, and the flattened-tomato-shaped Fuyu, which can be eaten crisp (we use the Hachiya for this recipe). | If you have some beautiful but hard Hachiya persimmons, and you want to make this wonderful fall dessert, put them in the freezer overnight. The next morning, thaw them and you'll have persimmons that are ready to be pureed (use nonreactive bowls made of glass, stainless steel, or plastic to keep from drawing out the acidic taste in the fruit).*

Makes 8 servings

PUDDING CAKES:
6 large, very ripe Hachiya persimmons (about 1½ pounds)
2 cups sugar
4 tablespoons unsalted butter, melted
1½ teaspoons vanilla extract
1⅓ cups bread flour
1½ teaspoons baking soda
¾ teaspoon salt
⅛ teaspoon freshly grated nutmeg
⅛ teaspoon ground cinnamon
¾ cup whole milk
6 tablespoons fresh orange juice

ORANGE SAUCE:
1 cup fresh orange juice
½ cup sugar
3 large eggs
1 teaspoon grated orange zest

RUM RAISINS:
1 cup water
1 cup sugar
¼ cup dark rum
½ vanilla bean, split lengthwise, or 1 teaspoon vanilla extract
1 cup dark raisins
1 cup golden raisins

ICE CREAM BASE:
2 cups heavy cream
⅔ cup milk
½ vanilla bean, split lengthwise, or 1 teaspoon vanilla extract
⅔ cup sugar
5 large egg yolks
3 tablespoons dark rum
Pinch of salt

Preparation

To make the pudding cake batter: Cut the stem out of the persimmons. In a food processor, process the persimmons until smooth, and then push the puree through a medium-mesh stainless-steel sieve to eliminate the skins. If you don't have a stainless-steel sieve, cut the persimmons in half, scrape the pulp from the skin, and puree the pulp in a food processor. You'll need 1½ cups puree. Pour the puree into a bowl and whisk in the sugar, 3 tablespoons of the melted butter, and the vanilla. In a medium bowl, stir the bread flour, baking soda, salt, nutmeg, and cinnamon together, then stir into the persimmon mixture. Whisk in the milk and orange juice.

To bake the persimmon cakes: Preheat the oven to 350°F. Brush eight 4-ounce ramekins, ovenproof molds, or individual brioche molds with the remaining 1 tablespoon melted butter and fill with the persimmon batter. Place the ramekins on a baking sheet. Bake until a skewer inserted in the center of a cake comes out clean, about 25 minutes.

To make the orange sauce: In a small saucepan, stir the orange juice and ¼ cup of the sugar together. In a small bowl, whisk the eggs and the remaining ¼ cup sugar together. Heat the orange juice mixture over medium-low heat until just warm, then whisk it into the eggs. Return the mixture to the saucepan and cook over medium-low heat, stirring constantly, until the mixture has thickened and reaches 170°F on an instant-read thermometer—be careful to not cook it further. Strain through a fine-mesh sieve into a bowl and set over an ice-water bath to stop further cooking. Stir in the zest and let cool completely. Cover with plastic and refrigerate until you're ready to serve the persimmon cakes, up to 1 day ahead.

To make the rum raisins: In a saucepan, combine the water, sugar, and rum. Scrape in the seeds and add the pod from the vanilla bean, if using. Bring to a boil and simmer for 5 minutes. Add the raisins and cook for 2 minutes to plump. Remove from heat and add the vanilla extract, if using. Remove the vanilla bean pod. Let cool and refrigerate for up to 4 days.

To make the ice cream base: In a heavy saucepan, combine the cream and milk. Scrape the seeds from the vanilla bean, if using, and add to the pan with the pod. Cook over high heat until bubbles form around the edges of the pan. Whisk the sugar into the egg yolks. Whisk the hot cream mixture into the egg mixture. Stir in the rum and salt. Return to the pan and cook over medium-low heat, stirring constantly, until the mixture thickens and coats the back of a spoon. Remove from heat and add the vanilla extract, if using. Strain through a fine-mesh sieve. Let cool, then refrigerate for at least 2 hours. Freeze in an ice cream maker to the manufacturer's instructions. Before the ice cream is completely frozen, drain the raisins from their liquid and fold them into the ice cream. Place in the freezer for several hours to allow the ice cream to harden. It will last for up to 4 to 5 days. Save the raisin liquid, refrigerated for another use, for up to 2 weeks.

To serve, place a warm persimmon cake on each of 8 dessert plates. Spoon some of the orange sauce around the cakes and serve with a scoop of ice cream on top.

IMPROVISATIONS *Because persimmons are only available for a short time each year, we also tested this recipe with pumpkin puree. Since it has a similar texture and moistness, it can be substituted for the persimmon puree. You can make your own by roasting a small sugar pumpkin and pureeing the flesh. Canned puree is acceptable, but be sure to use pure pumpkin, not pumpkin pie filling. Serve with the caramel ice-cream blend called dulce de leche (Häagen-Dazs makes one), or try a caramel sauce instead of the orange sauce. The reserved raisin liquid can be saved and poured directly over vanilla ice cream, used to flavor a crème anglaise, or tossed with some stone fruit.*

ADVANCE PREP *The cakes may be cooled completely, covered with plastic, stored at room temperature for up to 2 days, and then reheated in a preheated 350°F oven until warm, 5 to 8 minutes. The orange sauce can be made up to 1 day ahead and refrigerated in a covered container. The ice cream may be made several days ahead and kept in the freezer for up to 4 days.*

SIMPLIFYING *Good quality purchased rum raisin ice cream is perfectly acceptable. Instead of the ice cream and orange sauce, serve the cakes with a dollop of whipped cream that's been perked up with a little sugar and orange zest.*

WINE NOTES *The bracing acidity of Madeira, especially the sweeter, spicier style of Malmsey, would be perfect with these moist, autumn cakes.*

Profiteroles, little one- or two-bite cream puffs served with chocolate sauce, is a familiar item on French dessert menus. This a marvelous, comforting dessert perfect for entertaining because everything can be made in advance and assembled at the last minute. Profiteroles are also good candidates for improvisation; in this version I've flavored the choux pastry with cocoa powder, and instead of

COCOA PROFITEROLES *with* TOASTED-ALMOND ICE CREAM, CANDIED ALMONDS, *and* CHOCOLATE SAUCE

whipped cream or pastry cream, the puffs are filled with homemade almond ice cream. To contrast with the cold ice cream there's warm chocolate sauce, and for a nice little textural crunch there are candied almonds.

★ CHEF'S TIPS *Without the cocoa powder, this is a classic French choux pastry used in making éclairs. At Farallon, we create a slightly different texture and color by putting disks of plain short dough rolled in sugar on top of the pastries before they're baked, adding crispness to the profiteroles. | To keep the parchment paper from lifting as you pipe the profiteroles, put just a smear of the choux pastry (which acts a little like glue) in each corner of the baking sheet before pressing down the parchment. | The short-dough recipe makes more than you will need here. It freezes well for up to 2 months, and can be used for anything from tarts to cookies. | We use and highly recommend Silpat baking-tray liners made of ultra-nonstick silicone. They're hardy, heat resistant mats that have revolutionized professional baking.*

Makes 8 dessert servings

CANDIED ALMONDS:
1 large egg white
⅓ cup sugar
1½ cups (6 ounces) sliced almonds

SHORT DOUGH:
1¾ cups (3¼ sticks) unsalted butter at room temperature
¾ cup sugar, plus about 2 cups for rolling dough
1 egg
1 teaspoon vanilla extract
3 cups bread flour

PÂTE À CHOUX:
1 cup unbleached all-purpose flour
2 tablespoons unsweetened cocoa powder, preferably Dutch processed
Pinch of salt
1 cup water
2 teaspoons sugar
6 tablespoons unsalted butter
4 large eggs

CHOCOLATE SAUCE:
1¾ cups water
⅔ cup sugar
¼ cup corn syrup
½ cup cocoa powder, preferably Dutch processed
6 ounces bittersweet chocolate, chopped

Toasted-Almond Ice Cream (page 246)

Preparation

To make the candied almonds: Preheat the oven to 300°F. In a medium bowl, whisk the egg white until frothy. Whisk in the sugar. Stir in the nuts and evenly coat them with the egg-white mixture. Place them in a single layer on a non-stick or Silpat-lined baking sheet and bake for 10 minutes. With a metal spatula, stir the nuts and spread them out again into a single layer. Bake, stirring every 5 minutes, until the nuts are dry and golden brown, 5 to 10 minutes.

To make the short dough: In a heavy-duty electric mixer fitted with a whisk attachment, cream the butter and the ¾ cup sugar together until light and fluffy, about 5 minutes. Add the egg and vanilla and keep whisking, scraping down the sides of the container. Add the bread flour and mix until just combined. Remove from the machine. On a lightly floured board, roll the dough into a ball. Divide the ball into half and roll each piece out into a flat rectangle. Wrap well in plastic and refrigerate for 2 hours. Place the 2 cups of sugar onto the board and roll one piece of the chilled dough into a ⅛-inch-thick sheet. Using a 2-inch cookie cutter, cut into at least 12 rounds. Repeat with the second piece of dough. Place the rounds on a small baking sheet and put in the freezer while you make the profiteroles.

continued

To make the pâté à choux: Preheat the oven to 400°F. Sift the flour, cocoa powder, and salt together onto a sheet of waxed paper and set aside. In a medium heavy-bottomed saucepan, bring the water and sugar to a boil. Stir in the butter until melted. Remove the pan from heat and stir in the flour mixture. Return the pan to the stove and cook over medium-low heat, stirring constantly, until the mixture no longer sticks to the sides, about 2 minutes. Put the mixture in the bowl of a heavy-duty electric mixer fitted with a paddle attachment. On medium speed, beat until the dough is slightly cooled and no steam rises from it, 1 or 2 minutes. With the machine running, add the eggs one at a time, beating well after each addition. Continue beating until the dough is glossy and thick, about 4 minutes.

To make the profiteroles: Remove the short-dough rounds from the freezer. Put the choux dough in a pastry bag fitted with a ⅜-inch plain tip. Pipe at least 24 rounds several inches apart and about 1 inch tall onto parchment paper–lined baking sheets (the profiteroles will almost double in size in the oven). Or, drop tablespoonfuls of dough onto the sheets. Immediately press a short-dough round lightly onto the top of each profiterole, sugar-side up. Bake for 10 minutes. Reduce the oven temperature to 350°F and bake until crisp on the outside, about 20 minutes. When you cut one open, it should be hollow and just a little moist inside. The profiteroles will dry out as they cool. Let cool completely and place in an airtight container at room temperature. The profiteroles should be used the day they are made; leaving them overnight can make them soggy. Reheat in a preheated 300°F oven to recrisp them.

To make the chocolate sauce: In a large, heavy saucepan, combine the water, sugar, and corn syrup. Bring to a boil over medium-high heat. (A large pot is important here, because the mixture can boil over.) Whisk in the cocoa powder, reduce heat to a simmer, and cook, stirring frequently and scraping down the sides, until the mixture thickens slightly, about 10 minutes. Stir in the chopped chocolate until melted. Set aside in a warm place until serving, or let cool and refrigerate in a covered container for up to 3 days. Reheat over a saucepan of simmering water.

To serve, spoon some warm chocolate sauce in the center of each plate. Cut each profiterole in half horizontally. Place the bottom halves of 3 profiteroles in the center of each plate. Using a small ice-cream scoop, place a small scoop of ice cream in each half, then cover with the top half of each profiterole. Spoon the chocolate sauce liberally over the profiteroles and sprinkle the candied almonds around and on top. Serve immediately.

IMPROVISATION *Vanilla and coffee ice cream are popular fillings for traditional profiteroles, as are pastry cream and whipped cream. The chocolate sauce is almost universal. I've had a chocolate sauce laced with a crème de menthe that was terrific.*

ADVANCE PREP *The pâté à choux and short crust can be made, piped, rolled, and frozen for up to 1 week. Just pop them onto a baking sheet and bake when needed. After being baked, the profiteroles are best eaten the same day. The ice cream can be made 3 days ahead; the chocolate sauce can be stored in the refrigerator for up to 3 days and reheated; and the candied almonds can be kept for 1 week in an airtight container.*

SIMPLIFYING *Buy good-quality ice cream and chocolate sauce for this dish. The short-crust pastry tops can be omitted.*

WINE NOTES *Now is the time to check out the compatibility of chocolate and port. Choose a ruby port, either vintage or a house blend like Fonseca Bin 27. Or try, the sweet Grenache-based red wines of Banyuls from the South of France: a great match with chocolate. Whatever you decide on, make it full and sweet and bursting with deep fruit flavors.*

DOUBLE-CHOCOLATE PUDDING CAKE

"Seriously chocolate" is how I describe this cake. While many chocolate desserts cross the line from the sublime to the ridiculous, this one has a rich chocolate taste without being too much. When I've served it to guests in my home, they always clean their plates. The cinnamon cream keeps it from being too rich and is a nice complement to the chocolate flavor. This cake possesses a wonderful comforting quality—after all, it is a pudding cake—which makes it a perfect dessert for any occasion at home. In addition, it's easily assembled and can be made in advance.

★ *CHEF'S TIP Make the cake, creams, and glaze the day before serving the dessert. Assemble it to just short of glazing. Right before serving, rewarm the glaze and pour it over the cake.*

Makes 10 servings

PUDDING CAKE:

1 cup plus 3 tablespoons unsweetened cocoa powder

1½ cups unbleached all-purpose flour

½ teaspoon baking powder

¾ teaspoon salt

1 cup (2 sticks) plus 2 tablespoons unsalted butter, at room temperature

2¼ cups sugar

5 large eggs

¾ cup buttermilk

3 tablespoons water

1½ teaspoons vanilla extract

CHOCOLATE CREAM:

½ cup heavy cream

½ cup milk

2 large egg yolks

6 tablespoons sugar

6 ounces bittersweet chocolate, chopped

CINNAMON CREAM:

¾ cup mascarpone cheese at room temperature

1 teaspoon ground cinnamon

2 tablespoons sugar

6 tablespoons heavy cream

CHOCOLATE GLAZE:

¼ cup heavy cream

1 cup sugar

¾ cup water

½ cup unsweetened cocoa powder

1½ teaspoons plain gelatin

1 tablespoon water

Preparation

To prepare the cake batter: Preheat the oven to 350°F. Butter three 9-inch round cake pans and cut rounds of parchment paper to fit the bottom of the pans. Butter the parchment. Sift the cocoa powder, flour, baking powder, and salt together. In a heavy-duty electric mixer fitted with a paddle, cream the butter and sugar together until smooth. Beat in the eggs, one at a time. In a small bowl, stir the buttermilk, water, and vanilla together. Add one-third of the cocoa and flour mixture to the butter mixture, beating well to combine. Add half the buttermilk mixture and mix well. Repeat, alternating the wet and dry mixtures and beating well after each addition, ending with the cocoa mixture. Evenly divide the batter among the prepared cake pans.

To bake the cakes: Bake the cakes until a skewer inserted into the middle of a cake comes out clean, 20 to 25 minutes. Remove the cakes from the oven and let cool for 15 minutes before unmolding and assembling, or let them cool completely on wire racks, then wrap in plastic and store at room temperature for up to 2 days.

To make the chocolate cream: In a small saucepan, combine the cream and milk and cook over medium-high heat until bubbles form around the edges of the pan. Remove from heat. In a medium bowl, whisk the egg yolks and sugar together. Gradually whisk in the hot cream. Return the mixture to the saucepan and cook over low heat, stirring occasionally, until the cream has thickened and coats the back of a spoon. Stir in the chocolate until melted. Strain through a fine-mesh sieve into a bowl. Press plastic wrap directly onto the surface of the cream and refrigerate for at least 2 hours or up to 2 days.

continued

To make the cinnamon cream: In a small bowl, stir the mascarpone, cinnamon, sugar, and cream together until smooth. If the mixture seems too thick to spread, add 1 or 2 tablespoons of cream. Refrigerate, covered, for up to 24 hours.

To assemble the cake: Remove the parchment and put 1 cake layer on a large plate or serving platter with a rim. Spread the cinnamon cream on top, then top with another cake layer. Spread the chocolate cream on top of the second cake layer and then top with a third layer. The cake may be assembled to this point and refrigerated, covered with plastic wrap, for up to 8 hours.

To make the chocolate glaze: In a medium saucepan, stir the cream, sugar, water, and cocoa powder together. Bring the mixture to a boil, reduce heat to low, and simmer, stirring often, until it thickly coats the back of a spoon, about 10 minutes. Remove from heat and let cool slightly. Meanwhile, in a small bowl, stir the gelatin and water together and let sit for 2 minutes. Place the bowl of gelatin in a small saucepan of barely simmering water, stirring until liquid and translucent. Whisk the gelatin into the chocolate glaze. Refrigerate the glaze, stirring occasionally, until it has a thick pouring consistency, 15 to 30 minutes. It's important for the glaze to be at the right temperature before pouring it over the cake—if it's too warm it will run off, and if too cold it will be impossible to pour. Use your best judgment. It should be the consistency of a thick maple syrup. Either use the glaze immediately, or cover with plastic and refrigerate for up to 24 hours; reheat right before serving.

To serve, if the glaze is too thick to pour, or if you've made it ahead, rewarm it in a double boiler over warm water. Pour the chocolate glaze over the cake, letting the excess pool as a sauce in the bottom of the platter. Cut the cake into wedges and serve immediately, making sure to scoop up some extra sauce for each portion.

IMPROVISATIONS *For sour milk to use in place of the buttermilk, add ¾ teaspoon fresh lemon juice to ¾ cup room-temperature milk. Stir and let sit for 5 minutes.*

ADVANCE PREP *The cake can be assembled up to 8 hours in advance. The chocolate cream filling and the cake layers can be made separately 2 days in advance. The cake should be glazed right before serving.*

SIMPLIFYING *Flavor whipped cream with a little powdered sugar and liqueur and use to frost the cake right before serving.*

WINE NOTES *Got port? It seems to be everyone's favorite match with chocolate. True, there is nothing quite like a glass of well-aged, mature vintage port, but save that special bottle for sipping by itself. With this chocolate-chocolate dish, drink a dark ruby port with good fruit and not too much tannin.*

HONEY PANNA COTTAS *with* DRIED FRUIT *and* SAUTERNES COMPOTE

Panna cotta, or "cooked cream," seems to have replaced tiramisu as the current favorite Italian dessert, and with good reason. It's a sublime sweet that is easy to prepare and can be dressed up in endless ways. It originated in Piedmont, and basically it's an eggless custard that is thickened with a small amount of gelatin. Traditionally, it's served plain, but I love to give it a little twist. Here, it's sweetened with honey and garnished with bits of dried fruit that have been plumped in Sauternes.

★ CHEF'S TIP *This dessert can be very rich if you use a strong honey. Use a mild one, like acacia or sage.*

Makes 8 servings

PANNA COTTAS:
3¼ cups heavy cream
¾ cup whole milk
⅓ cup honey
Pinch of kosher salt
1 package plain gelatin
3 tablespoons water

DRIED FRUIT AND SAUTERNES COMPOTE:
¼ cup dried apricots, cut into
    ¼-inch pieces
¼ cup dried pears, cut into ¼-inch pieces
¼ cup halved dried sour cherries or pitted
    fresh sweet cherries
1 cup water
1 cup Sauternes or other sweet white
    dessert wine

½ cup sliced almonds, toasted
    (see page 236)

Preparation

To make the panna cottas: Lightly spray eight 4-ounce ramekins with nonstick vegetable-oil cooking spray, or use nonstick tartlet pans. In a large, heavy saucepan, heat the cream and milk over medium-high heat until bubbles form around the edges of the pan. Remove from heat. Stir in the honey and salt and set aside; don't whisk, to avoid making foam bubbles. In a small bowl, stir the gelatin and water together and let sit for 2 minutes. Place the bowl of gelatin over a small saucepan of barely simmering water until liquid and translucent. Test the cream mixture with your finger—it should be very warm, but not hot. Stir in the softened gelatin, then pour the cream mixture into the ramekins. Let cool, then cover with plastic and refrigerate until set, about 3 hours, or for up to 2 days.

To make the dried fruit compote: In a medium saucepan, combine the fruit, water, and wine and cook over medium heat until the fruit has softened, 3 to 4 minutes. Set aside, or cover and refrigerate for up to 4 days.

continued

To serve, fill a shallow bowl with very hot water and set aside. Dip a panna cotta ramekin into the water for 5 seconds (being careful not to get any water inside), wipe dry, then run a small knife around the edge of the ramekin and carefully invert onto a plate. Repeat with the remaining panna cottas. Spoon the fruit compote and its liquid around the panna cottas and sprinkle with the toasted almonds.

IMPROVISATIONS *Instead of honey, you can sweeten the panna cottas with an equal amount of sugar. Add spices like cinnamon or nutmeg, and serve them with fresh fruit instead of dried. Besides fresh berries, try sautéed apples or pears (apples are great with cinnamon panna cotta). Serve with crunchy cookies for a contrast in texture.*

ADVANCE PREP *The panna cottas must be refrigerated for at least 3 hours and can be made up to 2 days in advance. The fruit compote will keep for up to 4 days, refrigerated.*

WINE NOTES *This dessert is rich in texture and quite sweet. Try something aged in oak and tawny, like a sherry or Madeira, or something totally different that is packed with exotic dried fruits, butterscotch, and holiday aromas, like an Australian Tokay from Chambers Rosewood Vineyards in Victoria.*

MUSCAT GRANITA *with* SAUTÉED GRAPES *and* CHANTILLY CREAM

Depending on the variety of grape used, the flavors and colors of this granita can vary wildly. We often use Zinfandel or Concord grapes, which have their own distinctive flavors.

★ CHEF'S TIPS *The Muscat granita looks a little brown initially, but don't worry—the color of the granita will change as you mix it, as the air that is folded into it will lighten the hue as well as the texture. | The amount of sugar needed to make the syrup will depend on the sweetness of the fruit; taste the grapes and try to judge how much more sugar it will need.*

Makes 8 servings

GRAPE GRANITA:

4 pounds Muscat or Concord grapes, stemmed

¼ to ½ cup sugar

CHANTILLY CREAM:

1½ cups heavy cream

1 teaspoon sugar

½ teaspoon vanilla extract

1 to 2 tablespoons granulated sugar

2 tablespoons verjus, or 1 tablespoon fresh lemon juice

10 ounces grapes, halved

Preparation

To make the granita: In a medium saucepan, combine the grapes and ¼ cup sugar and cook over medium heat until the grapes have released their juice, about 40 minutes. Taste for sweetness and add up to another ¼ cup sugar if necessary. Remove from heat and let sit for 15 minutes. Strain the grapes through a fine-mesh sieve into a glass or ceramic baking dish and let cool completely. Transfer to the freezer until completely frozen, about 2 hours, stirring and scraping with a large fork every 15 minutes or so to give the granita a granular texture. Cover and freeze until ready for use. Stir and scrape once more before serving to fluff it up.

To make the Chantilly cream: In a deep bowl, combine the cream, sugar, and vanilla extract. Beat the cream until soft peaks form. Refrigerate for up to 2 hours.

To cook the grapes: In a medium sauté pan or skillet, bring the sugar and verjus or lemon juice to a boil. Add the halved grapes and cook until just soft, 3 to 4 minutes. Serve warm, or set aside at room temperature for up to 2 hours.

To serve, rewarm the grapes over low heat, if necessary. Spoon the grapes into a rough circle in the bottom of small, deep bowls. Mound the granita into the center of the grapes and top with a generous dollop of the Chantilly cream. Serve immediately.

IMPROVISATION *Replace the grapes with equal amounts of cantaloupe or another kind of melon.*

ADVANCE PREP *The granita can be made the day before you plan to serve. All the other components can be made up to 2 hours before serving.*

WINE NOTES *This light and fresh dessert will take well to sweeter styles of sparkling wine like a Moscato d'Asti. Also try Beaumes de Venise, a lighter, more floral style of dessert wine from the Rhône Valley in France.*

When Mark returned from a truffle hunting trip in Périgord, he was inspired to create a special menu that featured truffles in every dish—including dessert, which is not as adventurous as one might think. The French, whose passion for this extravagant commodity borders on fanaticism, have created thousands of recipes, sweet as well as savory, that employ truffles. Don Hall, our pastry chef, came up with the idea of presenting a plate of several small desserts, each including truffles, to show the many

TRUFFLED CRÈME BRÛLÉE

ways they can be used in sweets. The aromatic earthiness of truffles combines particularly well with dairy products, and our sampler plate included truffled panna cotta, truffled vanilla ice cream on a chocolate curl with a thin slice of whole truffle on top, and this unique crème brûlée.

★ CHEF'S TIPS *Truffle aroma tends to be diluted when baked in a custard, so we decided to add the fresh truffle at a later stage. The studding infuses the custard as it sets up, giving the brûlée a third textural dimension. | There are several different techniques for achieving the famous burnt crust of a brûlée. In most professional kitchens, a hand-held blowtorch is used when caramelizing something "to order"; you have more control over the process with a torch and are less likely to cook the cream. A very hot broiler is the next best method, with a rack placed 3 inches from the heat source. The most traditional method of all is heating a brûlée iron in a gas flame and searing the sugar.*

Makes 8 servings

6 tablespoons granulated sugar
1 large egg
3 large egg yolks
1¼ cups heavy cream
¾ cup whole milk
½ vanilla bean, split lengthwise, or
    1 teaspoon vanilla extract
1 ounce fresh truffle, finely julienned
4 tablespoons superfine or granulated
    sugar for caramelizing

Preparation

To make the custard: In a medium bowl, whisk the sugar, egg, and egg yolks together until pale yellow. Set aside. In a medium saucepan, combine the cream and milk. Scrape the seeds from the vanilla bean, if using, into the mixture and add the pod. Bring to a quick boil over high heat without letting it boil over—watch carefully! Remove from heat immediately and gradually whisk the cream mixture into the egg mixture. Add the vanilla extract, if using. Cool the custard over an ice-water bath. Strain the liquid through a fine-mesh sieve into a bowl. Bake now, or cover and refrigerate for up to 24 hours. Preheat the oven to 350°F. Pour the custard into 8 small soufflé dishes or ramekins and put them in a shallow baking dish. Add hot water to the baking dish to come halfway up the sides of the soufflé dishes. Bake until all but a ½-inch circle in the center of each custard is set, 30 to 45 minutes.

To stud the custards: Refrigerate the custards until slightly cooled, about 20 minutes. Remove from the refrigerator and gently slide 6 or 7 slivers of truffle into the custard. (Don't worry about the appearance of the surface of the custard; as long as it is flat the caramelizing will hide the places where the truffles show.) Immediately refrigerate for at least 2 hours or until ready to serve the same day.

To serve, sprinkle the tops of the custards evenly with a thin layer of sugar. Preheat the broiler to high. Broil 3 inches from the heat source until the tops of the custards are light brown and bubbling, 1 or 2 minutes (see Chef's Tips). Remove with tongs. Let cool slightly. Serve each custard on a folded napkin on a small plate.

IMPROVISATION *If you don't have a fresh truffle, mix 1 tablespoon canned truffle peelings or white truffle oil into the custard base just before pouring it into the soufflé dishes. If you use the truffle oil, sprinkle a few drops on top of each custard before caramelizing.*

ADVANCE PREP *The custard base can be made 1 day ahead and kept covered in the refrigerator. The custards can be baked and chilled earlier on the day of serving, then caramelized at the last minute.*

SIMPLIFYING *You can, of course, make the crème brûlée without the truffle.*

WINE NOTES *This may be a dessert to enjoy by itself, but if a wine is needed you might try to find the exotic sweet wines of Alsace: Vendage Tardive, or the even rarer Sélection de Grain Noble. They are made in Grand Cru vineyards, from Riesling, Muscat, Pinot Gris, and Gewürztraminer grapes, but only in select years when the weather cooperates, and boy are they expensive. But this dessert deserves a luxurious wine! Zind-Humbrecht, Domaine Weinbach, Trimbach, Albert Boxler, and Marcel Deiss are some of the producers from which to choose. The only problem will be finding them, so ask your local merchant for assistance.*

ROASTED NECTARINES FILLED *with* CINNAMON MERINGUE

Nectarines are a favorite stone fruit, and every summer when we receive perfectly ripe and juicy ones at their seasonal peak, we're tempted to simply serve them on porcelain plates, unadorned. While we have never gone that far, this recipe is only a couple of steps up from that. Of course, we also put nectarines in cobblers, ice creams, sherbets, pies, and tarts. After a morning at the Marin County Farmers' Market, I like to gather my willing and industrious friends to make nectarine preserves. But I have to admit that as wonderful as those preparations are, this is the recipe to choose when you want a simple and elegant presentation for this divine fruit.

★ CHEF'S TIP *If you need to cook these ahead and reheat for serving, remember that the meringue will puff up again the second time.*

Makes 8 servings

2 cups sugar syrup (page 246)
2 cups Riesling or sweet white wine
8 ripe nectarines

CINNAMON MERINGUE:
2 large egg whites
6 tablespoons sugar
2 tablespoons honey
⅛ teaspoon ground cinnamon

2 cups Crème Anglaise (page 239)

Preparation

To prepare the nectarines: In a medium saucepan, bring the sugar syrup to a boil and cook for 1 minute. Transfer to a bowl and let cool to room temperature. Stir in the Riesling and set aside. Cut a small slice from the bottom of the nectarines so they will sit flat on the plate. Remove the pits by cutting off the top of the nectarine so the pit is exposed, then cutting around the pit with a small paring knife. Be careful not to cut into the flesh of the nectarine. With your fingers, give the pit a twist to loosen it at the bottom, then pull it out. Put the nectarines in the Riesling mixture and marinate for 1 hour, rolling them around occasionally to make sure they are evenly saturated.

To make the cinnamon meringue: Preheat the oven to 400°F. Combine the egg whites, sugar, honey, and cinnamon in the bowl of an electric mixer and whisk for 3 minutes. Place the bowl over, but not touching, simmering water. Whisk the egg whites by hand until they are very warm, about 1 minute. Remove the bowl from heat and return to the mixer. Beat on medium-high speed until the meringue has thickened and cooled.

Put the meringue in a pastry bag that has been fitted with a large (No. 12) star tip. Pipe the cinnamon meringue into each nectarine. Put the nectarines in a baking dish (you can also place them in muffin cups to prevent them from falling over when they are moved in and out of the oven) and bake until the meringue is golden brown, about 10 minutes.

To serve, pour the crème anglaise into 8 warmed bowls and place a nectarine in each bowl.

IMPROVISATION *You could use peaches in this dish, with vanilla bean seeds scraped into the meringue instead of the cinnamon. Replace the crème anglaise with blueberry puree.*

SIMPLIFYING *Instead of making the crème anglaise, cook the Riesling sugar syrup to reduce it until thick (by about half) and serve this with the nectarines.*

ADVANCE PREP *The nectarines can be marinated up to 3 hours in advance. Keep them covered, in their liquid, until just ready to prepare.*

WINE NOTES *Although this unique presentation will pair with many dessert wines, look for something unique as well: maybe a Hungarian Tokai, or a well-aged Australian Muscat, or a vintage Malmsey from Madeira.*

STRAWBERRY-RHUBARB PAVLOVA

Debate rages in the Southern Hemisphere about the origins of the pavlova, and whether it was first created in Australia or New Zealand. It's still a bone of contention between the two countries, but there's no dispute that this light and ethereal meringue dessert was named for the famous Russian ballerina who visited both countries in the 1920s. A traditional pavlova is a little cake of meringue, crispy on the outside and slightly soft on the inside, said to resemble a tutu, and filled with whipped cream and fruit, usually strawberries, kiwis, and passion fruit pulp. I've played a bit here with tradition, and in this heavenly Farallon version little pavlova clouds simply sit atop mounds of whipped rhubarb cream (with crunchy pieces of meringue in it) and strawberries.

★ *CHEF'S TIP This recipe calls for a French meringue that, when cooked in a low oven for a long period of time, hardens on the outside but stays tender on the inside. Other versions are made with Italian meringue and are baked hard all the way through, or are soft and airy like the Swiss meringue that is used to top desserts like lemon meringue pie.*

Makes 8 servings

MERINGUES:
6 large egg whites
Large pinch cream of tartar
1 cup sugar
1 teaspoon vanilla extract

RHUBARB CREAM:
10 ounces rhubarb, washed, trimmed,
    and cut into ½-inch pieces
    (about 1½ cups)
¼ cup sugar
Pinch of salt
1½ cups heavy cream

STRAWBERY SAUCE:
4 cups fresh strawberries, hulled
2 tablespoons sugar

Preparation

To make the meringues: Preheat the oven to 200°F. Draw eight 2¾-inch circles on a piece of parchment paper, leaving about ¼ inch between each circle. Turn the paper over and put it on a baking sheet (the drawn circles should show through).

In the bowl of an electric mixer on medium-low speed, beat the egg whites until frothy, about 30 seconds. Add the cream of tartar and increase the speed to high. In a slow, steady stream, add the sugar. Beat the whites until thick and glossy, 3 to 4 minutes. Fold in the vanilla extract. Fit a pastry bag with a ⅜-inch star tip and fill with the meringue.

Using the drawn circles on the parchment paper as a guide, fill the circles with piped stars so they are all touching, pulling up on the bag as you're squeezing out the meringue so that the stars end up about 2½ inches tall. You will end up with a solid disk (a crown) made up of piped stars. Repeat for the remaining 7 circles. Pipe the remaining meringue into small ½-inch-diameter stars. (These will be used in the rhubarb cream.) You will need about 40 small meringue stars.

Bake until the stars are dry, about 1 hour; they should be a little chewy in the middle. Remove the tray from the oven and let sit for 2 minutes. Remove the stars from the baking sheet and return the meringue crowns to the oven. Bake the crowns until dry, another 15 to 30 minutes. Let cool for 2 minutes and then remove the crowns with a spatula. Set aside until ready to use, or let cool completely and store in an airtight container for up to 1 day.

continued

To make the rhubarb cream: In a small, heavy saucepan, combine the rhubarb, sugar, and salt. Cook over medium-low heat, stirring frequently, until the rhubarb is soft, about 15 minutes. Let cool, then puree in a food processor. Cover and refrigerate until cold. In a deep bowl, beat the cream until very stiff but not grainy peaks form. Fold in the chilled rhubarb puree, cover, and refrigerate for up to 4 hours.

To make the strawberry sauce: Puree one-third of the strawberries in a small food processor with the sugar until smooth. Add a little more sugar if the strawberry sauce is not sweet enough. Refrigerate, covered, for up to 1 day.

To serve, cut the remaining strawberries into thin slices. Set aside. Fold the meringue stars into the rhubarb cream. Divide the rhubarb cream among 8 dessert bowls, being careful to distribute the meringue stars equally. Place the sliced strawberries in a fan decoration around the rhubarb cream (see photo, page 214). Top each serving with a meringue crown. Pour strawberry sauce around each meringue.

IMPROVISATIONS   Depending on the season, the rhubarb and strawberries can be replaced with whatever fresh fruit strikes your fancy. Berries are the obvious replacement, but you can also use combinations like ripe peaches and nectarines, or passion fruit, mangoes, and kiwis.

ADVANCE PREP   The rhubarb cream can be made 4 hours in advance. The meringue stars and crowns can be made ahead and stored in an airtight container at room temperature for up to 1 day if it's humid, longer if it isn't. The strawberry puree can also be made up to 1 day ahead.

SIMPLIFYING   You could omit the stars and piping bag and simply spoon the uncooked meringue into mounds, depressing the centers slightly. To serve, fill with the rhubarb cream. Drizzle the fruit puree around the plate and place the cut strawberries on top.

WINE NOTES   This dessert is a natural for Brachetto, the rare late-harvest wine from the Piedmont region of Italy. Not only will the delicate, spicy, floral flavors complement those in the dessert, but the unusual dusty pink color will make for a visual feast as well.

LEMON RAVIOLI *in* THAI CONSOMMÉ *with* BASIL *and* MANGO

Don Hall is Farallon's superb pastry chef, and this unusual and extremely popular dessert is a perfect example of his imaginative talent. For some time, he had been trying to come up with a sweet pasta but couldn't get one to work to his liking. One night, Farallon's dinner menu featured ravioli in a shiitake mushroom consommé and the idea struck him that a sweet broth might be the perfect vehicle for sweet ravioli. But how to keep it from being too sweet? The answer was lemongrass in the consommé and the ravioli as well. The sake also helps to cut some of the sweetness in the broth. It's an inspired combination, and this dessert is, of course, a perfect ending to an Asian-inspired meal, but it would also make a light and unexpected finish to an Italian dinner.

★ *CHEF'S TIP* *The sake and star anise are important in this recipe; in fact, all the components of the consommé are essential to the final dish. Kaffir lime leaves are widely available in Asian markets these days, often in the frozen section, and they lend a much more distinctive flavor than the lime zest.*

Makes 8 servings

THAI CONSOMMÉ:
1 stalk lemongrass, chopped

2 cups water

1¼ cups sugar

2 tablespoons chopped fresh ginger

2 kaffir lime leaves, or 1 teaspoon grated lime zest

½ vanilla bean, halved lengthwise

Zest of ½ orange, cut into strips

Zest of ½ lemon, cut into strips

1 star anise pod

½ cup sake

LEMON CURD:
5 large eggs

1 cup plus 2 tablespoons sugar

¾ cup fresh lemon juice

½ teaspoon grated lemon zest

6 tablespoons unsalted butter, at room temperature

32 round wonton wrappers

1 large mango, peeled and cut into ¼-inch dice

4 fresh basil leaves, cut into thin shreds

Preparation

To make the consommé: Remove the tough outer leaves from the lemongrass. Roughly chop the lower third of the stalk and cut the remainder into 1-inch pieces. In a medium saucepan, combine all the ingredients except the sake. Bring to a boil. Remove from heat, cover, and let sit until cool. Add the sake and stir. Pour into a bowl, cover, and refrigerate for at least 4 hours or overnight.

To make the lemon curd: In the top of a double boiler, whisk the eggs with ½ cup of the sugar. In a small bowl, whisk the lemon juice, zest, and remaining ½ cup plus 2 tablespoons sugar together. Gradually pour the lemon juice mixture into the egg mixture, whisking constantly to incorporate. Set over barely simmering water in the bottom of the double boiler and cook, stirring frequently, until the curd thickens enough to stick to the back of a spoon without sliding off. Remove from heat and strain through a fine-mesh sieve. Stir in the butter. Place plastic wrap directly on the surface of the curd to prevent a skin from forming. Refrigerate for at least 4 hours or up to 2 days.

continued

To make the ravioli: Lay 16 of the wonton wrappers on a work surface. Place 1 heaping teaspoonful of lemon curd in the center of each wonton and brush the edges of the wrappers with water. Top each with another wrapper and firmly press the edges to seal, creating a small round mound in the center as you push out as much air as possible from the ravioli. Store, loosly covered, in the refrigerator for up to 8 hours. In a medium saucepan of very lightly salted boiling water cook several ravioli at a time until tender, 4 to 5 minutes. Remove with a slotted spoon, let most of the water drain off, and divide evenly among shallow bowls.

To serve, strain the consommé through a fine-mesh sieve. Spoon about ¼ cup of consommé into each bowl of ravioli. Sprinkle the diced mango and basil over the top of the ravioli.

IMPROVISATION   *Freeze the consommé and serve it as a granita or sorbet.*

ADVANCE PREP   *The curd can be made up to 2 days in advance. The consommé can be made 1 day ahead and quickly heated for serving. The uncooked ravioli can be loosely covered and refrigerated for up to 8 hours, or frozen for up to 5 days. Shred the basil just before serving.*

SIMPLIFYING   *Buy a jar of high-quality lemon curd at a specialty foods market. Taste it before using and adjust the sweetness of the consommé accordingly.*

WINE NOTES   *A light-bodied dessert wine, one that is delicate and floral, is called for with this unique dish. Cambria Winery makes a late-harvest Viognier that will pair nicely, as do some producers in the small French appellation of Condrieu. The rare and expensive late-harvest Vendage Tardive and Sélection de Grain Noble wines of Alsace are also worth finding and drinking, because they can be phenomenal.*

BUYING *and* STORING FISH *and* SHELLFISH

SHOPPING FOR A FISHMONGER

The first step in finding good-quality seafood is finding a reliable and reputable source. Whether you get your seafood from a specialty market or a supermarket, your first step in procuring fresh seafood is to find a fishmonger you can trust. A good fishmonger is also someone who appreciates the delicate and highly perishable nature of the product he sells and is conscientious about how he handles the fish after he receives it. Here are a few things you should look for when shopping for your fishmonger:

The market should have a clean, seashore smell—it should *not* smell like fish. The display cases and the floors should be spotless. The fish should be stored on ice and never be sitting in liquid or under ice. Better yet, fish fillets should be displayed in perforated trays above ice. Many good fish markets have visible temperature-gauge cases that register 29° to 32°F. Raw products should not be displayed next to cooked products where there is risk of cross-contamination.

Find out how knowledgeable the counter people are. The first and most obvious question to ask is "Which fish is freshest?" but then ask where it's from and when it came in. Find out if they cut their own fillets. Has this fish been previously frozen, and if so, how long has it been thawed? .

SHOPPING FOR FISH

Fish that is less than fresh is *bad* fish and there's no disguising it. Though the fish market may be well run and the counter person knowledgeable, freshness can vary from piece to piece and fish to fish in the display case. First, you need to know which fish will work in your recipe—sometimes your first choice won't be the freshest and you'll need to know which kind to substitute. Second, you should choose your own fish, rather than letting the counter person choose it for you.

WHOLE FISH: This is where it's easiest to discern freshness. Begin your inspection visually: First, lift up the fish and look into the gills; they should be bright red and without mucus or slime. Then, look at the skin; it should be shiny, bright, translucent, and unwrinkled. Some books recommend checking the eyes for cloudiness, but this is not always a reliable indicator (walleyed-pike eyes, for exam-

ple, are always cloudy); in general, though, look for eyes that are bright and not sunken. After your fish has passed the visual test, next give it a sniff test. Sniff the gills and the body cavity, and if it smells the least bit fishy or has an ammonia odor, put it back.

FILLETS OR STEAKS: If you find a market where they'll cut fillets or steaks to order from a whole fish, consider yourself lucky; most fish sold retail is precut, and although there are some obvious signs of freshness to look for, this is where you have to trust your fishmonger. Look for flesh that is shiny, moist, and almost translucent, with no dry edges or gaps in the muscles. In white- or ivory-fleshed fish, there should be no pink, red, or brown spots that indicate spoilage or age. Dark-fleshed fish like tuna should not have any opalescence, or "rainbows," on the surface. Just as for whole fish, trust your nose: Ask for a whiff of the fillet before you buy it. In the display case, fillets and steaks should not be sitting in liquid, and though good fishmongers never sell prepackaged fish, if that's all you can find make sure there's no liquid in the package and still give it the sniff test—fishy fish will smell even through plastic wrap.

FROZEN FISH: While truly fresh fish should always be your first choice, fish that's been flash-frozen at the source and then stored without defrosting can often be of better quality than the stuff that's labeled as fresh and has been kept in a holding tank at sea for a few days. Today, huge factory ships can clean and flash-freeze whole fish or fillets within minutes of being caught. In fact, most sashimi-grade tuna (and nearly all shrimp) has been frozen this way. While flash-freezing can preserve seafood with little flavor loss or damage to cells, it's important in terms of its final texture that the fish is properly defrosted. The key is that it should be done slowly, *always in the refrigerator, overnight for small fillets or up to 36 hours for a large whole fish.* In a pinch, you can defrost small fillets under cold running water, making sure that the fish is well wrapped and then cooking it as soon as possible. When choosing frozen fish at the market, look for solidly frozen fish, preferably vacuum-packed, without ice crystals, dry edges, white spots, or opaque flesh that indicates freezer burn. If your seller has defrosted the fish, ask politely when it was taken out of the freezer. Keep in mind that some fish freeze better than others: *salmon, swordfish, tuna, mahi-mahi, halibut, snapper, and smelt, because of their firm, dense flesh, suffer little if flash-frozen. On a final note, if you're freezing fish at home, invest in a vacuum sealer and make sure that your freezer is not overcrowded and is 0°F or colder.*

SHELLFISH: *The general quality of shellfish in this country is quite high, making it much easier to shop for than fish. All shellfish at the retail and wholesale levels is purchased alive, frozen raw, or cooked. Here are a few general rules for judging the freshness of the different categories of shellfish: crustaceans (lobster, crab, and shrimp), mollusks (scallops, clams, mussels, and oysters), and cephalopods (squid).*

CRUSTACEANS: *Choose your live lobsters and crabs from tanks in fish markets that do a brisk business—if kept more than 1 or 2 weeks in a tank, lobsters can lose weight and even flavor. Look for the ones that are lively and feisty—avoid any that appear lethargic, with drooping tails or claws. Ask your fishmonger to pick one up to see if its legs are moving. If not, it still may be okay, but take a closer look—it should pass the sniff test and be plump, shiny, and moist.*

MOLLUSKS: *With the exception of scallops, which are almost always sold raw and shucked, mollusks should be cooked live. Clams and mussels should be tightly closed, and if open (no more than ¼ inch), a live one will close within a few seconds of being tapped on the shell with a knife. Oysters must always be tightly closed. All mollusks like to breathe and should never be stored or displayed in plastic bags.*

OYSTERS: *The most obvious source for live oysters is a good, reputable local fish market. A second option, if you live near one of the coasts, is an oyster farm that sells to the public. In the San Francisco Bay Area, some oyster farmers have stalls set up at the local farmers' markets. More important than where you purchase your oysters is to find out when the oysters were harvested and observe how they've been stored, unless of course you're buying them at an oyster farm.*

Once you've gotten your oysters home, check them first to make sure that they're all tightly closed. Unlike mussels and clams, an open oyster is a dead oyster. Arrange them so that they're sitting with the rounded (cup) side of the oyster down. Fresh oysters are swimming in their liquid inside their shells. If they're upside down, they're more likely to start losing liquid. Store them in a cold part of the refrigerator in an open container covered with a damp towel or seaweed—oysters frequently come packed in it and it's great for garnishing. One of the reasons oysters could be shipped to inland areas in the nineteenth century is that they're not as perishable as other shellfish. If a live oyster is plucked from the ocean and stored properly (kept very cold) it will live for 5 to 7 days. If serving them on the half shell, however, shuck them within 2 days, while they're still juicy and moist.*

CEPHALOPODS: *This category includes octopus, squid, and cuttlefish, but in this book we use only squid. In local coastal markets, you can find fresh squid, both cleaned and uncleaned, but most of what you'll find across the country has been cleaned, frozen, and thawed. Fresh squid has a mottled gray transparent "skin" that is sometimes removed when it's cleaned. Whether or not the skin has been removed, look for a shiny, creamy, white flesh and give the squid the sniff test; and you'll know in an instant if they're old.*

STORING YOUR CATCH

The final link in the freshness chain is from the market to your refrigerator, and unfortunately this is where the chain is most often broken. Many good and conscientious cooks, who have spent a great deal of energy in finding some truly fresh fish, toss their purchase in their cart, shop for another half hour, check out, and then run a few errands before they get home. Once they get home, it takes another fifteen minutes or so to unload the groceries, the phone rings, and before you know it, the fish that's been perfectly handled since the time it's been caught has been unrefrigerated for a couple of hours. Fish are more perishable than any other food, and the longer they're exposed to temperatures higher than 32°F the quicker they deteriorate. Here are a few things to do at home to keep your fish and shellfish as fresh as possible until you're ready to cook it:

At the store, buy your seafood right before you're ready to check out. Many fish sellers will pack your fish on ice if you ask. Make sure that live shellfish are in breathable containers, not plastic bags.

On a warm day, or if you anticipate getting stuck in traffic, bring a cooler and some frozen gel packs with you to keep your purchase cool in the car. Put the seafood in the passenger compartment (if it's air-conditioned), rather than the trunk.

Put the fish in the fridge as soon as you get home, but first unwrap it, rinse it under cold water, and pat it dry. Because most home refrigerators are somewhere around 40°F, and fish will keep longer if held at 32°F, store both whole fish and fillets on a bed of ice or a gel pack that has been loosely covered with plastic wrap (fish fillets and steaks in particular should never come in direct contact with either ice or gel packs). Refrigerators also tend to dry things out, so keep your catch covered with moist kitchen towels or in a high-humidity produce drawer. Lobster, shrimp, crab, and crayfish can be kept in a bowl or a roasting pan, covered with seaweed, damp newspapers, or moist towels. Clams and mussels should be stored in a bowl, loosely covered with a towel, never on ice or in water. Oysters are stored the same way, but first make sure that they're sitting round-side down, so that their liquor doesn't leak out.

How long any particular fish can be stored depends on how fresh it was when it was purchased. As a rule, I like to cook fish the same day I buy it, but 2 to 3 days for very fresh fish that's been kept between 29° and 32°F is probably okay. Change the ice and toweling every day, however, because bacteria can collect in the liquid. Fresh-killed or live crabs should be cooked on the day of purchase, lobster within 24 to 36 hours, and mussels and clams within 2 days. Oysters should be consumed within 5 days of purchase.

SAFETY ISSUES

Only 5 percent of all the food-borne illnesses reported each year are from eating tainted fish or shellfish. If you follow all the steps above for finding high-quality seafood, then store it properly, you should be safe. Seafood that's been purchased from a reliable source and properly handled can be as safe as poultry, beef, or eggs, and is actually good for us too, as it's low in saturated fat and rich in vitamins and minerals. Keep a few things in mind when you're buying, cooking, and eating fish and shellfish:

If you have a compromised immune system, are pregnant, elderly, or very young, I would advise you to never eat anything raw, except vegetables. Shellfish is riskier than fish, but raw shellfish is riskiest of all. The tomalley and roe of shellfish carry the highest concentration of toxins and should be avoided by anyone in a high-risk category.

Never eat any fish or shellfish that has an off odor. If in doubt, throw it out, and this rule applies to everything, not just seafood.

Always purchase your seafood from a reliable source, someone who sells only fish and shellfish that has either been inspected, or is from a wholesaler that he trusts. In particular, clams, mussels, and oysters are sold with inspection tags assuring that the waters where they were harvested were free of toxins, and a good dealer should be willing to show you these if you ask. I rarely eat any fish that's not caught commercially, other that what I've caught myself. That goes double for harvested wild shellfish. The safest oysters, clams, and mussels are harvested from farms.

Cross-contamination is the most frequent culprit when it comes to food-borne illness. No matter what you're working with—fish, meat, or poultry—make sure that you wash your hands and use clean cutting boards, then wash your hands, cutting boards, and all utensils with hot, soapy water after working with raw meat or fish. Never allow raw seafood to come in contact with anything already cooked, or something that's not going to be cooked.

For raw preparations like tartares or carpaccios, it's safest to use fish that has been frozen because freezing kills parasites and some bacteria. In fact, most of the fish used in sushi bars has been frozen. The acid marinades used in ceviche will also kill some bacteria. Never use freshwater fish in raw preparations; they're too prone to parasites.

Infinitesimally small amounts of certain pollutants and poisons are present in many kinds of fish. The key is not to eat only one kind of fish from any one area in great quantity. Vary your seafood diet, and you shouldn't need to be concerned.

FISH and SHELLFISH GLOSSARY

ATLANTIC COD

Atlantic cod has an unparalleled historic significance to the American fishing industry, but unfortunately, it has been over-fished and is becoming a rarity in seafood markets. Its cousin, the Pacific cod (often called "true cod") is almost identical except that its flesh is not as white. At Farallon, we prefer to buy Atlantic cod from off the coasts of Maine and Massachusetts in the colder months, because in warmer water its flesh is softer and less consistent. Cod is a very lean, medium-firm, mild-tasting, large-flaked fish. Other members of the cod family include pollock, hake, grenadier, and scrod (which is actually small cod). Good substitutes include lingcod (a member of the rockfish family), sea bass, halibut, and rockfish.

BASS

The term bass can be very confusing, because for years fishmongers have been incorrectly applying it (as a marketing ploy) to several species that are not from the bass family at all. At Farallon, we use several kinds of bass, all having a lean, moderately firm, small to medium flake and white flesh. Black sea bass from the Atlantic has a very fine flake and a richer flavor than other bass, in part because it feeds on shrimp and crabs, and it has a particularly delicious skin. Because of its relatively small size, averaging around 2 pounds, it's often sold whole, particularly on the East Coast. Wild striped bass is fished commercially and for sport. Its flavor can vary depending on where it was caught, but generally it is delicate and lean. We also use Chilean sea bass, which is actually not a bass, but a Patagonian toothfish—a perfect example of the marketing angle. This flavorful fish is difficult to find fresh because of the distance it travels, but is well worth seeking out for its moderately fat, firm-textured, and large-flaked flesh. Frozen Chilean sea bass is found in many stores, but if you've ever had it fresh, you'll notice the difference in depth of flavor. Another type of bass used in the Farallon kitchens is the excellent New Zealand bluenose sea bass (another marketing example— this one is really sea bream). It has an oilier texture and is darker in color than other sea bass. Substitute halibut, pike, snapper, tilapia, grouper, or cod.

CLAMS

There are several species of clams, but I prefer the hard-shell East Coast littlenecks and cherrystones for serving raw because they're the most tender and sweet. Atlantic littlenecks are small and run 7 to 10 per pound, while cherrystones are mid-sized and run 5 to 7 per pound. We also use mahogany clams from Maine, which are dark brown and mainly served raw. Occasionally, we'll use hard-shell Pacific Manilas, which are small and very sweet. Particularly when serving them raw, always buy them from a reputable source and make sure they've been inspected for safety. Clams to be cooked may be stored, covered with a towel, in the refrigerator for up to 2 or 3 days. If you're serving them raw, they shouldn't be kept longer than a few hours. Before using, discard any that have opened and don't close when you tap them with a knife. After cooking, discard any that haven't opened. Some cooks soak clams in saltwater to rid them of their grit, but it's not necessary for hard-shell clams; most purveyors soak before they reach the market.

COCKLES

Farmed New Zealand cockles have a greenish hue and are about the size of a quarter; they're similar to small clams in flavor and texture. Wash them thoroughly before cooking to rinse off sand and grit.

CRAB

Although I'm partial to our own West Coast Dungeness crab, at Farallon we serve several of the kinds that are available in North American waters: soft shell, Alaskan king, rock, peeky-toe (also known as Jonah), and stone crab.

Dungeness crab is found up and down the Pacific coast. These crabs, when fresh, can rival lobster for sweetness. They're fairly large, anywhere from 1¼ to 3½ pounds, and have a high proportion of meat to shell. Dungeness season generally runs from December to August, varying from year to year.

Blue crabs are found all along the Atlantic coast, and soft shells are actually blue crabs in the process of molting shells and growing new ones. Maryland fishermen are experts at determining when this process is about to take place. Blues are in season from May to November, and soft shells can be purchased fresh from May to August. Both are available frozen throughout the year.

We have, on occasion, been able to get fresh Alaskan king crabs, which resemble huge daddy longlegs. The meat is all in the legs and claws and is almost always sold cooked and frozen, in long split shells.

Rock and peeky-toe crabs, related to the Dungeness, are from the North Atlantic. The latter, mostly caught off the coast of Maine, was given its name by Rod Mitchell of Browne Trading Company, supposedly because of the black tips on its large claws, similar to those on stone crab claws.

Florida stone crab claws are an incredible treat: rich, firm, and sweet. These distinctive white claws with their black tips are sustainable: Fishermen remove one claw and then throw the crab back to regenerate another one. They're sold fresh from October to mid-May and frozen during the rest of the year. They are harvested in Texas until June.

All crab is sold either live or cooked, and if cooked it's either fresh or frozen, whole or as crabmeat. Crabmeat is sold frozen or vacuum-packed and may be labeled "lump" for large pieces or "flake" for small pieces. Sometimes blue-crab meat is called "flake and lump." If you purchase live crab, it should really be lively. Reject any that are sluggish. See page 233 for information on killing, cleaning, and cooking live crab.

CRAYFISH

Whether you call them crayfish or crawfish, these freshwater crustaceans that resemble little lobsters have long been popular in the South and particularly in Louisiana, where they are farmed in huge numbers. At Farallon, we use both the greenish-brown crayfish from the Sacramento Delta, not far from San Francisco, and the bright red Louisiana crayfish. Crayfish are sold live, frozen whole, or as fresh tail meat. I think that most of the flavor is in the head and shell and recommend that you buy them either live or fresh-cooked and whole whenever you can, then freeze the shells to make a crayfish essence. Since 7 pounds of whole cray-fish only yield about 1 pound of meat, making use of their shells is nothing short of thrifty. The Louisiana season runs from March to May and the California season from May to October. The meat from crayfish tails is great for chowders and bisques.

FROG'S LEGS

Most of the frog's legs we get are from Florida or Louisiana and are similar in taste and texture to chicken, but fresh, meaty ones can even be compared to lobster. Fresh frog's legs can be found in many seafood markets in those states and throughout the South, and also in areas of the country where there are large Asian communities. Many butchers and fish purveyors can order frozen ones for you, and they're quite acceptable. Frog's legs are sold like shrimp: by the count, meaning the number in a pound.

HALIBUT

We use three types of this versatile flatfish: California halibut, which is soft and lean; Alaskan halibut, which is larger, thicker, and fattier from being in cold waters; and we also buy Atlantic halibut, which is the best of the three because of its firm texture, but it's less available to us on the West Coast fresh. While halibut has a clean, neutral flavor that works well in a number of preparations, because it's so lean you need to take care as it has a tendency to become dry if overcooked. A great deal of the true halibut sold in fish markets is frozen, either as steaks or fillets, and is thawed before display. While frozen halibut can be very good, if you can find fresh (I mean really fresh) halibut, snatch it up—it's a wonderful fish. Halibut is lean, dense, firm, mild, and very white. Greenland turbot is often sold as halibut but is technically neither a turbot nor a halibut (it's another species of flounder). It's fattier than true halibut and has a denser flesh. Good substitutes include grouper, sea bass, monkfish, salmon, swordfish, shark, and turbot.

LOBSTER

At Farallon, we mostly use American lobster, also known as Maine lobster, both for its high ratio of meat to shell, and its sweet, predictable flavor. American lobster is found in the waters of the Atlantic, from Newfoundland to South Carolina, though most of what we get is still primarily from New England and also now Canada. The greatest numbers of lobsters are caught between July and November, and prices fluctuate greatly depending on availability and demand but are most economical during spring and summer. The quality of lobster caught during the summer, however, when they're molting, is less than ideal. These "soft-shell" lobsters, although sweet-tasting and less expensive, tend to be watery, making them good for salads and soups, and less suitable for grilling or roasting.

As a consumer, you have several options when buying lobster: mail-order live lobsters; live ones from tanks; cooked whole, fresh or frozen; and cooked meat, fresh or frozen. You can also get frozen uncooked lobster tails, but these are usually from spiny lobsters, and though convenient, I think they tend to be somewhat tough. My first choice would be to buy them mail order, because they come quickly and directly from the source; second would be from a tank in a busy fish market where the turnover is high—lobsters that live too long in tanks lose weight and will have less meat. When choosing a live lobster, make sure it's alive and feisty; it should be swinging its claws and flapping its tail when you pick it up. If the tail curls under or the claws sag, pass it over. Store your lobster in a cool spot for no more than a few hours. Although they're expensive, the good news is that very little of a lobster is inedible (just the stomach, intestines, and gills), and you can use the shells to make lobster essence, giving you a much bigger bang for your buck. Lobsters come in sizes: chickens (about 1 pound), quarters (1¼ pounds), halves (1½ pounds), and selects (1½ to 2½ pounds). Culls, which are lobsters that are missing one claw, come in all sizes and are a good bargain if you're using the lobster for a salad or bisque. See page 233 for information on killing, cleaning, and cooking live lobsters.

MONKFISH

Monkfish has been called the poor man's lobster because of its similarity to lobster in texture and flavor. Monkfish is lean and mild, and its flesh is dense and doesn't flake. It is probably the ugliest fish on the planet, with a huge head and gigantic mouth; its edible portion is in the tail. Sometimes, you'll find whole tails with their central bone running through the middle, but most often the tail is sold cut into two long fillets. When preparing monkfish for cooking, peel off any membrane (usually the fishmonger does this) so that the meat is fully visible. Monkfish is an incredibly versatile fish that can be grilled, sautéed, steamed, or braised, but because it's so lean it can become dry if overcooked. Substitutes for monkfish include cod, grouper, scallops, shrimp, tilefish, or—lobster.

MUSSELS

I use several kinds of mussels, the ones from Prince Edward Island being my favorites. We also get them from the Northwest, depending on the season and price. Although I love mussels—they're meatier than oysters and not as chewy as clams—I'm not a fan of the green-lipped New Zealand mussels; they're too big and flabby. Store mussels covered with a damp towel in the refrigerator for up to 24 hours, but don't put them on ice, submerge them in water, or enclose them in plastic; mussels need to breathe and will die if too cold. Like clams, live mussels will close when tapped with a knife. Before cooking, use a paring knife to cut off the "beard," or fibrous mass, that protrudes from the shell. After cooking, discard any mussels that don't open. A word of caution: Mussels are more prone to pollution and toxic poisons than other bivalves, so I recommend that you buy those that have been commercially cultured and harvested. Wild mussels should only be gathered at times when local health authorities give you a green light. Serving raw mussels is a risky business.

ONAGA

See Snapper.

OYSTERS

If you're a novice purchaser of raw oysters, whether in a restaurant or at the market, and you're confused, don't feel bad. Even I get confused sometimes. Generally, oysters are named for the area where they're grown, but sometimes they're named for their producers, which makes it even more confusing. Blue Points, Wellfleets, Chincoteagues, Apalachicolas, Malpeques, Hama-Hamas, Kumamotos, Hog Islands, Colchesters—the list goes on. But although there are about ten species of oysters that are marketed in volume worldwide, there are only five kinds that are harvested off North American shores. Because the water conditions vary from region to region, oysters develop distinctive and unique flavors indicative of the areas where they grow and feed. Learning about oysters is a lot like learning about wine. If you're just beginning to become acquainted with oysters, it's less important to try to memorize all those different names than to learn about the five common oyster species and their general characteristics. Once you've familiarized yourself with the five species, you can start to taste them by region, say Blue Points or Malpeques from the Atlantic Coast, or Hog Island Sweetwaters or Kumamotos from the West Coast. Pretty soon, you'll be able to identify the ones you prefer. All oysters vary on a scale from very salty to sweet. The colder the water, the saltier the oyster, so as a general rule the oysters that come from northern waters will be briny and crisp, and oysters from southern and warmer waters will be sweeter and softer.

The five species of North American oysters are divided into whether they're from the East or West Coast:

PACIFIC OYSTERS
Crassostrea gigas: *Sweet and tender, these are the most widely cultivated of oyster species, from Alaska to California. They originated in Japan, and are sometimes referred to as Japonaise.*

Ostrea lurida, *or Olympia oysters: Crisp, briny, and slightly metallic, these super-tiny oysters from Puget Sound are the only species that is native to the West Coast. Most are grown in Washington, although some come from California and Oregon.*

Crassostrea sikamea, *or Kumamoto Oysters: Tender, fruity, and mild, this is another species of native Japanese oyster that is cultivated on the Pacific Coast. Some people lump these with the* C. gigas *oysters because of their Japanese origins, but they're actually a separate species.*

ATLANTIC OYSTERS
Crassostrea virginica: *Sweet, with a kind of vegetable flavor, this is the oyster species that most Americans are familiar with, the eastern oyster found from Canada to the Gulf of Mexico. The well-known Blue Points are* C. virginica.

EUROPEAN FLATS
Ostrea edulis: *Very briny, metallic, and rich, this oyster is recognizable by its unique shape: round, flat, and shallow. This is the same species of oyster as the famous Belons of France, and they're farmed in America on both the East and West Coasts.*

PERIWINKLES
Periwinkles are small muscles that look like miniature snails and come from the open ocean. We buy periwinkles from Cape Cod to be steamed and served on the Iced Atlantic and Pacific Shellfish Indulgence platter.

ROUGET
This prized Mediterranean fish is hard to come by in America, but it can often be found in Asian markets in New York and California. Rouget is a member of the goatfish family (talk about weird names) and is also called a red mullet. However, the mullet that is fished commercially in the Gulf and Southern Atlantic is an entirely different species. Rouget is a beautiful, bright red small fish that's moderately flavored, with firm but lean meat. Good substitutes are John Dory, red snapper, rockfish, croaker, and porgy.

SALMON
Salmon is probably the most familiar and popular fish in America, if not the world. There was a time when salmon was available only seasonally (in the spring and summer) or out of a can, but now, due to advanced farming techniques, high-quality fresh salmon is available year-round. There are primarily six kinds of salmon sold in American markets: one from the Atlantic, which is almost entirely farmed, and five from the Pacific, which are both farmed and wild. Their flavor and fat content vary according to season and where the salmon come from, but for consistency and high quality, we mainly buy Atlantic salmon, particularly for our own smoked salmon and gravlax. I also like to serve wild Pacific salmon when it's in season, from May to September, mainly as fillets and either pan-roasted or grilled. Salmon generally has a high fat content, flesh that varies from almost white to deep rosy red, and a delicate to full flavor. It's sold whole, in sections without heads or tails, cut into steaks, or as skin-on or skinless fillets.

SALT COD
Salt-cured Atlantic cod has been a staple food in Scandinavian and Mediterranean cultures for years, and although modern refrigeration has made this preservation process obsolete, I still love what the salt cure does to the flavor and texture of fish. Commercial salt cod has become a rather

expensive delicacy today. It can be found in supermarkets in little wooden boxes or as sides from whole fish in specialty ethnic delis, but quality varies wildly; some are drier and saltier than others. Salt cod needs to be rehydrated and soaked to remove excess salt before using. Plan on at least an 8-hour soak (and often as many as 24 to 36 hours), changing the water 4 or 5 times, to remove excess salt from commercially dried salt cod.

SEA URCHIN

The edible golden-orange meat that rests inside sea urchin shells is a wonderful gift from the sea, and only recently appreciated in the United States due to its popularity in sushi bars. The Japanese have long recognized that sea urchin meat, *uni* in Japanese, and sometimes called sea urchin roe, coral, or tongue, is a delicacy, briny and buttery rich. They vary in size between the Atlantic and Pacific coasts: East Coast urchins tend to be smaller—about the size of a tennis ball—compared to the larger California urchins, which are more like small softballs. Many Japanese food stores carry both whole fresh urchins and fresh or frozen roe, which we use for sauces and vinaigrettes.

SCALLOPS

Their sweet flavor and lush texture is what makes these bivalves so unique and so prized. Unfortunately, many consumers know only the ones that have been frozen or treated with preservatives and don't realize how truly wonderful they can be. At Farallon, we buy large sea scallops (my favorites are those from George's Bank, a huge reef many miles off the coast of Maine), and bay scallops from Nantucket Bay, which are in season between October and February. If you're on the East Coast, you can sometimes find live scallops in the shell—a real treasure—and often they'll have a roe sac that can be used as garnish, in sauces, or eaten along with the scallop. The best scallops are those that are labeled either "diver" or "day-boat," meaning that they're hand-plucked from the ocean by divers and then brought in on boats that go out and return on the same day. But the most important thing to look for when purchasing scallops is that they're "dry-packed," meaning that they're not treated with preservatives to prevent moisture loss and spoilage. It's difficult to distinguish dry-packed scallops by

appearance alone, and my best advice is to buy them from a respected source and ask if the scallops have been treated with phosphates (by law, their packing containers must state this information). Generally, dry-packed scallops are translucent, somewhat dull, and tend to stick together. The best way to tell is when you get them home: Untreated scallops will not shrink and will develop a nice caramelized crust when they're sautéed or grilled over high heat. All fresh scallops are extremely perishable; refrigerate them immediately after purchase, and use them within 24 hours.

SHRIMP

There are so many kinds of shrimp that they're worth an entire book (and there are several good ones out there). In brief overview, prawns and shrimp (the terms are used interchangeably) are sold by the "count," meaning the number per pound, and small shelled shrimp (bay shrimp) are sold by the pound. There are two classifications of shrimp, whether farmed or wild: warm-water shrimp and cold-water shrimp, and both kinds are sold either raw or cooked and shelled or unshelled. Most shrimp sold in the United States is imported and frozen, but occasionally you can get fresh shrimp if you live near where they're harvested. Also, fresh, live shrimp can sometimes be purchased from tanks in Asian fish markets. At Farallon, we buy white or pink shrimp from Florida and the Gulf of Mexico for all-purpose use, like mousses, stews, and soups. We also buy super-large (4-count) frozen tiger prawns, fresh spot prawns from various points on the West Coast and Hawaii, and rock shrimp from Florida. The spot prawns are a real treat: they have a sweet lobsterlike meat and often have roe attached. Rock shrimp have delicious meat, also, and we use them mainly in salads and soups. When purchasing shrimp, keep in mind that 99 percent of what you're going to find has been flash-frozen on the boat (also called IQF, or individually quick frozen), either in five-pound blocks or individually. Because defrosted shrimp deteriorate rapidly, I recommend that you pass on the ones that have been thawed—no telling how long they've been sitting in that display case, although you can always ask. If you're lucky enough to find whole shrimp with their heads still attached, it's much easier to determine freshness (the heads are first to go bad); any black spots are signs of deterioration. Also, if there's any whiff of ammonia, return the shrimp to your purveyor. I never, ever, buy shrimp that have been cooked and shelled (with the exception of rock and bay shrimp). If they are shelled, which isn't much of a time-saver anyway, they're also likely to have lost moisture and will turn to rubber when cooked.

SKATE

Skate has long been appreciated in Europe for its sweet flavor and gelatinous meat that resembles scallops, but it has only recently become popular here. A relative of the shark, the skate is a ray, and its edible part is in the wings. Skate is caught off both coasts and is primarily a byproduct of other commercial catches because it's been so undervalued. Skate wings yield 2 flat, triangular fillets on either side of cartilaginous ribs. We buy both Pacific and Atlantic skate year-round, but I tend to like the Pacific a little better—the fillets are larger and thicker. When purchasing skate, make sure that you buy skinned fillets, because you'll curse me forever if you have to skin your own. See page 134 for more tips on buying and cooking skate.

SNAPPER

Except for bass, I don't think there's a name that is more confusing in the fish world than snapper. In the United States, most people are familiar with "true" red snapper from the Gulf and Southern Atlantic waters, which is a delicious fish, distinctively sweet flavored, with a medium-firm texture and a small-to-large white flake. There are actually about 250 species of reef fish that are called snapper. The Pacific red snapper is really a rockfish and, though similar, is nothing like true red snapper. Much of what is passed off as red snapper is tasty, but the real stuff commands a high price and you should always ask where it's from. We use a lot of onaga, which is a Hawaiian red snapper that is great for serving raw. True red snapper is a beautiful red fish with red fins, about 4 to 6 pounds, and is often sold whole or as skin-on fillets. At the restaurant, we also get yellowtail snapper from Florida, which is yellow with a pinkish stripe; they average 1 to 3 pounds and are great for frying whole.

SPANISH MACKEREL

This oily fish has a strong, distinct taste similar to that of anchovies or sardines. We use Spanish mackerel almost exclusively, because they're the mildest and least oily of the species. Mackerel is a fish that migrates, so they're not readily or consistently available; Spanish mackerel is available mostly from December to March. We occasionally use Atlantic mackerel, which is available year-round, but rarely do we use the strong-flavored Pacific, or jack, mackerel. If you do get Pacific mackerel, be aware that they have a row of small bones on their exterior that must be removed either before or after cooking. Mackerel is a great fish for pickling and serving raw in sashimi or tartare, but because of their high oil content, they deteriorate rapidly, so use them soon after purchase.

SQUID

Squid have a sweet flavor and firm, chewy texture. While the ubiquitous fried calamari has made legions of American bar-and-grill patrons fans of this odd-looking cephalopod, few really appreciate squid for its incredible culinary versatility and great value. For the cook, the biggest negative about squid, and perhaps the reason it's taken so long for it to become popular, is that it is a pain in the neck to clean. Today, most of the squid we get is already cleaned. Squid is caught year-round on both the Atlantic and Pacific Coasts, although about 75 percent of the squid sold nationwide are from California, Monterey Bay in particular. At the restaurant, we're able to get fresh squid from Monterey, but most squid sold retail has been frozen, either whole or as cleaned bodies and tentacles. Fortunately, squid, like shrimp, freezes well; freezing even seems to break down the fibers, making them a little less chewy. But unfortunately, unlike shrimp, squid is not sold by size, so you have to take what you can get. Good-quality cleaned squid, even if thawed, will be firm and shiny, and the outer membrane will be gray rather than purple-pink. The flesh should be white, with no signs of yellow. If the squid is fresh, take a whiff—there shouldn't be even a slight smell of ammonia. Store squid, covered and refrigerated, for up to 2 days.

TILEFISH

Tilefish are found primarily in very deep waters off the Atlantic Coast from Nova Scotia to the Gulf of Mexico. They average 6 to 8 pounds and are sold primarily as fillets or steaks. Buy Atlantic tilefish when you're lucky enough to find it, but beware: The Pacific tilefish, or ocean whitefish as it is sometimes called, is inferior and can have a bitter taste. Substitute cod, sea bass, grouper, halibut, or rockfish instead. The mild flavor of tilefish is similar to that of lobster or perch, and its very low fat content and moderately firm flesh makes it good for sautéing or braising.

TUNA

Fresh tuna has become one of the more popular fish in restaurants today. Of the several different kinds of tuna (the largest member of the mackerel family), Farallon uses primarily bluefin, yellowfin (also called *ahi* or *hamachi*), and bigeye. Tuna is caught in both the Atlantic and Pacific Oceans; these big, strong, muscular fish winter in southern waters and are found in northern waters from late spring to fall, but are pretty much available year-round. All tuna is dense, meaty, and full flavored, and varies from lean to moderately fat, with bluefin being the fattiest. Most of the tuna for sale in retail markets is already cut into steaks from the large loin, although some of the better purveyors will slice them to order for you. A fresh tuna fillet will be translucent and have a subtle surface sheen with no brown color or rainbow opalescence. Because tuna flesh deteriorates when exposed to air, good markets often wrap the steaks in plastic. The darker part of the muscle should be cut off and discarded, because it has an unpleasant bitterness when cooked. Tuna is one fish that freezes well, and in fact much of the sashimi-grade tuna has been flash-frozen after being cleaned and cut into loins.

TURBOT

There are two types of turbot: the good kind and the imposters. The good kind is caught wild in Europe and is also farmed in Chile. The imposters are usually the so-called Greenland turbot, which is neither a turbot nor a halibut but a large flounder, and halibut, which is a wonderful fish but not anything close to turbot, either in flavor or texture. Turbot is an exceptional fish with a firm texture, a very sweet flesh, and gelatinous bones (which make a great stock). Farmed turbots from South America have a milder flavor than those from Europe, and wild ones from Europe have a delicate, distinct flavor, are more expensive, and are very difficult to get (see Resources, page 249). You can purchase whole turbot (make sure you save the bones for stock) or fillets, but make sure that if you buy fillets they've been skinned. If they're not, you can pull off the skin after they've been cooked.

WALLEYED PIKE

Here's a good example of where fish nomenclature gets really confusing. The walleyed pike is actually a member of the perch family, and the pike is another species entirely. Walleye is also called pike-perch, yellow pike, and of course walleyed pike. They're named for their large, bulging eyes and can weigh as much as 20 pounds, though they average from 2 to 5 pounds. This freshwater fish from the Great Lakes has a delicate, sweet flavor, a low fat content, and a very fine flake. They're available fall through spring; because they swim deeper in summer, they're harder to catch then. Small ones are sold whole, and fillets are sold both skin-on and skinless. Walleyed pike are unique in that their huge eyes are always cloudy, so ignore this freshness indicator if you're purchasing your pike whole. Good substitutes for walleyed pike are bass (striped or freshwater), halibut, pike (the real kind), rockfish, or snapper.

BASIC TECHNIQUES *and* RECIPES

In this chapter, you'll find some of the basic recipes and techniques you'll need to prepare the dishes in this book. I say "some of," because I think there's nothing more annoying than a cookbook where you have to turn to six other recipes to finish a dish. So we've tried to include as many "sub-recipes" as possible within the text of the dishes themselves. The recipes that we've gathered here are the ones that we refer to frequently or that are quite lengthy, like fish stock or duck prosciutto, for instance.

Basic Techniques

CUTTING BRUNOISE

This is the French term for ⅛-inch-diced vegetables. We use various combinations of tiny diced celery, onions, carrots, celery root, fennel, and parsnips sautéed in butter and served as an accompaniment to other dishes. You can, of course, cut the vegetables by hand with a sharp knife. A faster method is to first cut them into ⅛-inch-thick slices on a Japanese mandoline, then stack the slices and cut them into julienne strips, then cut the strips crosswise into ⅛-inch cubes. If using a French mandoline, use the special julienne blade, then cut into brunoise. A food processor can be used to finely chop the harder vegetables like carrots and celery, but it tends to turn onions into a puree, so I recommend that you always do onions by hand.

KILLING, CLEANING, AND COOKING CRAB

To kill the crab, turn it on its back and, keeping your fingers safely away from the claws, insert the point of a sharp chef's knife in a spot on its underside about 1 inch from the eyes. Quickly push downward with the knife, cutting through the eyes, then pull off and discard the triangular belly flap. Turn the crab over and, holding it by the legs, start from the rear of the crab and pull firmly to lift off the top shell. Remove the feathery gills and all the soft tissue from the inside. Rinse the crab well under running water. Cut the crab through the body into quarters, with 2 legs to each quarter. To cook the crab, bring a stockpot of cold, salted water to a boil over high heat. Drop the crabs into the boiling water and reduce heat to low. Simmer, covered, 15 to 20 minutes for up to 5 pounds live Dungeness, less for smaller crabs, until the shell is bright orange in color

and the flesh opaque throughout. Remove from water and put in an ice-water bath for several minutes. Drain, pat dry, and refrigerate until needed.

KILLING, CLEANING, AND COOKING LOBSTER

I think the least offensive way for a squeamish home cook to kill a live crustacean is by the cold-water method. To parboil a 1- to 1½-pound lobster, put it in a stockpot of cold, salted water, cover, and bring to a boil over high heat. Remove the lobster just as the shell turns pink, 1 or 2 minutes after the water boils. To cook the lobster completely, leave it in the boiling water for 8 to 10 minutes. This method is said to kill the lobsters as painlessly as possible.

To clean the cooked lobsters for the meat, set out 3 medium bowls and have a towel and a nutcracker or small sauté pan or skillet handy to break the shells. Begin by pulling the legs from the lobster over the first bowl to catch all the liquid, then the tails and head. Discard the mud sac inside the head, as well as the gills and lungs. Crack the tail and claws and put all the shells in the second bowl. Reserve the lobster meat and keep refrigerated until ready to use.

To kill and prepare a lobster for grilling: On a folded kitchen towel using a very sharp knife, cut the live lobster in half lengthwise, placing the tip of the knife in the middle of the head and bringing it down through the tail. Turn the lobster around and cut the rest of the head in half lengthwise. Separate the sides. Discard the brown-green mud sac inside the head and the white feathery gills and lungs. Keep any bright green coral with the liquid and reserve for lobster essence (page 245). Rinse under cold running water and pat dry.

PEELING AND SEEDING TOMATOES

Cut an X shape into the bottom of each tomato (not the stem end) using a sharp paring knife. Drop the tomatoes, 2 at a time, into a large pot of rapidly boiling water for 10 to 30 seconds, depending on the ripeness of the tomatoes (test one first to see if the skin peels easily but the flesh has not cooked too much and become mealy). Using a slotted spoon, transfer to a bowl of ice water. Using the X marks as your starting point, gently peel off the skin. Cut the stem end off and gently squeeze the seeds out of the tomato and discard. Rinse.

PEELING AND SEGMENTING CITRUS FRUIT

With a sharp paring knife, cut off the top and the bottom of the fruit down to the flesh. Stand the fruit up on one end and, working with slow, even stokes, cut off the peel down to the flesh from top to bottom, keeping as close to the shape of the fruit as possible. Trim away any remaining white pith. Hold the fruit over a small bowl with one hand and, with the knife in the other, carefully cut the segments from between the membranes using an angled "V" cut. Remove any seeds.

SHUCKING CLAMS

Shucking a clam is like shucking an oyster. Using a towel to protect your hands, insert the tip of an oyster knife into the edge of the clam and wiggle it until you feel the shells begin to pop apart. Run the blade around the perimeter of the shells to separate completely, then scrape the clam from the top shell into the bottom one, trying to keep as much liquor in the shell as possible. Scrape the meat to detach it from the bottom shell before serving.

SHUCKING AND SERVING OYSTERS

While it takes some practice to get the hang of it, shucking an oyster is much easier to do than to describe. Remember that during the whole process you always want to keep the oysters as flat as possible to prevent the liquor from spilling out. If you're right-handed, put the oyster on the left side of your work surface, wrapped in a heavy kitchen towel. Hold the oyster with your left hand, wrapped in the towel, with the flat side of the oyster up, the deeper, rounded (cup) side down, and the hinged, or pointy, end toward your right hand. Insert an oyster knife into the hinge, trying to find the little crevice where the top and bottom shells are attached. Once you locate the spot where you can insert the knife, push it in with a little forward pressure and twist the knife until you can feel a little "pop." That means that the top and bottom shells have separated. Without removing the knife, run it against and parallel to the top shell to cut the muscle that connects the oyster to its shell. After you've shucked your oyster, take a whiff. Bad oysters smell bad and need no further description. If you've opened it properly, with the least amount of spillage, your oyster should be swimming in a clear, not milky, white liquid. The longer an oyster is out of water, the drier it gets. Shriveled or dry oysters in the shell should be discarded.

Discard the top shell, then take the knife and run it under the oyster to separate it from its bottom muscle. With your finger, carefully wipe away any broken pieces or bits of shell. Place the opened oysters, still in their bottom shells and surrounded by their liquor, on a platter of crushed ice or rock salt and refrigerate until serving time.

Shucked oysters can also be purchased by the pound or in containers, and here on the West Coast they're usually sold in 10-ounce jars. Shucked and jarred oysters are okay for certain cooked preparations, like stews or chowders.

To serve oysters raw, put them on a platter with a few lemon wedges, figuring on about 6 oysters per person for an appetizer or first course. If you want to go a little further, make a mignonette sauce. This classic French sauce is a combination of crushed black pepper with wine vinegar and minced shallots. At Farallon, we serve oysters two ways: with or without caviar. Either way, we serve a mignonette sauce made with Champagne vinegar and also put lemon wedges on the platter. If you really want to educate yourself about the different flavors of oysters, however, I highly recommend that you taste your oysters au naturel. If you're feeling ambitious and you have access to a variety of oysters, think about hosting an oyster-tasting party. Put out the different kinds, on different platters, and compare the oysters side by side. Have some oyster crackers to munch on between gulps, and ask your guests to comment on the flavors of the different oysters. It's great fun and also a fantastic way to educate your own oyster palate.

TOASTING NUTS, SEEDS, AND SPICES

To extract the full flavor from many nuts, seeds, and spices like saffron and cardamom, I recommend toasting them. In a small sauté pan or skillet over medium heat, toast the nuts, seeds, or spice until fragrant, stirring constantly. Immediately turn out onto a plate to cool. Alternatively, place on a baking sheet and toast in a preheated 350°F oven for 2 minutes for saffron and most seeds, about 5 minutes for pine nuts, and up to 8 minutes for almonds, walnuts, and pecans. Watch carefully for burning.

BRIOCHE

Makes about 5 pounds dough, or two 9-by-5-inch loaves

1 teaspoon active dry yeast
½ cup warm (105° to 115°F) water
3 tablespoons sugar
6 eggs, at room temperature
5 cups unbleached all-purpose flour
2 tablespoons kosher salt
1 cup (2 sticks) plus 6 tablespoons unsalted butter,
   cut into tablespoon-sized pieces, at room temperature

In the bowl of a heavy-duty mixer fitted with the paddle, combine the yeast and water. Stir in the sugar and let stand until the yeast is dissolved and the mixture has thickened, about 10 minutes.

On medium-low speed, add the eggs, one at a time. Add the flour and salt in 2 batches and continue to mix on medium-low until the flour is completely incorporated. Change to the dough hook and, on low speed, gradually add the butter, 1 piece at time. When all of the butter has been incorporated, increase the speed to medium and knead until the butter has been absorbed and a nice, soft dough has formed around the hook, about 5 minutes. Put the dough in a large bowl and cover with plastic. Let rise in a warm place until doubled in volume, about 2 hours, or let rise overnight in the refrigerator. Punch the dough down and roll out as instructed in the recipe or divide into 2 greased 9-by-5-inch loaf pans and let rise again in a warm place until doubled, about 2 hours. Bake the loaves in a preheated 350°F oven until golden, about 30 minutes.

CANDIED ORANGE SLICES

We use these as a garnish for citrus desserts, like the Blood-Orange Gratins on page 188. Using a mandoline or very sharp slicing knife, cut several oranges into paper-thin crosswise slices and spread them out in one layer on a rimmed baking sheet lined with a lightly oiled parchment paper. Heat 1 cup sugar syrup (page 246) until hot, then pour the hot syrup over the orange slices and let sit for a few minutes to cook and slightly soften. Pour off any extra syrup and put the pan in a preheated 250°F oven to dry the slices for about 2 hours. Remove from the oven. If you'd like to curve the slices as in the photo on page 189, place them on a rolling pin or wine bottle while still warm. Let cool and harden, then store in a covered container for up to 2 weeks.

CLARIFYING BUTTER

There are two ways to make clarified butter, one to use when making a large amount of butter, and the other when only a small amount is needed. For a large amount: Cut 2 cups (4 sticks) of butter or more into cubes and place them in a medium saucepan over very low heat. Let the butter melt on the lowest heat setting or over a pilot light for 2 to 4 hours, or until the milk solids have fallen to the bottom. With a spoon, carefully skim any of the crusty white foam off the top and discard, then gently ladle out all of the clear butterfat without disturbing the milk solids on the bottom. When all the liquid fat has been removed, discard the solids on the bottom of the saucepan. For a small amount: put 1 cup (2 sticks) of butter in a small saucepan and melt over low heat. Increase heat to medium and boil until the solids begin to turn golden, 10 to 15 minutes. Let cool slightly, then strain through a fine-mesh sieve lined with a double layer of cheesecloth or a coffee filter, discarding the solids. The clarified butter can be cooled and refrigerated for up to 2 days or frozen for up to 3 months.

CONSOMMÉ

Makes about 4 cups

The process of clarifying a stock to produce a sparkling-clear, greaseless broth is one of the miracles of the kitchen, and not as difficult as you might think. Consommé may be made with any kind of base stock, substituting equal amounts of ground meat, such as chicken, for instance, if you're making chicken consommé, for the fish in the following recipe. You can also use only egg whites, but the consommé will be less flavorful. It is important to remember that you must begin with *cold* stock, so make a stock, then chill it before clarifying it. Never allow the stock to boil once you've added the protein and vegetable mixture; bring it to a slow simmer.

1 cup egg whites (about 8 to 10 large eggs)
1½ pounds pike (or other white-fleshed fish) fillets, cut into chunks
2 cups coarsely chopped carrots
2 cups coarsely chopped onions
2 cups coarsely chopped celery
1 teaspoon freshly ground pepper
1 tablespoon chopped fresh tarragon (optional)
4 quarts cold fish stock (page 243) or shellfish stock (page 244)

In a food processor, combine the egg whites, fish, carrots, onions, and celery. Puree until the mixture begins to form a ball on the blade, about 30 seconds. Add the pepper and the tarragon, if using, and pulse for a few more seconds just to combine. Put the cold stock in a large saucepan and whisk in the egg white mixture. Over medium heat, bring the liquid to a low simmer, stirring occasionally. As soon as the mixture of proteins, called a "raft," begins to coagulate, use a ladle or spoon to break a hole in the raft that's big enough for you to see the liquid below (don't disturb the raft after this point). Maintain the stock at a low simmer until it looks clear, about 45 minutes. Remove from heat, let cool slightly, and strain through a fine-mesh sieve lined with a double layer of cheesecloth, being careful to not disturb the raft, which might cloud the stock.

CORNMEAL BLINI

Serves 8 to 16, depending on size of blini

1 cup yellow cornmeal
1½ cups boiling water
2 eggs
1 cup milk
½ teaspoon kosher salt
½ cup unbleached all-purpose flour
2 tablespoons unsalted butter, melted
Clarified butter (see page 237) for frying

Put the cornmeal in a medium bowl. Pour the boiling water over the cornmeal, cover with plastic wrap, and set in a warm place until the water has been absorbed, 10 to 20 minutes. Using a whisk, beat in the eggs, one at a time, then gradually stir in the milk. Add the salt, flour, and melted butter. Whisk until the mixture is fairly smooth. If the batter is too thick, whisk in a little more milk until it's the consistency of heavy cream.

To cook the blini: Heat an 8-inch nonstick crepe pan over medium-high heat until a drop of water dances over the surface without evaporating instantly. Add 1 teaspoon clarified butter to the pan, heat for a few seconds, then ladle in a scant ¼ cup batter and tilt to cover the bottom of the pan. Cook until bubbles begin to appear on the surface and the edges start to look a little dry, about 1 minute. Gently lift the pancake with a spatula to see if the underside is lightly brown. Flip the pancake over and cook for about 1 minute longer on the other side. Transfer to a 250°F oven to keep warm while making the other blini.

COURT BOUILLON
Makes about 8 cups

A traditional court bouillon, sometimes confused with stock, is a flavorful and aromatic broth used for poaching fish, shellfish, or vegetables. It keeps in the refrigerator for a few days, or can be frozen for months. You can poach food in it several times and it becomes more flavorful with each use (although oily fish will make it too strong). Once it's been used for poaching, it can stand in for fish stock in other recipes. Court bouillon should include some acid, and many chefs like to add vinegar, but I prefer the subtler flavor of white wine with a little kick of lemon juice added at the end.

½ large onion, chopped
1 carrot, peeled and chopped
1 small leek, white part only,
    thinly sliced crosswise and rinsed well
1 small stalk celery, chopped
1 bay leaf
1 sprig thyme
2 sprigs parsley
2 teaspoons kosher salt
10 black peppercorns
8 cups water
1 cup dry white wine
Fresh lemon juice to taste

In a large saucepan, combine all the ingredients except the lemon juice. Bring to a boil over high heat, then reduce heat and simmer for 15 to 20 minutes. Taste for seasoning—it should be quite flavorful—and add lemon juice as desired. Strain through a medium-mesh sieve into a bowl, discard the solids, and reserve the liquid. Let cool. Refrigerate for up to 3 days, or freeze for up to 4 months. Experiment with other herbs; ginger, garlic, and lemongrass, for example, would be good additions if using this in an Asian dish.

CRÈME ANGLAISE
Makes 1½ cups

5 large egg yolks
1½ tablespoons sugar
Pinch kosher salt
1½ cups whole milk
½ vanilla bean, halved lengthwise, or 1 teaspoon vanilla extract

In a medium bowl, whisk the eggs, sugar, and salt together. Pour the milk into a medium, heavy saucepan. If using the vanilla bean, scoop out the seeds and add with the pod to the milk. Heat over medium-high heat until bubbles form around the edges of the pan. Gradually whisk the hot milk into the egg mixture. Return the milk mixture to the saucepan and cook over low heat, stirring constantly until the custard coats the back of a spoon and a clean track remains when a finger is drawn through (160°F on an instant thermometer). Stir in the vanilla extract, if using. Put the saucepan in a large bowl of ice water and stir frequently until the crème anglaise has cooled. Strain through a fine-mesh sieve. Transfer to a covered container and refrigerate for at least 2 hours to chill or for up to 1 day.

CRÈME FRAÎCHE
Makes about 3 cups

Similar in texture and taste to sour cream, crème fraîche has a higher butterfat content, which makes it more rich and velvety. It can be used in place of sour cream for added character and depth and will take a slightly higher temperature without breaking, but should still never be boiled. There are many excellent brands available, though they are expensive. A great alternative is to make your own.

1½ cups heavy cream (not ultrapasteurized)
1 cup sour cream
½ cup buttermilk

Combine all the ingredients and refrigerate, covered, until thickened, about 1 week. As it ages, the crème fraîche will give off a watery liquid; either stir it back in or spoon it out and discard. Use within 1 week.

DRIED BREAD CRUMBS
Put slices of day-old bread (with or without crusts) on a baking sheet in a 200°F (or lowest setting) oven until completely dry, 1 to 2 hours. Remove and let cool completely. Break into large pieces and pulse in a blender or food processor until the bread is broken into either coarse or fine crumbs, as desired.

DUCK PROSCIUTTO
At Farallon, we purchase two kinds of fresh duck from local suppliers: Muscovy and Mulard. Most of the ducks that are sold in supermarkets across the country are the common Long Island or Pekin ducks, which are relatively small with a high proportion of fat. Muscovy ducks, originally from South American jungles, are lean and flavorful but not gamey. Mulards, a sterile cross between Muscovy and Pekin, are bred in the United States primarily for foie gras, but have large breasts (called *magrets* in French). For this recipe, it's important to use a Muscovy or Mulard because of their larger, meatier breasts; the process of curing and drying for prosciutto causes a tremendous loss of moisture, and small thin duck breasts will shrink to almost nothing.

1 large whole Muscovy or Mulard duck breast, halved, skin on
2 cups kosher salt
4 bay leaves, crumbled
1 tablespoon juniper berries, lightly crushed
1 tablespoon dried thyme, crumbled

Trim away any ragged edges of skin from the duck breasts and put the breasts in a glass baking dish. In a small bowl, stir the salt, bay leaves, juniper berries, and thyme together. Evenly coat both sides of the duck breasts with the salt mixture, then cover the breasts loosely with plastic wrap. Place another plate or dish on top of the duck breasts and weight them with some large cans. Refrigerate for 3 days, turning once a day, making sure that the breasts are always coated with the salt. Rinse the breasts of the curing mixture and put the breasts on a rack over a plate. Store in the refrigerator for at least 7 days. After the 7 days, the duck is ready to use. Wrap in plastic and refrigerate for up to 2 weeks. Cut into very thin slices to serve.

FOIE GRAS BUTTER

Makes about 1 cup

This is a recipe made to use up scraps of foie gras, whether raw or cooked. My preference is using the cooked product, for the flavor, but both work well. You could replace the foie gras with cooked chicken livers but the flavor will be stronger.

6 ounces cooked or raw fresh foie gras
4 tablespoons unsalted butter, softened
½ teaspoon Cognac
½ teaspoon chopped fresh thyme
Kosher salt and freshly ground pepper to taste

In a food processor, combine all the ingredients and process until very smooth, about 2 minutes, scraping the sides of the container down as needed. Using a rubber spatula, transfer to a sheet of plastic wrap on a work surface. Roll tightly into a sausage shape, using the plastic wrap, and store in the freezer for up to 2 months.

GRAVLAX

Makes 4 appetizer servings

Here is our take on the classic recipe for cured salmon. Gravlax originated in Scandinavia and refers to an age-old method for preserving salmon. The fish was coated with a mixture of salt, sugar, and dill and buried in the ground ("in the grave," as it were). The salt and the weight preserved the fish. We no longer have to worry about having no refrigeration, but we still love the flavor and satiny quality of this salmon. The curing mixture adds a subtle but tart, salty complement to the fish. It's nice to serve some bread, like rye, pumpernickel, toasted brioche, or of course, blini alongside the cured salmon. Try a creamy sauce accented with preserved lemons (page 242), or just crème fraîche with a little grated lemon zest.

CHEF'S TIPS I like to use less sugar in proportion to salt, which gives the finished salmon a firmer texture. Add more sugar, and you'll have a softer fish. | This recipe is easily scaled up if you want to prepare a 10-pound side of salmon for a party of 24. Increase the cure mixture by 4 times or more, so that you have enough salt mixture to generously coat your salmon.

1 cup kosher salt
2 tablespoons sugar
1 tablespoon peppercorns, lightly toasted (see page 236) then crushed
1 small bunch dill, stemmed and coarsely chopped,
   or 1 small fennel bulb with leaves, very thinly sliced
1 pound center-cut salmon fillet, skin on, pin bones removed (see Chef's Tips, page 46)

In a small bowl, combine the salt, sugar, pepper, and dill or fennel. Spread half of the mixture in a glass baking dish. Put the salmon fillet, skin-side down, on top of the salt mixture and completely cover the fish with the remaining salt mixture. Loosely cover the dish with plastic wrap and place another baking dish or plate on top to weight it down. Cure the fish in the refrigerator for 3 days, checking once a day. Pour off any liquid that accumulates in the dish, and turn the fillet over once. Rinse the fish under cool water to remove all the salt, sugar, and dill or fennel. Pat dry and wrap the fillet tightly with plastic wrap. Keep refrigerated until ready to serve, for up to 7 days. Serve by slicing very thinly on the diagonal.

INFUSED HERB OIL

Makes 1 cup

Leaves from 1 bunch parsley, basil, tarragon, or chives
1 cup grapeseed, canola, or olive oil
1 teaspoon fresh lemon juice
Pinch of kosher salt

In a saucepan of lightly salted water, blanch the herb leaves for 4 to 5 seconds. Drain and plunge immediately into a bowl of ice water for 1 minute. Drain and pat dry on paper towels. Put the herb leaves in a blender. With the machine running, gradually add the oil. Season with the lemon juice and salt. Pour the mixture through a fine-mesh sieve lined with a double layer of cheesecloth or a coffee filter and set over a bowl. Let drain at room temperature for at least 8 hours or overnight. Store in an airtight container in the refrigerator for up to 4 days.

INFUSED LEMON OIL
Makes 1 cup

Zest of 5 lemons, preferably Meyer lemons
1 cup grapeseed, canola, or olive oil
Pinch of salt

In a small food processor, combine all the ingredients and puree to make a thin sauce, about 2 minutes. Transfer to a small container and refrigerate overnight, allowing the flavors to infuse and the sediment to settle on the bottom. Carefully pour off the clear, top portion of the oil, discarding the cloudy part at the bottom. Store in an airtight container in the refrigerator for up to 4 days.

INFUSED MUSTARD OIL
Makes 1 cup

2 tablespoons dry mustard
1 cup grapeseed, vegetable, or olive oil
Pinch of salt

In a small food processor, combine all the ingredients and process for about 2 minutes. Transfer to a small container and refrigerate overnight, allowing the flavors to infuse and the sediment to settle on the bottom. Carefully pour off the clear, top portion of the oil, discarding the cloudy part at the bottom. Store in an airtight container in the refrigerator for up to 4 days.

MOROCCAN PRESERVED LEMONS

4 lemons, scrubbed and dried
⅔ cup kosher salt
½ teaspoon red pepper flakes
2 bay leaves, crumbled
1 teaspoon black peppercorns
1¼ cups fresh lemon juice

Thinly slice off the blossom and stem ends of the lemons, then cut them lengthwise into eighths. In a medium bowl, toss the lemon wedges thoroughly with the salt, red pepper flakes, bay leaves, and peppercorns. Pack the wedges into a sterilized 1-quart glass mason jar. Pour in the lemon juice, making sure there is enough to cover the lemon wedges, leaving ½ inch of space at the top. Tightly screw on the top of the jar and gently turn the jar over a few times to distribute the salt. Let it sit on the counter at room temperature for 7 days, turning the jar occasionally. Unscrew the cap once in while and check to see if any scum has formed; if it has, remove it with a spoon. After 7 days, refrigerate the preserved lemons. They will keep for months; in fact, they get more flavorful as they age. Keep in mind when using preserved lemons in a sauce or vinaigrette that they're really powerful and a little goes a long way.

24-HOUR SALT COD
At Farallon we've found that commercial salt cod varies a great deal in quality and decided to make our own. This is incredibly easy and though you may not want to make it simply to use it as a garnish for a dish like the Asparagus Soup (page 83), it's wonderful in the brandade on page 116. Next time you buy some really fresh cod, get a couple extra fillets and preserve them with this method. Keep in mind though that a 24-hour salting is not really a preservation method, it's more of a flavor enhancement, and after it's rinsed it will only keep for 2 days in the refrigerator. If you leave it in the salt for 3 days, however, you can probably keep the cod for up to 3 weeks after it's been rinsed.

Fresh Atlantic or Pacific cod fillets, skinned, and pin bones removed
Kosher salt

Put the cod fillets in a shallow glass or stainless container, and liberally coat the fish on all sides with at least a ¼-inch layer of salt. Refrigerate (uncovered is okay) for at least 24 hours and up to 72 hours. Rinse well and pat dry with paper towels before proceeding with the recipe, or wrap in plastic for 2 days or up to 3 weeks (see note above).

CHICKEN STOCK

Makes about 4 quarts

We primarily use a "blond" chicken stock, or one in which the bones haven't been roasted first to make a brown stock. This is an all-purpose stock that can be used in many dishes, even ones including fish. I think if I had to choose only one stock to keep on hand at home, this would be it.

4 to 5 pounds chicken backs, necks, wings, and bones
6 quarts cold water
1 tablespoon kosher salt, plus more to taste
1 unpeeled yellow onion, halved
2 large carrots, peeled and coarsely chopped
2 stalks celery, coarsely chopped
2 bay leaves
2 sprigs thyme
4 sprigs parsley
3 sprigs tarragon
20 black peppercorns
Freshly ground pepper to taste

Trim any visible fat from the chicken pieces and rinse well. Put in a stockpot with the water. Add the 1 tablespoon salt and bring the liquid to a medium simmer. Cook, skimming occasionally, for 3 minutes. When the surface scum seems to have stopped accumulating, add the vegetables, herbs, and peppercorns. Reduce heat and cook, uncovered, at a very low simmer for 3 to 4 hours, skimming frequently (the more scum you remove during cooking, the clearer the finished stock). Let the stock cool for 10 to 15 minutes, then strain through a fine-mesh sieve into another container. Season with salt and pepper. Let cool completely and refrigerate overnight. Remove the congealed fat from the surface. Cover and refrigerate for up to 3 days or transfer to small containers and freeze for up to 2 months.

FISH STOCK

Makes about 4 quarts

This is a very lightly flavored fish stock; if you'd like a stronger stock for, say, a fish stew or soup, double the proportion of bones and heads to water. The key to making a good fish stock is to use bones and heads from mild-tasting white-fleshed fish. (Although you could use oilier salmon bones if you're using the stock in a salmon dish.) As a variation, consider replacing the bay, thyme, and parsley with ginger and lemongrass for an Asian flavor.

4 pounds bones and heads (gills removed) from non-oily, white-fleshed fish like turbot, halibut, sea bass, cod, rockfish, snapper, or sole
2 tablespoons unsalted butter
2 onions, coarsely chopped
2 stalks celery, coarsely chopped
2 leeks, green tops only, sliced and rinsed well
Tops of 1 fennel bulb, coarsely chopped (optional)
6 unpeeled cloves garlic, lightly smashed
1 cup dry white wine
4 quarts water
1 bay leaf
2 sprigs thyme, or 1 teaspoon dried thyme, crumbled
4 sprigs parsley
3 to 4 sprigs tarragon
10 black peppercorns
Kosher salt and freshly ground pepper to taste

Rinse the bones and heads well to remove all traces of blood and chop any large ones. In a large stockpot, melt the butter over medium heat and add the bones, heads, and vegetables. Reduce heat to low and cook until the vegetables are soft and translucent, about 5 minutes. Add the wine and increase heat to medium-high; cook for 1 minute to evaporate the alcohol. Add the water. Bring to a simmer for a few minutes. Skim off any scum. Add the herbs and peppercorns. Reduce heat to a low simmer and cook, uncovered, for 30 minutes; do not allow to boil. Skim off the scum frequently. Remove from heat and strain through a fine-mesh sieve lined with a double layer of cheesecloth or a coffee filter set over a bowl. Season with salt and pepper. Let cool. Cover and refrigerate for up to 3 days or transfer to small containers and freeze for up to 2 months.

SHELLFISH STOCK
Makes about 8 cups

If you already have some fish stock on hand, this is a snap to make, but if you don't, make the Quick Shellfish Stock that follows instead. You can use any combination of mussels, clams, and oysters, or all mussels or all clams. Because this recipe uses fish stock as its liquid, there is no need to add other seasonings.

1 tablespoon olive oil
12 ounces mussels, scrubbed and debearded
12 ounces clams, scrubbed
12 ounces oysters
8 cups fish stock (page 243)

In a large saucepan or small stockpot, heat the oil over high heat for 2 minutes. Add the shellfish, cover, and cook for 4 minutes, shaking the pot a few times to redistribute the shellfish. Remove the lid and add the fish stock. Reduce heat to medium-low and bring the liquid to a simmer. Cook, uncovered, for 30 minutes. Strain through a fine-mesh sieve lined with a double layer of cheesecloth or a coffee filter set over a bowl. Let cool in an ice-water bath. If there seems to be a lot of sediment on the bottom, pour the stock into another container, leaving the sediment behind, then let cool. Cover and refrigerate for up to 3 days or transfer to small containers and freeze for up to 2 months.

QUICK SHELLFISH STOCK
Makes about 4 cups

This recipe is simpler than the previous one, because you don't have to have fish stock to make it. You can use clams or mussels, or a combination of both.

1 tablespoon olive oil
1 onion, chopped
1 carrot, peeled and chopped
1 stalk celery, chopped
3 to 5 cloves garlic, lightly crushed
2 pounds debearded mussels, clams, or a combination, scrubbed
1 cup dry white wine
10 black peppercorns
1 sprig thyme
2 sprigs parsley
3 cups water

Heat the oil in a large saucepan or small stockpot over medium-low heat. Add the onion, carrot, celery, and garlic and cook, stirring occasionally, until the vegetables are soft but not browned, about 6 minutes. Add the shellfish, cover, and cook for 2 minutes. Uncover, increase heat to high, and add the wine. Boil for 1 minute. Add the peppercorns, thyme, parsley, and water. Reduce heat to low, cover, and cook for about 4 minutes. Remove from heat. Strain through a fine-mesh sieve lined with a double layer of cheesecloth or a coffee filter set over a bowl. Let the stock sit for a few minutes. If there seems to be a lot of sediment on the bottom, pour the stock into another container, leaving the sediment behind. Let cool. Cover and refrigerate for up to 3 days or transfer to small containers and freeze for up to 2 months.

Shellfish Essences

A shellfish essence is a stock made by breaking down the shells. This draws out the flavor of the shellfish and reduces it to its purest flavor, or "essence." This then forms the base of a sauce, or it can be used as a flavoring by itself.

CRAYFISH ESSENCE
Makes about 4 cups

The shells of crayfish are different from those of lobsters and so require a different technique to get the essence.

1 tablespoon grapeseed or canola oil
2 pounds whole crayfish, coarsely chopped
1 onion, coarsely chopped
1 carrot, peeled and coarsely chopped
1 stalk celery, coarsely chopped
1 bay leaf
2 sprigs thyme
2 sprigs tarragon
¼ cup Cognac
¼ cup dry white wine
6 cups fish stock (page 243)

Heat the oil in a medium saucepan over high heat for 1 minute. Add the crayfish, being very careful, as they will pop and spit oil, and cook, stirring, for 1 minute. Stir in the onion, carrot, celery, and herbs. Cover and let steam for 4 to 5 minutes. If you want some of the whole crayfish for garnish, remove and reserve them at this point. Remove the lid, add the Cognac, wine, and fish stock, and cook for 2 minutes. Strain the broth and reserve both liquid and solids. Put the solids in the bowl of a heavy-duty mixer fitted with a paddle attachment. Put a kitchen towel over the top or plastic wrap around the mouth to avoid spattering. Mix on low speed for 15 minutes, then on medium-high speed for another 15 minutes. Add the reserved liquid and mix on low speed for 5 minutes. Pour through a fine-mesh sieve lined with a double layer of cheesecloth or a coffee filter set over a bowl. Transfer to small containers and refrigerate for up to 3 days or freeze for up to 2 months.

LOBSTER ESSENCE
Makes 4 cups

Shells from 3 cooked whole lobsters
2 tablespoons grapeseed, canola, or olive oil
4 cups fish stock (page 243), shellfish stock (page 244),
    or equal parts clam juice, water, and dry white wine

Preheat the oven to 400°F. In a roasting pan, toss the lobster shells with the oil. Roast until the shells are dark red and brittle when you press on them with a spoon, 20 to 25 minutes. Transfer to the bowl of a heavy-duty mixer fitted with a paddle attachment. On the lowest speed, crush the lobster shells for 20 minutes, covering the mixer with a large kitchen towel or plastic wrap to prevent spattering. Increase the speed to second from lowest and continue to crush for 10 minutes. Add the stock, reduce speed to low, and mix for 5 minutes. Pour through a fine-mesh sieve lined with a double layer of cheesecloth or a coffee filter set over a bowl. Let cool. Transfer to small containers and refrigerate for up to 3 days or freeze for up to 2 months.

VEAL STOCK
Makes about 4 quarts

This is a basic recipe for a brown stock, where the bones and vegetables are roasted first to give the finished stock its characteristic golden brown color. Use this technique with any kind of bones: beef, duck, chicken, or lamb. The recipe may be cut in half if you have fewer bones.

2 tablespoons canola oil
10 pounds veal, knuckle, breast, or neck bones, or a combination
2 onions, halved
2 large carrots, peeled and cut into 2-inch pieces
2 stalks celery, cut into 2-inch pieces
4 quarts cold water
2 bay leaves
2 sprigs thyme
4 sprigs parsley
2 tablespoons kosher salt
20 black peppercorns

Preheat the oven to 425°F. Add 1 tablespoon of the oil to a large roasting pan and spread out the veal bones in the pan. Drizzle the remaining 1 tablespoon of oil over the bones. Roast the bones for 45 minutes, turning once to ensure even browning. Add the onions, carrots, and celery and continue to roast until the vegetables have browned but not burned, another 45 minutes. (Don't let them scorch or the stock will taste bitter.) Put the bones and vegetables in a large stockpot. Place the roasting pan over a burner on medium-high heat. Add 1 cup of the water and, using a wooden spoon, stir to scrape up any browned bits from the bottom of the pan. Pour the juices into the stockpot and add the remaining water. Over high heat, bring the liquid to a boil for 3 minutes, then reduce heat to low. Skim off the impurities and add the herbs and salt and pepper. Cook, uncovered, at a very low simmer for 6 to 8 hours, skimming frequently (the more scum you remove during cooking, the clearer the finished stock). Add more water as necessary to maintain the same level. Let the stock cool for 10 to 15 minutes, then strain through a fine-mesh sieve into another container. Let cool completely and refrigerate for up to 3 days or transfer to small containers and freeze for up to 2 months.

SUGAR SYRUP
Makes about 5 cups

2½ cups sugar
3 cups water

In a small saucepan, combine the sugar and water. Bring the mixture to a boil over medium-high heat. Boil until all the sugar is dissolved and the mixture is clear, about 30 seconds. Let cool to room temperature. Store in an airtight container in the refrigerator for up to 4 months.

TOASTED-ALMOND ICE CREAM
Makes a generous quart

½ cup sliced almonds, toasted (see page 236)
1⅔ cups milk
1⅔ cups heavy cream
1 vanilla bean, halved lengthwise, or 2 teaspoons vanilla extract
¾ cup sugar
6 large egg yolks

In a heavy saucepan, combine the almonds, milk, and cream. If using the vanilla bean, scoop out the seeds and add with the pod to the milk mixture. Heat over medium-high heat until bubbles form around the edges of the pan. Turn off heat and let sit for 30 minutes. Stir in the sugar. Heat again until bubbles form around the edges. In a medium bowl, gradually whisk the hot milk mixture into the egg yolks. Return to the pan and cook over medium-low heat, stirring constantly with a rubber spatula, until the mixture thickens and coats the back of a spoon. Remove from heat and add the vanilla extract, if using. Pour into a bowl set in an ice-water bath and stir until cool. Cover and refrigerate for at least 2 hours to chill. Strain through a fine-mesh sieve. Freeze in an ice cream maker according to the manufacturer's instructions.

TOMATO CONCASSÉ

Cut peeled and seeded tomatoes (see page 233) into ⅛- to ¼-inch dice. Use as a garnish or as an ingredient in many dishes.

TOMATO CONSOMMÉ

Makes 2 cups

The riper the tomato, the more flavor the extracted juice will have. If you can, use a peak-season heirloom variety.

6 very ripe red tomatoes (not Romas), stemmed and coarsely chopped
1 to 1½ cups water
Pinch of kosher salt
Freshly ground pepper to taste

Put the tomatoes in a blender or food processor and puree for about 3 minutes, adding water as necessary. Season with salt and pepper. Pour into a fine-mesh sieve lined with damp cheesecloth and placed over a bowl. Refrigerate for 2 to 4 hours to allow the tomato water to drain. Discard the solids and reserve the liquid. Taste and adjust the seasoning. Cover and refrigerate for up to 2 days.

SLOW-ROASTED TOMATOES

Makes about 1½ cups chopped tomatoes

This technique will intensify even out-of-season tomatoes, so consider making a large batch—they're great to have on hand to add to pastas and sauces. If you're going to chop them for a rustic sauce or puree them, you can leave the skins on after roasting. The skins will slip off easily if you want a more refined look to the dish.

4 pounds Roma (plum) tomatoes, halved lengthwise
¼ cup extra-virgin olive oil
Kosher salt and freshly ground pepper to taste

Place the tomatoes, cut-side up, on a baking sheet, drizzle with the olive oil, and sprinkle with salt and pepper. Bake in an oven set at 100°F for 8 hours, or preheat the oven to 200° to 250°F, put the tomatoes in, then turn the oven off

and let sit overnight. If you want to speed up the process, roast the tomatoes cut-side up for 2 to 3 hours at 225°F. They will keep, covered, in the refrigerator for up to 5 days.

SMOKED TOMATOES

These smoky tomatoes give a depth of flavor to all kinds of vinaigrettes, sauces, salsas, and soups. If you have a stove-top smoker, it's a quick 20- to 30-minute technique. Otherwise, have some tomatoes ready to put on the outdoor smoker or grill after you've finished cooking another dish.

12 vine-ripened red tomatoes, halved crosswise
Olive oil for drizzling
Kosher salt and freshly ground pepper to taste

Drizzle the tomatoes with olive oil and sprinkle with salt and pepper. Prepare a stovetop smoker according to the manufacturer's instructions. Smoke the tomatoes for 20 to 30 minutes. They will keep, covered, in the refrigerator for up to 5 days.

VINAIGRETTE

Makes ¼ cup

This is a basic vinaigrette to use as an all-purpose dressing for greens; it's simple and light, and you can adjust the proportions of acid and oil to suit your taste. Try adding minced shallots, garlic, or fresh herbs to the mixture.

1 tablespoon fresh squeezed lemon juice or white, red, Champagne, or sherry vinegar
3 tablespoons extra-virgin olive oil
Kosher salt and freshly ground pepper to taste

Put the lemon juice or vinegar in a small bowl and gradually whisk in the olive oil to form an emulsified sauce. Season with salt and pepper and set aside. Or, put all the ingredients in a clean jar and shake vigorously. A vinaigrette like this, without garlic or shallots, will keep, tightly covered and refrigerated, for up to 10 days. If there are any solids, the vinaigrette will keep for up to 3 days.

RESOURCES

Here's a list of suppliers for many of the foodstuffs and much of the special equipment mentioned in this book. By no means is this meant to be an exhaustive list of all the wonderful food purveyors out there—new resources are springing up on the Internet every day—it's simply a list of our favorites. Although we give a very general description of what they offer, their products often overlap. Most of them have Web sites, but in some cases you can only request a catalog and order by phone or e-mail.

ASSOULINE & TING
800-521-4491
www.caviarassouline.com
Caviar, aged balsamic vinegars, and Moroccan lemons.

BALDUCCI'S
212-673-2600 (in New York)
800-225-3822
www.balducci.com
Specialty foods, spices, oils, and vinegars.

BRIDGE KITCHENWARE
212-838-6746 (in New York)
800-274-3435
www.bridgekitchenware.com
A huge selection of professional cooking equipment, from ring molds to Flexipans.

BROKEN ARROW RANCH
800-962-4263
www.brokenarrowranch.com
Wild boar and venison products.

BROWNE TRADING COMPANY
800-944-7848
www.browne-trading.com
Seafood, including lobster, dayboat scallops, peeky-toe crab, yellowfin tuna, turbot, and caviar.

CAVIARTERIA
800-4-CAVIAR
www.caviarteria.com
An emporium of caviar and related products.

CYPRESS GROVE
707-839-3168
www.cypressgrovechevre.com
Artisan goat cheeses, including Cypress Grove chèvre and Bermuda Triangle Blue.

D'ARTAGNAN
800-327-8246
www.dartagnan.com
Foie gras, truffles, and wild mushrooms.

DEAN & DELUCA
800-221-7714
www.dean-deluca.com
Specialty-food products, including Valrhona chocolate, cheese, vinegars, oils, and spices, plus kitchen and tableware.

ETHNIC GROCER
www.ethnicgrocer.com
An international selection of food products.

FARMERS' MARKETS
www.ams.usda.gov/farmersmarkets
Information on and locations of farmers' markets nationwide.

FARM-2-MARKET.COM
800-663-4326
www.farm-2-market.com
An online source for fresh seafood, including lobsters, striped bass, PEI Penn Cove mussels, crayfish, oysters, and caviar.

FRESH FISH 4 U
877-474-FISH
www.freshfish4U.com
Fresh lake fish, including walleyed pike as well as salmon, halibut, and yellowfin tuna.

FRIEDA'S
800-421-9477
www.friedas.com
An extensive selection of fresh specialty produce.

FULTON STREET LOBSTER AND SEAFOOD
718-433-4540
www.fultonstreet.com
Fresh and frozen seafood, and kitchenware.

GARDEN AND VALLEY ISLE SEAFOOD
808-524-4847
www.gvisfd.com
Hawaiian seafood.

GOURMET MUSHROOMS
800-789-9121
www.gourmetmushrooms.com
Fresh wild and cultivated mushrooms.

HOME CHEF
415-927-3290
www.homechef.com
Cooking equipment and tableware for the home.

HUDSON VALLEY FOIE GRAS
516-773-4400
www.hudsonvalleyfoiegras.com
Foie gras and duck products, including duck fat.

JAMES HOOK LOBSTER CO.
617-423-5500
www.jameshooklobster.com
Live Maine and Canadian lobster and other fresh fish and shellfish.

J. B. PRINCE
800-473-0577
www.jbprince.com
A huge selection of professional cooking equipment, including hemisphere Flexipan molds.

J. J. BRENNER
253-929-1562
www.jjbrenner.com
Fresh oysters and shellfish from Puget Sound in Washington State.

JOIE DE VIVRE
707-938-1229
www.frenchselections.com
Sonoma foie gras and French gift items.

KALUSTYAN'S
212-685-3451
www.kalustyans.com
Moroccan lemons, spices, and ethnic foods.

KATAGIRI
212-755-3566
www.katagiri.com
Japanese specialty foods, including shiso leaves and yuzu juice.

KING ARTHUR FLOUR
BAKER'S CATALOG
800-827-6836
www.kingarthurflour.com
Specialty baking products and cookware.

KYLE LEBLANC CRAYFISH FARMS
504-537-6444
www.crawdads.net
Louisiana crayfish.

LEGAL SEAFOODS
800-477-LEGAL
www.legalseafoods.com
Live Maine lobsters.

OAKVILLE GROCERY
800-973-6324
www.oakvillegrocery.com
Specialty foods.

PEARL PRODUCTS
888-303-1111
www.pearlsea.com
Live British Columbia oysters, clams, and scallops.

PERFECT PUREE
707-967-8700
www.perfectpuree.com
Common and unusual fresh fruit purees.

PETROSSIAN, INC.
800-828-9241
www.petrossian.com
Caviar, smoked fish, foie gras, and other specialty foods.

POLARICA
415-647-1300
www.polarica.com
Venison, wild boar, rabbit, foie gras, truffles, and caviar.

SAINTE ALVÈRE TRUFFLE MARKET
www.sainte-alvere.com/uk_accueil.asp
Truffles from Périgord.

SOFTCRAB.NET
www.softcrab.net
Fresh Chesapeake Bay soft-shell crabs.

SPANISH TABLE
206-682-2827
www.tablespan.com.
Squid ink.

SUMMERFIELD FARM
800-898-3276
Lamb and veal, including veal cheeks.

SUR LA TABLE
800-243-9852
www.surlatable.com
Cooking equipment and tableware for the home.

TAVOLO
www.tavolo.com
A Web site linked to the Culinary Institute of America, with a wide selection of food products and equipment.

TAYLOR SHELLFISH
360-426-6178
www.taylorshellfish.com
Fresh shellfish from Puget Sound: clams, oysters, Dungeness crab, scallops, and mussels.

URBANI TRUFFLES & CAVIAR
800-281-2330
urbaniusa@aol.com
Truffles from Italy, caviar.

UWAJIMAYA
800-889-1928
www.uwajimaya.com
Asian foods.

WILLIAMS-SONOMA
800-541-1262
www.williams-sonoma.com
Specialty foods, cookware, and tableware.

TABLE OF EQUIVALENTS

The exact equivalents in the following tables have been rounded for convenience.

LIQUID/DRY MEASURES

U.S.	METRIC
¼ teaspoon	1.25 milliliters
½ teaspoon	2.5 milliliters
1 teaspoon	5 milliliters
1 tablespoon (3 teaspoons)	15 milliliters
1 fluid ounce (2 tablespoons)	30 milliliters
¼ cup	60 milliliters
⅓ cup	80 milliliters
½ cup	120 milliliters
1 cup	240 milliliters
1 pint (2 cups)	480 milliliters
1 quart (4 cups, 32 ounces)	960 milliliters
1 gallon (4 quarts)	3.84 liters
1 ounce (by weight)	28 grams
1 pound	454 grams

OVEN TEMPERATURES

FAHRENHEIT	CELSIUS	GAS
250	120	½
275	140	1
300	150	2
325	160	3
350	180	4
375	190	5
400	200	6
425	220	7
450	230	8
475	240	9
500	260	10

LENGTH

U.S.	METRIC
⅛ inch	3 millimeters
¼ inch	6 millimeters
½ inch	12 millimeters
1 inch	2.5 centimeters

INDEX